Global Economics

Capitalist Thought: Studies in Philosophy, Politics, and Economics

Series Editor: Edward W. Younkins, Wheeling Jesuit University

Mission Statement

This book series is devoted to studying the foundations of capitalism from a number of academic disciplines including, but not limited to, philosophy, political science, economics, law, literature, and history. Recognizing the expansion of the boundaries of economics, this series particularly welcomes proposals for monographs and edited collections that focus on topics from transdisciplinary, interdisciplinary, and multidisciplinary perspectives. Lexington Books will consider a wide range of conceptual, empirical, and methodological submissions, Works in this series will tend to synthesize and integrate knowledge and to build bridges within and between disciplines. They will be of vital concern to academicians, business people, and others in the debate about the proper role of capitalism, business, and business people in economic society.

Advisory Board

Books in Series

The Ontology and Function of Money: The Philosophical Fundamentals of
  Monetary Institutions by Leonidas Zelmanovitz
Andrew Carnegie: An Economic Biography by Samuel Bostaph
Water Capitalism: Privatize Oceans, Rivers, Lakes, and Aquifers Too by Walter E. Block
  and Peter Lothian Nelson
Capitalism and Commerce in Imaginative Literature: Perspectives on Business from
  Novels and Plays edited by Edward W. Younkins
Pride and Profit: The Intersection of Jane Austen and Adam Smith by Cecil E. Bohanon
  and Michelle Albert Vachris
The Seen, the Unseen, and the Unrealized: How Regulations Affect Our Everyday Lives
  by Per L. Bylund
Money, Interest, and the Structure of Production: Resolving Some Puzzles in the
  Theory of Capital by Mateusz Machaj

Global Economics

A Holistic Approach

Clifford F. Thies

LEXINGTON BOOKS

Lanham • Boulder • New York • London

Published by Lexington Books
An imprint of The Rowman & Littlefield Publishing Group, Inc.
4501 Forbes Boulevard, Suite 200, Lanham, Maryland 20706
www.rowman.com

Unit A, Whitacre Mews, 26-34 Stannary Street, London SE11 4AB

British Library Cataloguing in Publication Information Available

Library of Congress Cataloging-in-Publication Data

Names: Thies, Clifford F., author.
Title: Global economics : a holistic approach / Clifford F. Thies.
Description: Lanham : Lexington Books, [2018] | Series: Capitalist thought: studies in philosophy, politics, and economics | Includes bibliographical references and index.
Identifiers: LCCN 2018012211 (print) | LCCN 2018013594 (ebook) |
    ISBN 9781498546164 (electronic) | ISBN 9781498546157 (cloth : alk. paper)
Subjects: LCSH: International economic relations. | International trade. |
    International finance. | Globalization—Economic aspects. | Economic history.
Classification: LCC HF1359 (ebook) | LCC HF1359 .T447 2018 (print) |
    DDC 337—dc23
LC record available at https://lccn.loc.gov/2018012211

Dedicated to Elinor Ostrom

Contents

Preface

The past thirty years have been the greatest period in the world's history for the spread of market economics and democratic government and for the reduction of poverty. It is a privilege to document and give context to this progress especially since many people are only vaguely aware of what preceded the Industrial Revolution and only see the challenges posed by the integration of national economies into the emerging global economy.

This book is titled *Global Economics* because it looks beyond the inter-action of national economies as is implied by the term "international eco-nomics." The concern of this book includes *both* the integration of national economies into the global economy *and* the interaction of these national economies. A generation ago, Frank Sinatra said if you can succeed in New York City, you can be successful anywhere. Today, if it can be made any-where, it can be sold everywhere. All markets are increasingly part of the global economy.

It is a momentous time for yet another reason. We are involved in a great experiment to see if the advantages of economic integration can be achieved by nations each retaining their sovereignty. The old way of achieving the advantages of economic integration involved empires and colonies. But economic integration came at a severe cost in terms of wars of conquest. The results, thus far, of our experiment have been enormously beneficial, but have also involved dislocation. We do not yet know how our experiment will turn out.

With advances in transportation and communication, and also with certain bilateral and multilateral agreements, trade has been growing as a percentage of global GDP even as global GDP has been fast growing. Capital and labor have also been crossing national borders, so have business organizations and other social institutions.

This book is subtitled *A Holistic Approach* because it embraces the roles of technology, politics, law, natural resources, climate change, social institutions, and values in the emerging global economy, in addition to the role of economics (narrowly defined). In fact, recourse to abstract economic analysis is restrained, and discussion is replete with concrete examples and case studies.

Acknowledgments

I thank my coauthors of scholarly papers from which materials were adapted for this book, also the editors and referees, discussants, and other readers of those papers and of chapters of this book. I also thank my colleagues and students at Shenandoah University, my son Daniel Thies for his many fine illustrations, and my wife Barbara Thies for helping me, encouraging me, and putting up with me.

Chapter 1

Genesis

In the beginning, God created the heavens and the Earth.

Genesis 1:1

As we currently understand it, the universe began as a singular event called "The Big Bang." With the Big Bang, there was space, matter, energy, and time. Within the first tiny moments, the universe began organizing itself. The stuff of atoms began to be formed, and then atoms. The atoms accumulated sufficiently in certain places to begin the process of forming stars. And all the while there was motion, both within the atoms and without, and the universe was expanding.

The first stars were different from those of subsequent generations. In particular, they consisted almost exclusively of hydrogen (one proton and one electron) and helium (two protons and two electrons). These stars were powered by the fusion of hydrogen atoms into helium atoms. Even today, fourteen billion years later, the mass of the universe consists mostly of hydrogen (75%) and helium (24%).

Because of their enormous size, the first generation stars were relatively short-lived. When they exploded in supernova, heavier atoms—such as iron, carbon, nitrogen, and oxygen—were formed and spread through the universe. Carbon, nitrogen, and oxygen are also formed by older stars as they exhausted their initial supply of hydrogen, and start to "burn" helium. In this regard, carbon, nitrogen, and oxygen are like ash resulting from the "burning" of helium. These heavy atoms and others formed in the explosion of dying second-generation stars were spread through the universe.

ORIGIN OF THE EARTH AND SOLAR SYSTEM

Nine billion years after the Big Bang, or five billion years ago, our solar system was formed. Because it is a third-generation star system, the material gathered featured heavier atoms. The heavier atoms concentrated in the disk emanating from the center, out of which the planets of the solar system were formed. By mass, our planet consists mostly of iron and oxygen.

Nine and a half billion years after the Big Bang, or 4½ billion years ago, the Earth was formed. The Earth's core is solid iron surrounded by a mantle consisting of a liquid iron-nickel alloy. By reason of its core and mantle, the Earth projects a strong magnetic field, shielding it from the most dangerous emissions from the Sun even though the Earth is relatively close to it. The characterization of the Earth as a rocky planet comes from the crust of the planet, a relatively thin layer of silicon-based compounds, rich in mineral deposits.

The water and atmosphere of the young Earth were very different from what they are today. Water that wasn't trapped in the crust was mixed with the atmosphere, possibly forming a thick cloud over the Earth. This Earth was incapable of supporting advanced forms of life, in part because its thick cloud cover prevented sunlight from supporting photosynthesis. Nevertheless, the Earth was quite warm due to volcanism and radioactivity. Without attempting a point-by-point reconciliation with contemporary science, here is how the Bible accounts for the history of the planet through to the emergence of mankind:

- DAY 1: From the Big Bang through the early Earth, cloud cover becomes translucent (Hadean geological age);
- DAY 2: Separation of the waters (sky from seas) (early Archean geological age);
- DAY 3: Formation of the continents, emergence of plant life (from Archean to Proterozoic geological age);
- Day 4: Sky becomes clear, the Sun, Moon and stars become visible;
- Day 5: Animal life (Phanerozoic period age) (current geological age, beginning about 500 million years ago);
- Day 6: Human life (beginning perhaps 100,000 years ago).

ORIGIN OF HUMANS

According to the Bible, the whole human race is descendant from a common ancestry. Adam and Eve were placed in the Garden of Eden and, then, because they sinned, they were expelled. As to where was the Garden of

Eden, nobody knows. But, as to where Adam and Eve went following their expulsion, we have a good idea. Genetic research, supported by other data, indicates that the human race originated in Africa, and relatively recently.

In the first great migration out of Africa, humans traveled along the southern edge of Asia, and eventually arrived in Australia. Because of its isolation, Australia best preserved the genetic trace. Along the route, for example, in southern India, the genetic material of current inhabitants reflects their inheritance both from the first and subsequent arrivals of humans.

In a second great migration, humans split into several directions, forming the peoples of Europe; of North Africa and west Asia; and the peoples of east Asia and the Americas. The extent of the glaciers of the last ice age, and then their receding; the giant lakes that were formed when the glaciers receded, and then the bursting of the ice dams and earthen berms holding back these lakes; the rising of sea levels in certain places, and of land in other places during and subsequent to the last ice age—all may have affected these two migrations.

As a result of these migrations, humans came to populate most of the planet and confronted very different climatic challenges: in the temperate and arctic zones—long, cold winters; and in the tropics—amazingly hot days, with dryness in deserts and humidity in jungles. Through natural selection and differences in culture, humans adapted themselves to these very different circumstances.[1]

The most obvious way in which humans adapted to different climatic conditions was in skin color. Nearer the equator, humans are darker. Nearer to the North Pole, humans are lighter. Differences in skin color help humans, who are mostly hairless, better deal with sunlight and associated maters. Few northern Europeans are lactose intolerant, but many humans in the tropics are. Being able to digest milk as an adult used to be crucial for survival in the harsh winters of the north.

In addition to physical differences, humans are differentiated by culture. These cultural differences include dress, manners, and work habits. Humans who live in the dry heat of deserts traditionally wear long, loose-fitting garments that facilitate cooling by sweating. Humans, who live in the humid heat of jungles, wear very little clothing. During the winter, northern Europeans dress in layers and stay indoors when it is particularly cold. Some of these cultural differences continue to this day, as traditions.

Humans are famous not only for using tools, but also for fashioning tools. Indeed, human history is broken into three ages based on certain tools: (1) the Stone Age (circa 100,000 BC to 3000 BC), (2) the Bronze Age (circa 3000 BC to 1000 BC), and (3) the Iron Age (circa 1000 BC to 500 BC).

But, "tools" should be broadly defined. During the Stone Age, humans were making great strides in developing many kinds of tools. Among these other tools were the domestication of fire and clothing, counting and the domestication of animals and of plants, ceramics, the invention of the wheel, and writing.

And human life was not merely concerned with work, but with expression and religious observance. Early humans expressed themselves in art, such as in cave paintings, and often buried the dead with ceremony, such as burying the dead with several elongated flint stone knives arranged in a pattern. They also adorned themselves with feathers, bones, shells, and colored pebbles. Often, when archeologists discover bones, the co-location of artifacts evidencing toolmaking, counting, religious observance, and cultural expression clinches the argument that these are human bones.

With the advances made during the Stone Age, the stage was set for the emergence of cities and of civilization.

THE RISE OF CIVILIZATION

During the last ice age, glaciers covered much of the temperate zone of the northern hemisphere, and the sea level was considerably lower. In the north, there were wooly mammoths, saber-toothed tigers, and other fearsome creatures. To survive in the cold among these creatures, men fashioned clothing, lived in caves, made knives and spears using stone tools, and hunted in teams consisting of men and dogs. Because of the land bridges that existed back then, men migrated not only from Africa to Europe and Asia, but also to Australia and to the Americas.

With the end of the last ice age, the glaciers receded, and man embarked on a new age, the age of civilization. In the first section of this chapter, three periods of human history were identified: the Stone Age, the Bronze Age, and the Iron Age. In this section, a new trichotomy is presented, with its focus being the contemporary economy: (1) the Agricultural Age (circa 10,000 BC to 1776), (2) the Manufacturing Age (1776 to 1984), and (3) the Information Age (1984 to present).

The introduction of new toolmaking technologies marked the transitions of the Stone to the Bronze Age, and the Bronze to the Iron Age. The three new periods are marked by the publication of *The Wealth of Nations* by Adam Smith and by the introduction of the Apple computer—to explain why would be premature.

With the warming of the Earth and with the increase in carbon dioxide (CO_2) in the atmosphere following the end of the last ice age, plant life flourished, as did animal life. As the glaciers receded, much of the liquid water collected into giant lakes behind ice dams and earthen berms that had been formed by the glaciers when they pushed south. Even as sea levels were rising, land that had been under the glaciers rose up, in a process known as post-glacial rebound. For both reasons (rising sea levels and post-glacial rebound), coastlines changed through much of the world.

The melting of the ice dams and the erosion of the earthen berms by rain eventually ended in catastrophic floods in the northern hemisphere. Clear evidence of these floods can be found in the Hudson River valley of New York State. In that part of North America, pro-glacial lakes formed in the regions of the Great Lakes and the St. Lawrence River of today. When the earthen berms holding back the waters of these lakes burst, there was an enormous rush of water through the Hudson River valley. The flood swept up everything in its path, dropping debris, including boulders well past the harbor of New York City, into the Atlantic Ocean.

There is also clear evidence of such a cataclysmic flood in the Columbia River valley on the west coast of the United States. Stories of a great flood are found in the ancient histories of many peoples of the northern hemisphere, including the people of the Middle East.

The Emergence of Agriculture

Perhaps the first great civilization in the world was that of Sumer, located on the alluvial plain in the southern region of present-day Iraq. An alluvial plain is a broad and relatively flat region, formed by the deposit of sediment over many thousands of years, by one or more rivers originating in mountainous regions upland from the plain. In the case of Sumer, the rivers are the Tigris and the Euphrates. See Table 1.1. These rivers originate in the mountainous regions to the northwest, in present-day Turkey. The rivers not only formed the plain, they provided the region with a relatively dependable source of water, since they are fed through most of the year by the slowly melting snow at their headwaters (as opposed to being fed by torrential rains during a wet season and being without water during a dry season). Moreover, the rivers provide the region with a means of transportation.

Table 1.1   First Civilizations

Civilization	Beginning	River(s)	Headwaters of River(s)
Sumer	3500 BC	Tigris and Euphrates	Turkey
India	3300 BC	Indus	Tibet
Egypt	3100 BC	Nile	Blue Nile—Ethiopia; White Nile—Burundi
China	3000 BC	Yellow	Western China
China	3000 BC	Yangtze	Tibet

Note: All dates are approximate.

Man's transition from a hunter-gatherer society to an agricultural-based, civilized society was preceded by the development of certain tools, as described in the first section of this chapter, as well as by the end of the last ice age. Among these "tools" were the domestication of animals and agriculture. The first animal to be domesticated was the wolf, which, once domesticated, became the dog.[2] Together, men and dogs formed hunting teams in which the abilities of each complemented the other. Dogs were later bred and trained for other purposes, such as herding.

Dogs and other advanced animals are capable of developing relations with others, even outside their species, at least when their supply of food is made secure. By controlling their breeding, man can select those whose temperament and other characteristics are suitable for the purposes intended by man. After several generations, the animals themselves raise their young to embrace their new relationship.

The dog is a carnivore and a pack animal by inclination. It was relatively easy to include dogs in man-dog hunting parties. Once accustomed to being among humans, reorienting dogs to other purposes became possible.

The sheep was the second animal to be domesticated. An herbivore, the sheep was the first animal to be domesticated for its products (meat, milk and skins, and later wool). It is thought that the wild sheep from which came the domesticated sheep represented an animal of manageable size, sociable enough, with a high enough reproduction rate to be profitable to domesticate. As to how sheep came to be domesticated, it is thought by the adoption of lambs by human children, when the lambs became orphans when their parents were hunted by the parents of the human children.

By foraging on leaves and grass, sheep convert vegetation that humans cannot digest into milk and meat that humans can digest. Furthermore, sheep gain moisture from the vegetation they eat, which is important in arid climates.

By the late Stone Age, man began to cultivate crops, initially by planting seeds harvested from wild vegetation. Over time, through plant breeding and through advances in cultivation, crop yields increased. These advances included crop rotation, fertilizer, and irrigation. All of these things were evident in the ancient civilization of Sumer. In particular, Sumer featured intensive cultivation of the land "between the rivers" (the meaning of "Mesopotamia"), with irrigation provided by a vast system of canals.

The Emergence of a Market Economy

Agriculture in Sumer was enormously productive, releasing many people from the production of food for other purposes. The most obvious of these "other purposes" was the construction of cities. An increasing array of occupations emerged, including the artisans who made stone and latter bronze tools, along with manufacturers of bricks, ceramic pottery, boats made out of reeds, and wooden furniture; merchants who bought and sold products originating within Sumer and originating outside of Sumer; the architects who designed and built the cities and canals; and, a class of priests and rulers.

Sumer, while productive in agriculture, had to obtain wood, metal, and other things from the outside, as it had no internal supply of them. With regard to the animals and their products, and certain products of agriculture, Sumer might have been able to supply itself with these. But, it was more efficient for Sumer to produce wheat and barley and trade for them. From what we can tell, merchants from Sumer bartered with people from the outside, using the Tigris and Euphrates to trade with people to the northwest, and caravans otherwise.

Within Sumer, it is clear that coined money eventually came to be used, facilitating indirect exchange. A common form of payment throughout the history of Sumer was barley. Archeologists have recently uncovered token money, made of clay, dating much further back than it is believed that coined money came into use. The tokens represent different amounts of grain, human labor, and livestock such as goats and sheep. It is supposed that the tokens facilitated counting as in the keeping of financial records, and perhaps that they enabled merchants acting as bankers to extend credit to their customers.

The people of Sumer developed a deep sense of ownership and private property. Merchants carefully recorded transactions, using rollers to impress their cuneiform alphabet onto clay tablets. Since their written language was deciphered, it has been exciting to learn more about their society from the thousands of tablets recovered from beneath the sand.

Among the things we have learned is the world's first recorded tax revolt, in the Sumerian city of Lagash. Once relatively free farmers, fishermen, merchants, and craftsmen, the people of Lagash found that they had lost their political and economic freedoms to heavy taxation and exploitation. A clay tablet, illustrated in Figure 1.1, speaks of their demand for reform,[3] which

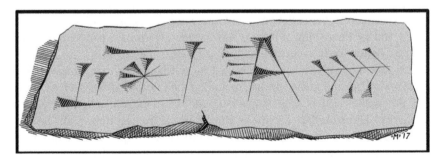

Figure 1.1 Amagi ("return to mother"). *Source*: Daniel Thies.

they characterized as *amagi*, literally, "return to the mother." It is the first recorded expression of the idea of freedom.

GOLDEN AGES

According to Dan Smith of the British indie rock band Bastille, the song "Pompeii" is about two of the people killed in the eruption of Mount Vesuvius in AD 79. The people of Pompeii died in the tremendous heat of the ash cloud emitted by the volcano. Their bodies were then buried in the ash, and remained undiscovered until the site was excavated centuries later. During the excavation, it was realized that empty spaces in the ash containing human remains represented where bodies had long decomposed. To capture the shape of these bodies, plaster was injected into the spaces. These casts are on display in the Archeological Museum of Naples. The plaster casts make it look as though the people who died in the eruption had been immobilized. The singer imagined a conversation between two people frozen in the same position forever.

The prior section of this chapter tells the story of Sumer, an ancient civilization situated between the Tigris and Euphrates in present-day Iraq. The fact is, throughout the world, almost everywhere there were humans, there were cities. Through the course of human history, many of these cities and some entire civilizations went into decline or were completely destroyed. Some were destroyed by natural disaster, such as Pompeii. Others were destroyed by war.

The Sumerian civilization survived many hundred years. As a political entity, it was succeeded by other kingdoms and empires. Through several thousand years, the land between the rivers remained highly productive. Then, in the 13th century, the Mongols utterly destroyed Baghdad and the canals, killing and enslaving much of the population, and leaving the survivors destitute.[4] It would be centuries before the place recovered. Table 1.2 lists a few of the cities that have come and gone in human history.

For the historian Ibn Khaldun (1332–1406), there is a cycle for great nations.[5] The cycle consists of a period of growth, followed by a period of decline. During the period of growth, the great nation features economic progress, military power, and the flourishing of the arts and sciences. During the period of decline, the great nation features corruption, both economic and moral.

The period of growth is characterized by self-confidence, openness, tolerance, optimism, and many virtues, including the martial virtues such as courage, the market virtues such as honesty, and the compassionate virtues such as charity. The period of decline is characterized by uncertainty, defensiveness, and suspicion of others. The ruling class comes to prefer the enjoyment of leisure to the creation of wealth, and the deterioration of living conditions of the working class. The government relies more on coercive force for

Table 1.2 "Lost Cities"

City	Place	Centuries	Reason for Decline
Angkor Wat	Cambodia	AD 12–16	Sacked by Thailand
Baghdad	Iraq	AD 8–13	Sacked by Mongols
Carthage	Tunisia	8–1 BC	Sacked by Rome
Chichen Itza	Mexico	AD 6–12	Sacked by Mexico
Machu Picchu	Peru	AD 15–16	Abandoned after Spanish conquest
Mesa Verde	Colorado	AD 10–13	Climate change
Pompeii	Italy	6 BC–AD 1	Volcano
Samarkand	Uzbekistan	5 BC–AD 16	Declined after change in trade routes
Timbuktu	Mali	AD 12–17	Declined after change in trade routes
Troy	Turkey	30–12 BC	Sacked by Greece

obedience, instead of relying on the willing consent of the people. During the period of growth, the government enjoys increasing revenue from low tax rates. And, during the period of decline, the government obtains decreasing revenue from increasingly high tax rates.

Ibn Khaldun's theory of history was based on his study of all the world's great nations through his time. In a simplistic version of his theory, the time from growth to decline is set at four generations. Yet, it is clear from history that the time from growth to decline is much longer and variable—around 200 to 400 years. Also, a simplistic version of his theory is that mankind is caught in a vicious circle, merely repeating the pattern, with no real progress. But, the cycle of great nations can be a happy helix instead of a vicious circle.

Instead of merely repeating the pattern, the cycle can involve progress. Possibly, countries can break out of the vicious circle of growth and decline, and instead have a more complex pattern involving growth, decline, revival, and then a new cycle at a higher level. John Wesley, the founder of the Methodist Church, was a revivalist preacher. He said that virtue leads to work and saving, which in turn leads to wealth, which in turn can lead to laziness and moral corruption, which in turn leads to decline, which in turn can lead to revival, which in turn can bring the country back to virtue.

While groups of humans located from the Mediterranean to China periodically fell into decline, their knowledge was generally shared with others around them. Their knowledge survived, even though they did not. When the Europeans fell into the Dark Ages, their knowledge was preserved and further developed in the Islamic world. When the Islamic world was ruptured by the Mongols, their knowledge was preserved and further developed by the Europeans. Thus, the earliest manuscripts we have of Aristotle are written in Arabic. Thus also, the European scholars of the late Dark Ages, such as Thomas Aquinas of Italy, were in conversation with the scholars of the Islamic world of that time, such as Ibn Rushd of Spain and Moses Maimonides of Egypt. Famously, Marco Polo's travels to China sparked the imagination of the people of Europe.

The sharing of knowledge among the people located from the Mediterranean to China was instrumental in the development of knowledge, as ideas from one place lead to further ideas in another place. Consider the development of mathematics. The Egyptians and Greeks were well aware of arithmetic and geometry. The Indians developed zero and the placeholder number system. The Persian al-Khwārizmī (c. 780–c. 850) developed algebra, based in part on older works from India and Greece. The Italian Fibonacci (c. 1170–c. 1250) introduced the Hindu-Arabic number system to the Western world, along with accounting and many business calculations that he learned from his contacts with the Islamic world.

In contrast to the interconnection of the people located from the Mediterranean to China, the people of Australia, the Americas, and Africa south of the Sahara desert were isolated or nearly so. Accordingly, the opportunities they had for sharing knowledge were limited.

Power and Subjugation

As shown in Table 1.3, golden age of China is associated with the Han dynasty, from 202 BC to AD 220, particularly the fifth and sixth emperors of the this dynasty, Emperor Wen, who ruled from 180 to 157 BC, and Emperor Jing, who ruled from 157 to 141 BC. During this period, China was unified, taxes were low, there was peace, and there were great advances in art, culture, and science. This was followed by wars and increased taxes, economic stagnation, and decline.

In Rome, the period of Pax Romana, from 27 BC to AD 180, is recognized as a golden age. The beginning was marked by the consolidation of Rome's rule over most of the Mediterranean. While certain wars followed, these wars were mainly in the outlying regions. Within the region, Roman law prevailed, piracy was suppressed, and commerce flourished. The end of the period is usually marked by the death of Marcus Aurelius, the last of "the five good emperors." A remarkable aspect of Rome is its long period of decline, from AD 180 to 410, when Rome was sacked by barbarians; and, to 1453, when Constantinople fell to the Ottomans.

In the case of Islam, a golden age prevailed from AD 786 to 1258. The beginning is marked by the call of Harun al-Rashid, the fifth Caliph of the Abbasid dynasty, for a gathering of scholars to translate all of the world's knowledge into Arabic. The ending is usually marked by the utter destruction of Baghdad at the hands of an invading Mongol army.

During the long decline of Rome, corruption extended to all the classes of the capital city.[6] The ascension of new rulers came to involve internal wars

Table 1.3 Golden Ages

Golden Age	Period	Rise	Decline
China Han Dynasty	202 BC–AD 220	Unification, low taxes, peace, advances in art, culture, and science	War, high taxes, conscription and forced labor, economic stagnation, dissolution
Rome Pax Romana	27 BC–AD 180	Consolidation of empire, civil liberties, advances in art, architecture and engineering	Long period of corruption and decline, incessant wars with barbarians, "tax farming," farmers reduced to serfs
Islam	AD 786–1258	Advances in science and philosophy, Islamic art, law and justice, trade and commerce	Wars in India and Europe, then the Mongol invasion, stifling of free thought, moral decay

in which teams of rivals offered larger and larger bribes to army units. The winners expected to pay the bribes from plundering the wealth of those they defeated. As the bribes got larger, there wasn't enough wealth of those who were defeated to cover the bribes, and some of the members of the winning team were also plundered.

During the rule of Caesar Augustus (27 BC–AD 14), taxes were based merely on a count of the population, and were relatively low. By the time of the rule of Diocletian (AD 284–305), taxes were assessed on practically everything, and required an extensive bureaucracy. The right to tax provinces ("tax farming") was offered to the highest bidder, and came to involve many abuses. To provide bread and circuses to the people of Rome, producers were organized into guilds that were assigned quotas.

During the rule of Constantine (306–337), peasants and their children were reduced to serfs. That is, they were legally bound to the place of their birth, not free to travel or to pursue an occupation of their choice, and made subject to the will of their lord. Serfdom continued in much of Europe until the late Middle Ages. In Eastern Europe, serfdom continued yet longer, being ended in Russia only in 1861. Serfs were not slaves in one very important way: they could not be alienated from the place of their birth.

Until recently, slavery was ubiquitous. There was slavery in Sumer, in ancient Egypt, in ancient China, and in Rome. There was slavery in the Americas and in Africa south of the Sahara prior to the arrival of the Europeans. To be sure, the law and practice of slavery varied significantly from time to time and from place to place. Nevertheless, some tendencies can be stated. People could be reduced to slaves upon conviction of a crime, for nonpayment of debt, or when taken as prisoners in war. Indeed, persons taken as prisoners in war could simply be killed or held for ransom, freed or reduced to slaves. When enslaved, they were often carried off to a far-away land. The prospect of reducing the defeated people to slaves was often an inducement for war. Concern for being reduced to slavery is reflected in moral codes forbidding kidnap-slavery of compatriots.

> If a man is found kidnapping a person from among his fellow Israelites, and regards him as mere property and sells him, that kidnapper must die. In this way you will purge evil from among you. (Deuteronomy 24:7)

By the late Middle Ages in Europe, slavery of fellow Christians was largely abolished, along with serfdom, although the enslavement of non-Christians was condoned, and millions of these slaves were Muslims and Africans. Islam similarly prohibited the enslavement of fellow Muslims, although the enslavement of non-Muslims was condoned, and millions of slaves were taken from Europe, India, and Africa.

Through the 18th century, the only place in the world where slavery was abolished was Europe. During the 19th century, the abolition of slavery proceeded through various means. Toward the end of the 19th century, a great international agreement was joined by the Christian and Islamic nations of the world to put an end to slavery. These nations included the nations of Europe, the United States, the Ottoman Empire, Persia, and Zanzibar. At about the same time, there was another international agreement concerning prisoners of war. The people defeated in war would no longer be reduced to slaves or otherwise treated inhumanely.

While we can identify certain times and places of relative freedom in mankind's history, the truth is that the history of mankind has mostly been one of wars and oppression. The golden ages of the past were short-lived, and were succumbed by corruption and decline. For most people, for most of the time, the standard of living was subsistence or maybe a bit higher or a bit lower. It was only toward the end of the 18th century that there began sustained economic development.

Spotlight: Lao-tzu

Wei Wu
by acting without direction, all things will be in spontaneous order

Lao-tzu (c. 5th–6th century BC) is thought to have been a contemporary of Confucius. Lao-tzu is associated with non-action. But, according to some, his philosophy was one of a free society (this interpretation is reflected in the translation). Disappointed with the corruption of his time, Lao-tzu withdrew from society. Thus, he is depicted as sitting on a water buffalo, heading west.

Summary

- Genetic research, supported by other data, indicates that the human race originated in Africa, and relatively recently.
- In the first great migration out of Africa, humans traveled along the southern edge of Asia, and eventually arrived in Australia.
- In a second great migration, humans split into several directions, forming the peoples of Europe, of North Africa and west Asia; and, the peoples of east Asia and the Americas.
- Through natural selection and differences in culture, humans adapted themselves to very different circumstances.
- Archeologically, human remains are distinguished from nonhuman hominid remains by evidence of (1) tools, (2) cultural expression, (3) counting, and (4) religious observance.
- Among the first "tools" developed by humans were stone tools, clothing, and the domestication of fire. Other early tools include the domestication of animals and agriculture.
- The emergence of civilization was facilitated by the productivity of agriculture on alluvial plains, as well as by the steady supply of water provided by the slow-moving river or rivers that formed those plains.
- By the late Stone Age, civilizations were springing up in many places in the world. The first of these civilizations was Sumer located in what is today southern Iraq.
- Sumer was initially characterized by a market economy, with many farmers, artisans, and merchants who were at least relatively free, and governed by rulers dedicated to justice.
- However, after a while, the freemen of Sumer came to be burdened by high taxes and restrictions on their freedom.
- Studying the histories of all great nations through his time, Ibn Khaldun developed a theory of history involving a cycle of rise and decline.
- During the period of rise, taxes were low and revenues were increasing. These were times of military power, cultural expression, and scientific advance.
- During the period of decline, taxes were high and revenues were decreasing. These were time of corruption and decline.
- For most people, for most of human history, life was at the subsistence level or maybe a little higher or a little lower.
- While the conditions of slavery varied from time to time, and from place to place, until recently, slavery was normal.

- Various moral codes restricted slavery of fellow countrymen or coreligionists. But, enslaving the soldiers and civilian populations of defeated countries was allowed. In such manner, conquerors enslaved millions upon millions of people through the ages.
- By the 18th century, slavery had ended in one place in the world. Then, during the 19th century, there was an abolitionist movement that culminated in an international agreement to end slavery. There was also a parallel agreement for the honorable treatment of soldiers and civilian populations of all nations joining into the agreement, and for the humane treatment of all soldiers and civilian populations.

NOTES

1. Sara Stinson, Barry Bogen and Jennis O'Rourke, ed., *Human Biology: An Evolutionary and Biocultural Perspective* (Hoboken, NJ: Wiley-Blackwell, 2012).

2. John R. Walton, "Animal Husbandry," in *Oxford Encyclopedia of Economic History*, vol. 1, ed. Joel Mokyr, 127–130 (New York: Oxford University Press, 2007).

3. Samuel Noiah Kramer, *From the Tablets of Sumer, Twenty-five firsts in Man's Recorded History* (Indian Hills, CO: Falcon's Wing Press, 1956).

4. Svat Soucek, *A History of Inner Asia* (New York: Cambridge University Press, 2000).

5. Ibn Khaldun, *The Muqaddimah: An Introduction to History*, transl. Franz Rosenthal (New York: Pantheon Books, 1958 [1377]).

6. The classic reference is Edward Gibbon, *The History of the Decline and Fall of the Roman Empire* (New York: Modern Library, 1983 [1906]). See also Gary M. Pecquet, "The Original Road to Serfdom: From Rome to Feudal Europe," *Journal of Private Enterprise* 12 (2017): 45–62.

Chapter 2

Rise of the Market Economy

In the story of Hansel and Gretel,[1] their mother leads them into the woods, to lose them, as the family does not have enough to eat. Because the idea that parents would put out their children to deal with a shortage of food became alien, later editions have the children's stepmother—not their biological mother—put the children out. Today, it sounds unbelievable even for a stepmother.

After the European people were converted from pagans to Christians, the former practice of infanticide became unacceptable. But, what were Christians to do when food was short? The answer was that they would let their excess children go, the ones they could not feed. God would provide for them. Europe became the land of the wandering children. During the Little Ice Age in Europe, millions of people died of famine.

The impact of climate change on northern Europeans is shown in their heights, presented in Figure 2.1. The earlier heights have been inferred from skeletons exhumed from graveyards. More recent heights are determined by direct measurement. Prior to the Little Ice Age, the average height of adult northern European men was something like 172 centimeters (5' 8"). During the Little Ice Age, it fell to 166 centimeters (5' 6"). By 1900, the Europeans recovered their prior height. Today, adult northern European men average 181 centimeters (5' 11"). Height, today, reflects both climate change (the recovery from the Little Ice Age) and a fundamental change in the standard of living of the mass of people.

When my late friend Roger MacBride brought the *Little House on the Prairie* to television, he and Michael Landon, the leading actor in the series, had disagreements over historical accuracy. Roger wrote the last three *Little House* books, taking over from Rose Wilder Lane as she had taken over from Laura Ingalls. Roger wanted the depictions of frontier life to be accurate. In particular, he wanted the children to be shown without shoes. But, Michael Landon said

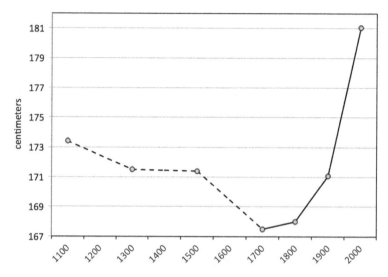

Figure 2.1 Average Height of Northern European Adult Males 1100–1500—inferred from skeletons. *Source*: Created by author. Adapted from: Richard H. Steckel, "New Light on the 'Dark Ages': The Remarkably Tall Stature of Northern European Men during the Medieval Era." *Social Science History* 28 (2004): 211–230.

that the television audience would incorrectly surmise from the children being without shoes that the parents were neglectful and didn't love their children.

Those of us who live in advanced market economies have little or no direct experience with famine or epidemic, whether due to drought, floods, locust swarms, cattle disease, or plague. Beyond knowing that they happened in the past, and still happen in certain places in the world today, we don't have any direct knowledge of them. When, for example, was the last locust swarm in this country, such as periodically devastated the prairies of the West? And, why haven't we had any of them since? When was the last outbreak of contagious disease such as yellow fever that periodically devastated the cities of the east coast? When was the last time a major snowstorm actually killed thousands of people? Or, a major heat wave that actually killed hundreds? By reason of modern farming and ranching, public sanitation, modern housing, heating, and air conditioning, people in the advanced economies of the world are largely insulated from the ravages of nature.

The world changed in a very fundamental way during the Industrial Revolution, first in Holland,[2] then in England, and since spreading in an uneven fashion across the world. Before the Industrial Revolution, the overwhelming majority of people lived at the edge of subsistence. Sometimes, they had a little more than they needed to survive. Sometimes, a little less. When the standard of living was higher than the subsistence level, more children survived until reproductive age and population increased. With more people relative to available resources, wages fell until the masses of people were returned to the subsistence level. When the standard of living fell below the subsistence level, the population fell. With fewer people relative to available resources, wages rose until they reached the subsistence level. This tendency of wages to equal the subsistence level was known as the iron law of wages and is associated with Thomas Malthus.[3] Following the Industrial Revolution, as nations joined into the new system, there was sustained growth raising standards of living and quality of life.

> But, prior to the Industrial Revolution, wges tended to be the minimum neces-sary to enable workers to sustain their number. This wage rate is necessarily higher than what is needed by workers individually to sustain themselves as, over time, workers would need to support their families and raise enough chil-dren to replace their number.

For Malthus, life involved a struggle between the resourcefulness of the Earth and the size of the human population. Humans, not having a predator to keep their numbers in check, grow to the limit of their surroundings. Once at that limit, there would be tension between the human population and the resourcefulness of the Earth. A positive fluctuation in the resourcefulness of the Earth would induce an unsustainable increase in the human population. When the Earth returned to its normal resourcefulness, some form of depriva-tion would return the human population to its normal level.

Conversely, a negative fluctuation in the resourcefulness of the Earth would lower the human population from its norm. Then, when the Earth returned to its normal resourcefulness, the human population would rebound to its prior level. Thus, there would be times of relative plenty and times of deprivation. In a very real sense, wars, famines, and other catastrophes kept the human population in check.

> These vices of mankind are active and able ministers of depopulation. They are the precursors in the great army of destruction, and often finish the dread-ful work themselves. But should they fail in this war of extermination, sickly seasons, epidemics, pestilence, and plague advance in terrific array, and sweep off their thousands and tens of thousands. Should success be still incomplete, gigantic inevitable famine stalks in the rear, and with one mighty blow levels the population with the food of the world.[4]

BREAKING THE IRON LAW OF WAGES

At the time that Malthus wrote, his ideas were not controversial. They were deeply imbedded in the experience and consciousness of the European people. During the prior several hundred years, there had been a discernable negative correlation between the size of the population and the standard of living. Following the Black Plague, when the population was decimated, wages and the standard of living were high. When population recovered, wages and the standard of living fell. At a later time, with statistics compiled using historical methods, the relationship could be shown as with the black dots in Figure 2.2. The underlying data of this chart are records of wages paid to farm laborers by manors throughout England.

Even as Malthus was writing, things were changing. The negative correlation between population and standard of living was being destroyed. At first, the new experience simply deviated from the old pattern. This intermediate pattern is shown in the gray dots in Figure 2.2. Eventually, a new pattern emerged. One featuring both increasing population and standard of living. This relationship is not shown in Figure 2.2.

What was causing this fundamental change? Was it breaking the so-called iron law of wages, and ushering in a new era of rising population *and* rising standard of living? In two senses of the word, it was capitalism. It was capitalism in the sense of using capital in addition to labor and land in production; and, it was capitalism in the sense of the breakdown of the old systems of serfdom and slavery in Europe and elsewhere, and the emergence of a market-oriented economy and liberal, democratic government.

In hindsight, it is clear that Malthus made a fundamental mistake in thinking there were only two factors of production—labor and land. If labor and

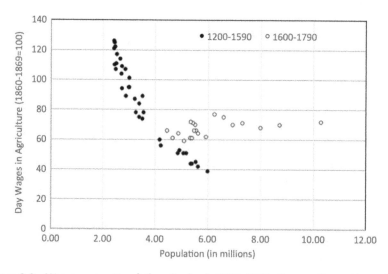

Figure 2.2   Wages versus Population, England, 1200–1790. *Source*: Created by author. Adapted from: Gregory Clark, "The Long March of History: farm wages, population and economic growth, England 1209–1869." *Economic History Review* 60 (2007): 97–135.

land were the only factors of production, then it would be true that more labor would result in less land per worker, and a fall in productivity. In a world of fixed resources, a larger population impoverishes the community.

With the possibility of adding to the resources provided by nature through the accumulation of capital—factories and such—there is no necessary connection between population and standard of living. The standard of living with a larger population can be higher if there is *more land and capital* per worker.

Why would there be more land and capital per worker? This is where capitalism as an economic system comes into play. If those who produce own what they produce, they have an incentive to produce more. If those who save own what they save, they have an incentive to save more, that is, to add to the stock of capital. Furthermore, if those who produce and save own what they produce and save, they will try to produce and save in the most productive way given the information that is available. Indeed, it is not so much that people work more hours that their standards of living increase under capitalism. It is that the hours they work are more productive.

Figure 2.3 shows the progress of wages during the eight hundred years from 1200 to 2000 in southern England. The underlying data for this chart come from church records. As churches were constructed and repaired, workers were hired. Some of these workers were skilled craftsmen, such as masons and carpenters. Others were common laborers. Furthermore, the churches

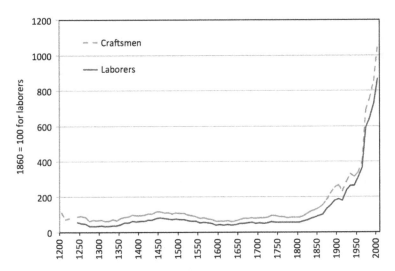

Figure 2.3 Construction Wages in Southern England, 1200–2000. *Source:* Created by author. Adapted from Gregory Clark, "The Condition of the Working Class in England, 1209–2004." *Journal of Political Economy* 113 (2005): 1307–1340.

regularly purchased commodities such as wheat and butter. The transactions were recorded in journals many of which have survived to the present day. From these records, the purchasing power of wages could be tracked over time. These records are probably the best continuous source of data for tracking the standard of living of ordinary people over a long period of time.

As can be seen, there was no systematic progress in wages prior to about 1800. Wages merely fluctuated about a flat trend line. We can suppose that the trend line prior to 1800 equals something like the subsistence level of income. It's difficult to make a one-to-one correspondence because households often feature more than one worker. For example, a male adult who was a skilled worker and an older child who was an apprentice or an unskilled worker. In any case, following 1800, wages start to rise.

It is possible to look at the course of wages even further back in time. However, the data are scattered and the sources diverse. From the ancient world, the Code of Hammurabi gives us the wages of free workers directly in terms of bushels of grain. When coined money came into use, the equivalent wages of free workers can be determined by comparing money wages to the money price of a bushel of grain. From such exercises, monthly wages in grain ranged from 7½ to 10 in the ancient world. A quotation of ten bushels in ancient Greece is thought to reflect a shortage of labor due to the Peloponnesian War.

Fast forward to Massachusetts during the 17th and 18th centuries. During the 1630s, the colony of Massachusetts made several attempts to fix wages and prices from which the monthly wage is indicated to equal 7⅔ bushels of wheat. Through the next century, scattered quotations in probate records[5] show that monthly wages in money ranged from about 7½ to 11 bushels of wheat in terms of the purchasing power of that money. As far as most people were concerned, hardly anything had changed over 5,000 years. The next section explores why, after 5,000 years, there started to be progress in the standard of living of ordinary people.

THE INDUSTRIAL REVOLUTION

Adam Smith was quick to notice the changes that were taking place toward the end of the 18th century.[6] He described the additional productivity obtained by specialization and trade in the case of sewing pin manufacture.

> One man draws out the wire, another straightens it, a third cuts it, a fourth points it, a fifth grinds it at the top for receiving the head; to make the head requires two or three distinct operations; to put it on, is a peculiar business, to whiten the pins is another; it is even a trade by itself to put them into the paper; and the important business of making a pin is, in this manner, divided into about eighteen distinct operations. (Adam Smith, *The Wealth of Nations*, 1776)

According to Smith, a team of 10 workers could produce 48,000 pins a day or 4,800 pins per worker per day. Smith could not imagine that a single worker, performing all the tasks himself, could produce anything like 4,800 pins per day. The increase in productivity was due to workers performing the same task over and over again, so that each worker becomes very quick and skilled at his particular task.

But, where would 48,000 pins per day be sold? To obtain the greater productivity associated with mass production, the market would have to expand. Thus, Adam Smith said, the degree of specialization is determined by the extent of the market. Advances in transportation and the breakdown of local monopolies were necessary.

As insightful as Adam Smith was into the advances in productivity occurring in his day, further advances in productivity in the next century were astounding. The following are news items describing machines developed early during the 19th century for pin manufacture:

> The small machine for making pins, originally of American invention, has been so far improved by H. Whitmore that he makes from the simple wire 30 per minute, completely holed and pointed, entirely by machine, with one hand only to turn the crank. They are better than any other pin because the head and shank is one piece.[7]

> Brown & Elton of Waterbury, Connecticut, have in operation an improved machine for the manufacture of pins, which turns out two barrels per day. A barrel contains 4,000,000 pins.[8]

For Smith, it was impressive that a person could produce 4,800 pins per day, by joining into a team of workers each of whom specialized in a particular task. With the machine developed in 1823, a worker could produce three times as many pins per day. Then, using the machine developed in 1848, eight million pins could be produced per day. How extensive must the market have been to absorb such an enormous quantity?

The Industrial Revolution is often characterized as ushering in the factory, or mass production using industrial machinery. Therefore, it could be said that the Agricultural Age was succeeded by the Manufacturing Age. But, the Industrial Revolution also involved advances in transportation, new sources of energy, and certain political arrangements to increase productivity and to expand the markets in which mass-produced goods could be sold.

Powering the Industrial Revolution

During the Stone Age, man tamed fire, domesticated the dog, and invented clothing. At a later point, man began fashioning soft metal found in outcroppings into tools, and the Stone Age transitioned into the Bronze Age. By applying heat to iron, to soften it, man was able to work with the black metal, and the Iron Age was born.

Iron softens, becoming plastic, at a relatively high temperature, higher than the temperature at which untreated wood burns. Therefore, for many centuries, man's metalworking was restricted to the soft metals. Then, the Hittites discovered a process for transforming wood into charcoal. Basically, the wood is partially burned to remove its water content. The resulting charcoal burns at a sufficiently high temperature for a blacksmith to work iron. Through the Agricultural Age, wood served as fuel not only for cooking and heating homes, but also for making tools.

Wood was not the only source of power during the Agricultural Age. Animals started to be domesticated for work and transportation. The first such animal was the donkey. Later work animals included the horse, camel, ox, water buffalo, Indian elephant, and llama. We continue to this day to honor these animals by measuring the capacity of a machine to work as its "horse power."

As shown in Table 2.1, the sources of energy developed during the Agricultural Age were limited relative to the needs for energy that would be developed during the Manufacturing Age. Indeed, there was concern for the exhaustion of the supply of wood in Europe at the start of the Industrial Revolution.[9]

Waterpower provided some of the energy needed. Through an intricate system of gears, the power provided by a waterwheel was transferred to the looms of early textile factories. Necessarily, these textile factories were located near rivers, and only ran when the water flowed. Often located in isolated places, company towns sprang up around the early textile factories, and workers had to be attracted to these company towns from distant places. The use of waterpower goes back to ancient times, for milling grains and

Table 2.1   Sources of Energy

Source	Early Use	Industrial Revolution
Wood	Heat, metalworking	
Donkey, etc.	Work, transportation	
Olive oil	Lighting (lamps)	
Animal fat	Lighting (tallow candles)	
Whales	Lighting (sperm candles and lamps)	
Wind	Mill grain, pump water, sail ships	
Water	Mill grain, pump water	Textile factories
Coal	Heat, metalworking	Factories, railroads, steam power, electricity
Oil		Lighting (kerosene lamps), fuel
Natural gas		fuel

Source: Created by author.

for pumping water into irrigation canals. Its use became linked to industrial machinery during the Manufacturing Age.

The use of coal, like the use of waterpower, predates the Industrial Revolution. In 1700, three million tons of coal were produced in Great Britain;[10] by 1770, six million; by 1815, fifteen million; and, by 1830, thirty million.[11]

The United States did not produce one million tons of coal until 1832. But, by the early 20th century, the Unites States surpassed Great Britain. In recent years, the United States has produced an average of about a billion tons of coal per year, about 10 percent of which is exported.

During the 1850s, a new form of energy was developed—one involving the refining of crude oil. Crude oil and other mineral oil had been used in ancient times for pitch, in order to waterproof roofs and ship hulls and such. It was known that a liquid could be distilled from mineral oil that could be burned for light, but no one had yet to develop a practical process. Indeed, there usually are concepts and impractical prototypes prior to the development of products that can be produced and sold at a profit. Then, several inventors in the United Kingdom, United States, and Canada simultaneously developed practical processes to obtain fuel from crude oil and a new industry was formed. In the United Kingdom, the inventor named the distilled liquid "paraffin" and in Canada, "kerosene." Until the early 20th century, the main use of the products refined from crude oil was lighting. Then, the main use became fuel for vehicles.

During the 1860s, the new oil industry was characterized by many small producers, products of varied quality and availability, and high prices. John D. Rockefeller's company, Standard Oil, was merely one of many companies in the business. In 1870, the price of a gallon of kerosene was 58 cents (equal to $10.90 in today's money), and Standard Oil had a 4 percent market share.

Standard Oil grew quickly by the acquisition of rivals, and by lowering cost and price and, thereby, expanding the market. Standard Oil relentlessly cut costs through economies of scale and through vertical integration. By 1880, the price of a gallon of kerosene was 9 cents ($2.15), and Standard Oil had a 90 percent market share. In 1890, the price was 7 cents ($1.88), and Standard Oil still had a 90 percent market share.[12] With his tremendous success, Rockefeller became the richest man in America of his day.

Spotlight: John D. Rockefeller

John D. Rockefeller (1839–1937) is best known for the development of the oil industry. Being a devout Christian, he tithed regularly, taught Sunday school at his church, and became a great philanthropist. Among his many benefactions was the Rockefeller Sanitary Commission.

The Rockefeller Sanitary Commission was established in 1909 to prevent and cure hookworm disease. From 1909 to 1914, the organization sponsored research and disseminated information, working with health professionals, school officials, churches, and others. Hookworm disease is contracted by barefoot children in the vicinity of outhouses with pits not dug sufficiently deep. Parasitic worms germinating in the pit can climb out unless the pit is at least six feet deep. Children infested with hookworm are listless and inattentive in school. Prior to the suppression of the disease, the rural people of the American South, both white and black, were tarnished by a prejudice that they were lazy and stupid. This prejudice continues to this day. The truth is that the rural people of the American South were often poor and afflicted with hookworms.

Spectacular Creation of Wealth

A short list of people widely known in their time to be the richest men in the United States might begin with George Washington of Virginia. Washington was not only "first in war, first in peace, and first in the hearts of his countrymen," he was, in his day, first in wealth. George Washington, a planter, was worth $500,000 in the money of his day, or $7 million in today's money. Next might be John Jacob Astor of New York. Astor was an immigrant to this country from Germany, and the son of a butcher. He made a great fortune in the fur trade. His fur trading business established a network that gathered in bear and deer skins, beaver pelts, and other furs from the frontier regions of the continent, for sale in the eastern cities, in Europe and in China. When he died, he was worth the then enormous sum of $20 million, or, in today's money, $350 million.

The next two might be Jay Gould and Rockefeller, one the son of an upstate New York farmer, and the other the son of a traveling salesman. Gould's estate was estimated to be worth $250 million ($4.5 billion in today's money), and Rockefeller's $1.4 billion ($18.4 billion in today's money). Gould made his fortune in the railroad industry and in his financial dealings. Rockefeller, as discussed above, made his fortune in the oil industry. Each amassed wealth, an order of magnitude greater than his predecessor as the richest man in the United States. The fifth and last person on the list might be Bill Gates, the first person in the world's history to break the $100 billion mark in private wealth.

Along with growing fortunes, GDP has been growing. From $5 billion in 1790 (in money of today's purchasing power), GDP has grown to $12 trillion. While there are recessions, all but seem to be minor fluctuations in this 200-year perspective. The one recession that stands out is the Great Depression of the 1930s. But, when you are out of a job and the country is in a recession, whether big or small, you may have a different perspective.

Through the Manufacturing Age, productivity increased tremendously because of the following:

- The accumulation of capital in the form of factories and equipment, through saving and investment;
- The development of new sources of energy;
- A series of inventions, not only of tools useful in production, but also "tools" useful in communication and transportation;
- New forms of business; and
- A wide expanse in which trade was relatively free.

In a sense, the above reasons are superficial. More like the "how" than the "why" of sustained economic growth. The real reasons were more fundamental. They include:

- Unleashing of the potential of an expanding number of people by securing to them their rights to own property and to trade in the marketplace;
- Scientific curiosity, the desire for achievement, and the entrepreneurial spirit on the part of a relatively small number of people of enormous capacity;
- The profit incentive within the context of a marketplace governed by law and ethical self-restraint; and
- The role of prices and profits in coordinating the activities of the many decision-makers of a market-oriented economy.

The next section examines the spread of market-oriented economics throughout the world.

THE INFORMATION REVOLUTION

Apple introduced its personal computer with an iconic commercial during the 1984 Superbowl. A heroic woman runs with an oversized hammer into a theater where propaganda is being broadcast. As she smashes the screen, a voice comes on: On January 24, Apple Computer will introduce Macintosh. And you'll see why 1984 won't be like "1984."

The reference was to the George Orwell's novel *Nineteen Eighty-Four*.[13] The novel portrays a dystopian future featuring a totalitarian state in which individualism is suppressed and independent thinking is made into a "thought crime." As the calendar year 1984 approached, two movies were put into production. One, "1984," was meticulously true to the book. Some scenes were shot on the very days laid out in the book (e.g., on April 4, 1984), even in some of the same locations. This is a difficult movie to watch because of the torture used to twist a man's mind. The other movie, "Brazil," was almost the opposite, funny and comedic, that is, until the end of the movie.

An upstart company, Apple, was in production of a new kind of computer— a personal computer. Previously, computers were very specialized pieces of equipment. Even for the few who could access computers, computers were physically remote, kept in separate, climate-controlled rooms. You accessed the computer via a terminal (not itself a computer). Data also are kept in these climate-controlled rooms. With centralized control of the data processing equipment and also the data, the possibility of totalitarian central government must have felt very real. The new Apple computer was going to change all that. It was going to put computers and data into the hands of the masses of people.

The choice of a heroic woman by Apple was no accident. She is a manifestation of Athena, the Greek goddess of courage and liberty. According to one myth, her father, Zeus, was warned that his wife would bear a child more powerful than him. So, he swallowed his wife whole, but it was already too late. Athena was already conceived. She grew within him, and then burst from him fully grown and armed, and slew him. The Commonwealth of Virginia depicts Athena on its state flag, standing in victory over the oppressor. "Sic Semper Tyrannis," thus always to tyrants.

As the goddess Columbia, Athena is Americanized. In the statue atop the capital building, she is represented as an Indian warrior. Her sword is shown in its scabbard. While we are the land of the free and home of the brave, we had just been through our Civil War.

Political and Economic Freedom

At the turn of the 19th into the 20th century, it was not clear what was to be the future of the human race. The Enlightenment put an end to the idea that there are some among us who are descended from gods. We are, all of us, mere human beings. In our Declaration of Independence, we put the idea this way: "We hold these truths to be self-evident, that all men are created equal and endowed by their Creator with certain inalienable rights." Yet, if no man could claim to rule by divine right, what was the basis for government? Was it, as the Declaration of Independence says, the consent of the governed; or, was the exercise of power self-justified by the gaining of power?

At the beginning of the 20th century, most all the world was governed by absolute monarchs or was organized into colonies.[14] There were no true democracies, and only a few places had "restricted democratic practice." By mid-century, the world had changed. At that time, it was mostly divided into two parts: (1) the democratic countries and (2) the authoritarian and totalitarian countries. All that was really clear is that the old world order, dominated by absolute monarchs and colonial empires, was coming to a conclusion. It was not yet clear what would be the new world order.

At the end of the 20th century, the future of mankind seemed clear. Freedom had gone "from zero to sixty" (meaning from 0% to 60% of mankind) in a mere one hundred years. In the 19th century, we practically ended serfdom and slavery, and in the 20th century we practically ended absolute monarchy, colonialism, and totalitarianism. What tremendous accomplishments!

Granted, many challenges are before the human race. Countries that are making the transition from authoritarian and totalitarian regimes to liberal, democratic capitalism have to deal with the economic ruins left by decades of neglect and abuse by the former regimes. Certain people cannot stand the idea that people of diverse ethnicities, cultures, religions, genders, and lifestyles can live and work together in harmony. Some people are afraid that the changes put into motion by capitalism will cause irreparable harm to the environment. Small minorities are reacting violently to the changes taking place in the world, among these being religious fanatics and anarchists. Even those who embrace the progress of freedom in the world are concerned about problems such as pollution, over-specialization, and excessive stress. The difference is that they believe that these problems can be adequately addressed through democratic government and the social institutions of a free society.

Economic freedom means that the masses of people have the right to make meaningful decisions about economic matters. This includes things such as choice of occupation and of how long and how hard to work, the decisions to save and to invest, to accumulate property including one's residence and other real estate, business property and financial assets, to borrow, and to provide for life's contingencies through pensions and insurance. Where can a distinction be made between these kinds of decisions, and decisions such as joining into or leaving a family unit, pursuing an education beyond primary school, and contributing to charities and community service? As the masses of people come to see themselves as decision-makers, it would seem that, inevitably, they will demand personal autonomy and that their society will value self-expression and tolerance of others.[15] The next several sections look at the causes of economic growth including (1) its preconditions and (2) its policies, and the rate of economic growth in emerging economies relative to the rate of economic growth in advanced economies.

Causes of Economic Growth: Preconditions

In *Economic Growth in the Third World, 1850–1980*, Lloyd G. Reynolds examined economic growth in all the large underdeveloped countries of the world that joined the march of progress. During the late 19th century and the 20th century, a number of originally underdeveloped countries clearly attained developed status, while others began sustained economic growth. Examining these countries, Reynolds identified a number of essentially political *preconditions* for sustained economic growth: national unification, continuity of government, external peace, and internal order.

In addition, Reynolds found that Third World countries tended to begin sustained economic growth during certain periods of time. The first period he identified lasted from 1850 to 1914, which is a period when international trade and finance was based on the gold standard. During that period, a number of Third World countries—some of them colonies at the time—began sustained economic growth. The second period he identified lasted from 1915 to 1945. This period was characterized by world wars, severe recessions, and the breakdown of the gold standard. During this period, few Third World countries began sustained economic growth.

The third period Reynolds identified lasted from 1946 to 1973. During this period, international trade and finance were based on the U.S. dollar through the Bretton Woods fixed exchange rate system. This period featured a number of Third World countries beginning sustained economic growth. The fourth and final period that Reynolds identified lasted from 1974 to 1980. This period was characterized by severe recessions, the breakdown of the Bretton Woods Agreement, and rates of inflation that ranged from moderate to hyper. Few Third World countries began sustained economic growth during this period.

In most cases, sustained economic growth began when a Third World country started to participate in world trade that was expanding at the time. Economic growth was marked by the growth of exports and an integration of the domestic economy into the world economy. Employment tended to shift from the household economy (which includes self-sufficient farming) into the market economy.

The major Third World countries that, as of 1980, had not yet begun sustained economic growth are informative. These countries were Afghanistan, Nepal, Bangladesh, Ethiopia, Sudan, Mozambique, and Zaire. Most or all of these countries are characterized by geographic remoteness, a lack of infrastructure, internal political turmoil, and primitive or abusive governments. Of these countries, only Bangladesh has, since the publication of Reynolds's book, started sustained economic growth.

Causes of Economic Growth: Economic Freedom

By definition, production is dependent on the available supply of factors of production—land, labor, and capital—and the efficiency with which these resources are utilized. The fundamental questions are why are some countries able to accumulate more factors of production, specifically additional capital, and why do they become more efficient in utilizing their factors of production?

In slave-based economies, serf-based economies and centrally planned economies, the supply of capital and the efficiency of factors of production are functions of the ability of a relatively few decision-makers to force people to work and to save. Adolph Hitler is known, among other things, for his slave-labor camps, yet Nazi Germany's industrial production did not approach pre-Nazi levels.[16] In a market economy, the supply of capital and the efficiency of factors of productions are functions of the choices made by all of those involved in working and saving. When people have property rights, and can keep what they earn and what they save, they tend to work more and to save more, and to do both more efficiently.

Figure 2.4 illustrates this tendency. It correlates GDP per capita against an index of economic freedom compiled by the Fraser Institute of British Columbia, Canada, and the Cato Institute of Washington, DC.[17] The index of economic freedom takes into account such things as property rights, the level of taxation, government regulations, trade policy, and the rate of inflation. It is clear that there is a strong positive correlation between economic freedom and overall productivity.

In 1956, Soviet Premier Nikita Khrushchev said, in a famous speech at the United Nations, "We will bury you." By this, he meant that centrally

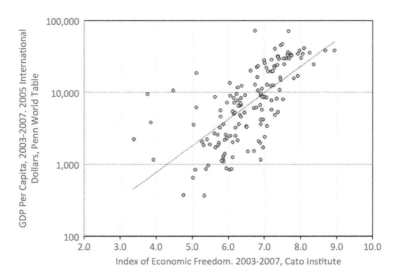

Figure 2.4 GDP per capita versus Economic Freedom, 148 Countries, 2003–2007. *Source:* Created by author. Data from Penn World Table and Cato Institute as given in the axes.

planned economies would not only catchup to market-oriented countries in production, but would far-exceed them. He said this because he believed central planning would apply scientific management to the problem of production. At the time, most of the intellectuals in the world believed that this would come to be true. But, the problem of inducing work, saving, and efficiency in the utilization of factors of production is—it is now obvious—too complex for any small number of central planners to manage. A market-oriented economy is more productive because it enables everybody to be a decision-maker for the resources under his or her control, and gives them good incentives to work, save and invest, and to do these things efficiently.

Economic Growth in Emerging Economies

The rate of economic growth appears to differ systematically across countries that have achieved sustained economic growth, according to their stage of development. *Highly developed economies* grow at relatively modest rates, and *emerging economies* that adopt policies of economic freedom tend to grow at a faster rate, enabling their people to catchup to the standard of living of those in highly developed economies.

Figure 2.5 compares the rate of growth in several countries and regions of the world. In "Year 0," to the extent it can be determined, all people

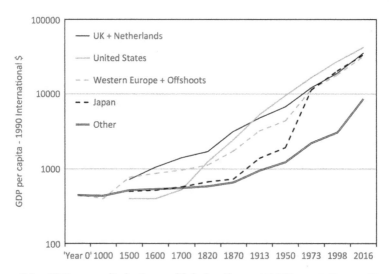

Figure 2.5   GDP per capita in the world during the past 2,000 years. *Source:* Created by author. Adapted from Angus Maddison, The World Economy: A Millennial Perspective. OECD, 2001. Updated by author.

everywhere had something like a subsistence level of GDP per capita. By 1500,Western Europe and especially the countries of the United Kingdom and the Netherlands started to separate themselves from the rest of the world. By 1800, the United States caught up to Western Europe, and by 1900, the United States caught up to the United Kingdom and Netherlands. Since 1900, among the larger countries of the world, the United States has set the pace.

By the late 1800s, Japan began to separate itself from the rest of the world, and by the late 1900s, Japan caught up to Western Europe (but not the United States). The rate of growth exhibited in the rest of the world since the late 19th century masks wide variation among the countries in that category. Notice that when the United States and Japan began sustained economic growth they, first, grew at a relatively fast rate and, then, grew at a moderate rate. Robert J. Barro, examining a large data set of countries during the post–World War II period, finds a similar pattern.[18]

As to why the rate of growth might vary in such a way across countries, the following can be said: In highly developed economies, economic growth comes from exploration, invention, business innovation, and other inherently risky investments. Only a fraction of these investments will turn out to be profitable as, by definition, it cannot be known in advance which of these risky investment projects will be successful. In contrast, in an emerging economy, investment can be made in proven technologies, almost all of which can be successful.

Forty years ago, the newly independent island nation of Singapore was poor relative to the United States, with a GDP per capita less than half of ours. Singapore embarked on a policy of economic freedom. Being an emerging economy, its economy was growing at a faster rate than ours, and it was catching up. When the index of economic freedom was developed, Singapore was found to have about the same level of economic freedom as we had. During the 1990s, it caught up to us in terms of GDP per capita, and moved up in terms of economic freedom while we slipped a bit. Today, Singapore is rated #1 in economic freedom, and we are rated #17, and Singapore has a GDP per capita that is much greater than ours. You can say that Singapore has buried us.

Summary

- Prior to the Industrial Revolution, wages and the standard of living of common people tended to the level of subsistence.
- By subsistence is meant enough for workers to reproduce their number.
- If wages are higher than the subsistence level, more children survive until reproductive age, and population increases. With a larger population (and fixed resources), the greater supply of labor drives wages down.

- If wages are lower than the subsistence level, fewer children survive until reproductive age, and population decreases. With a smaller population (and fixed resources), the reduced supply of labor drives wages up.
- Because common people live at the level of subsistence, negative fluctuations in the productivity of the Earth due to climate change are devastating. Examples include the famines of Europe during the Little Ice Age and the famines in South Asia during the El Niño Holocaust of the 1890s.
- With the Industrial Revolution, productivity growth began in certain places to outpace population growth, and wages and the standard of living began sustained growth.
- The growth of productivity is made possible by (A) the accumulation of capital in the form of factories and equipment, (B) the development of new sources of energy, (C) a series of inventions, not only of tools useful in production, but also "tools" useful in communication and transportation, and (D) new forms of business.
- In other words, resources are no longer fixed, so that an increase in the population no longer results necessarily in more workers per available resources. Instead, available resources are the result of saving and investing, the discovery of new forms of energy, inventions, and innovations.
- As to whether the possibility that the resources will be increased, this is dependent on the rights of common people. The tendency is that countries with greater economic freedom have higher standards of living.
- During the past half century, political and economic freedom has increased in the world, with prosperity spreading to more and more countries.
- The rate of economic growth of countries is dependent on whether they are advanced or emerging economies. The rate of economic growth of advanced economies is relatively slow, since investment is focused on invention, innovation and other forms of creativity, in which investments are inherently risky. In contrast, the rate of economic growth of emerging economies is relatively fast, since they can focus their investment on proven technologies.
- Because emerging economies grow faster than advanced economies, once countries begin sustained economic growth, wages, and standards of living in those countries tend to catchup with wages and standards of living in the advanced economies.

NOTES

1. Jacob and Wilhelm Grimm, *The Complete Grimm's Fairy Tales* (New York: Pantheon Books, 1972 [1812]).
2. In Holland, they would say the Commercial Revolution.

3. Thomas Malthus, *An Essay on the Principle of Population*, ed. Gertrude Himmelfarb (New York: Modern Library, 1960 [1798]).

4. ibid.

5. George Francis Dow, *The Probate Records of Essex County, Massachusetts* (Salem, MA: Essex Institute, 1917–1920).

6. Smith, Adam, *The Wealth of Nations*, ed. Edwin Canaan (New York: Modern Library, 1970 [1776]).

7. *National Gazette* [of Philadelphia], June 19, 1823.

8. *Galveston Civilian and Gazette*, June 2, 1848.

9. John U. Nef, "An Early Energy Crisis and Its Consequences," *Scientific American*, Nov. 1977: 140–150.

10. Emma Griffin, *A Short History of the British Industrial Revolution* (New York: Cambridge University Press, 2008).

11. Peak coal was reached in the United Kingdom in the early 20th century, averaging 258 million tons per year from 1903–1912. Coal production fell to 20 million tons per year by 2003–2012. Nowadays, the United Kingdom imports coal.

12. Standard Oil's production continued to grow strongly through 1911, in which year it was broken into several companies. However, because of the growth of other companies in the industry, Standard Oil's market share fell to 82 percent in 1899, 70 percent in 1906, and 64 percent in 1911. See: David I. Rosenbaum, *Market Dominance: How Firms Gain, Hold, or Lose It and the Impact on Economic Performance* (Westport, CT: Praeger, 1998), p. 32. In the United States, peak oil was hit in 1970, at 9.6 million barrels per day. After a low point of 5.0 million barrels per day in 2008, oil production rebounded to 8.7 million in 2014.

13. The book was published in 1949. Orwell had previously written *Animal Farm* (1945). Two other novels that could be mentioned along with Orwell's are Aldous Huxley's *Brave New World* (1932) and Ayn Rand's *Atlas Shrugged* (1957). F. A. Hayek's popular economics book *The Road to Serfdom* (1944) might also be mentioned.

14. Adrian Karatnycky, "A Century of Progress," *Journal of Democracy* 11 (2000): 187–200.

15. Careful analysis shows that while economic freedom and economic development may bring about a greater degree of political freedom, the connection is not strong. For further discussion, see: Clifford F. Thies, "Political and Economic Freedom Reconsidered," *Journal of Private Enterprise* 22 (2007): 95–118.

16. See Albert Speer, *Inside the Third Reich* (New York: Macmillan, 1970).

17. A similar index is produced by the *Wall Street Journal* and the Heritage Foundation of Washington, DC.

18. Barro, Robert, "Economic growth in a cross-section of countries," *Quarterly Journal of Economics* 106 (1991): 407–443.

Chapter 3

Trade Theory

Under a system of perfectly free commerce, each country naturally devotes its capital and labor to such employments as are most beneficial. This pursuit of individual advantage is admirably connected with the universal good. By stimulating industry, by ingenuity, and by using most efficaciously the peculiar powers bestowed by nature, it distributes labor most effectively and most economically: while, by increasing the general mass of productions, it diffuses general benefit, and binds together the universal society of nations.[1]

David Ricardo (1772–1823) was a businessman, investor, politician, and economist. Intellectually, he is generally seen as a successor of Adam Smith. He had a great ability to surmise some of the most important laws of economics through nonmathematical reasoning (however, he wasn't always correct). Perhaps his greatest contribution to economics is the law of comparative advantage.[2] It was Ricardo who made clear that even if one country was superior in production in every way to another, it would benefit both countries for the first to specialize in producing the goods in which it had the greatest relative advantage, and for the other to specialize in producing the goods in which it had the least relative disadvantage.

Ricardo used the example Great Britain and the United States to illustrate his theory. At the time, Great Britain was far superior to the United States in wealth, as well as in developing the factory system, in canal building, and in the application of then modern techniques to farming, mining, forestry, shipbuilding, and many other industries. Nevertheless, he said, both Great Britain and the United States had much to gain from trade. And, Ricardo was no armchair economist. He advocated his position in widely read publications and in parliament, although, it would be his successors—Richard Cobden and John Bright—who put an end to Great Britain's restrictions on international trade.

This chapter presents the theory of international trade, beginning with Ricardo's theory of comparative advantage and continuing through the contemporary theories developed by Paul Krugman and Michael Porter. The first theory explains trade through differences in productivity as might be reflected in different ratios of capital-to-labor. The contemporary theories explain more complex patterns of trade, as when two countries with similar ratios of capital-to-labor both export apparently similar products to the other.

This chapter shows the mutual benefit involved in international trade, as well as the profit available to those who act first to take advantage of opportunities for gains from trade. The chapter also identifies those who, in the short run, are losers with free trade, everyone being a winner in the long run.

THE CASE OF TWO GOODS AND TWO COUNTRIES

The law of comparative advantage was originally developed by Ricardo to support the repeal of Great Britain's restrictions on international trade known as the Corn Laws. Ricardo argued that it did not matter that Britain had an absolute advantage in the production of both manufactured and agricultural goods relative to the United States. Instead, he said, both Britain and the United States stood to gain from specializing in the production of the goods in which each had a comparative advantage.

> *Law of Comparative Advantage*: In free trade, countries will specialize in the production of the goods in which they have the lowest opportunity cost (loss of other goods not produced).

At the time, Great Britain was one of only a few highly developed economies in the world. The United States was an emerging economy. In Great Britain, the Industrial Revolution was already underway, factories dotted the landscape, canals crisscrossed the country, and banking and finance were well developed. The United States was mostly an agricultural country.

Ricardo, who had retired from business to become a politician, argued in parliament to lower Great Britain's restrictions on the importation of food. He said even though Great Britain was superior to the United States in agriculture, Great Britain had a greater superiority in the production of manufactured goods. Because of this greater superiority, Great Britain stood to gain from cutting back its production of agricultural goods and increasing its production of manufactured goods. Great Britain should import its resulting deficiency in agricultural goods and export its resulting surplus of manufactured goods.

Was Great Britain, in the early 19th century, actually superior to the United States in agriculture as well as in manufacturing? It may not be possible to say.

Ricardo, it should be kept in mind, was making a political argument, and wouldn't want to offend any of his constituents. Nevertheless, his point is perfectly valid.

To illustrate the theory of comparative advantage, Figure 3.1 uses the example Ricardo used, involving Great Britain ("GB," shown in black) and the United States ("US," shown in gray). Great Britain, we will assume, had a greater ability to produce manufactured goods (in terms of units of agricultural goods given up), and the United States, a greater ability to produce agricultural goods (again, in terms of units of manufactured goods given up). Without trade, each country's consumption would be restricted to its own production. Assuming the people of each country share the same preferences (given by the curved lines), the figure shows the best each country can do on its own (Black A for Great Britain and Gray A for the United States).

In Figure 3.1, the straight lines show each country's ability to produce agricultural and manufactured goods. Great Britain, for example, can produce 600 units of agricultural goods and 0 units of manufactured goods, or 0 units of agricultural goods and 240 units of manufactured goods, or any linear combination thereof. Given its preferences, shown in the curved lines, Great Britain would, in autarky (or, isolation), choose to produce and consume at the point Black A. Point Black A attains the highest level of utility, represented by the curved lines, attainable by Great Britain in autarky, given its production possibilities. By similar reasoning, the United States would, in isolation, choose to produce and consume at the point Gray A. In equilibrium,

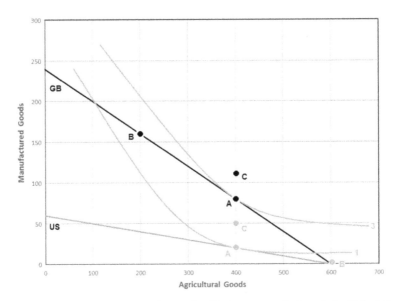

Figure 3.1   Production, Consumption and Utility in Great Britain and the United States with and without trade. *Source:* Created by author.

Great Britain produces and consumes 400 units of agricultural goods and 90 units of manufactured goods, and achieves the utility level 3. The United States produces and consumes 400 units of agricultural goods and 20 units of manufactured goods, and achieves the utility level 1.

With trade, the restriction that consumption must equal production in each country is lifted. Countries may, instead, specialize in producing one or another good, and trade its surplus production for the surplus production of other countries in goods in which they have specialized. To be sure, there is still a restriction that consumption of each good must equal production of each good. But, this restriction now operates on a global basis. Global consumption of each good must equal global production of that good.

Figure 3.1 illustrates a possible solution with trade, assuming that the cost of transportation is zero and that there are no tariffs or other interferences with trade. In the figure, the United States produces 600 units of agricultural goods and 0 units of manufactured goods, shown as point Gray B. The United States trades 200 units of agricultural goods to Great Britain for 50 units of manufactured goods. As a result of this trade, the United States consumes 400 units of agricultural goods and 50 units of manufactured goods, shown as point Gray C. Comparing point Gray C to point Gray A, by specializing and trading, the United States is able to consume 30 units more of manufactured goods at no sacrifice in agricultural goods. The United States necessarily achieves a higher level of utility (which can be thought of as level 2).

Analogously, Great Britain produces 200 units of agricultural goods and 160 units of manufactured goods, shown as point Black B. Great Britain trades 50 units of manufactured goods to the United States for 200 units of agricultural goods. As a result of this trade, Great Britain consumes 400 units of agricultural goods and 110 units of manufactured goods, as shown in point Black C. Comparing point Black C to point Black A, by specializing and trading, Great Britain is able to consume 20 more units of manufactured goods at no sacrifice in terms of agricultural goods. Great Britain also achieves a higher level of utility (which can be thought of as level 4).

Mutual Benefit

As illustrated in Figure 3.1, trade is mutually beneficial. Each country improves its utility by specializing in the production of the good in which it has a comparative advantage and trading its surplus production for the surplus production of other countries. All countries engaged in free trade improve their utility relative to autarky.

The Law of One Price

Returning to the solution without trade illustrated in Figure 3.1, the trade-offs in production between manufactured and agricultural goods in the two countries are very different. In Great Britain, anywhere along the black line, increasing the production of manufactured goods requires reducing the production of agricultural goods by a little more than 2.14 units (i.e., by two and one-seventh). In the United States, increasing the production of manufactured goods requires reducing the production of agricultural goods by ten units. If the price of a unit of agricultural goods is 1£ in Great Britain, then a unit of manufactured goods would cost 2.14£ there. If the price of a unit of agricultural goods is $5 in the United States, then a unit of manufactured goods would cost $50 there.[3] The difference in the ratio of prices of manufactured to consumption goods—1:2.14 in Great Britain and 1:10 in the United States—indicates there is an opportunity to gain from trade.

A trading company need only follow the rule "buy low, sell high" to bring about the solution with trade illustrated in Figure 3.1. In the first transaction, an enormous profit would be possible. A trading company would simultaneously buy, say, 100 units of agricultural goods in the United States for sale in Great Britain, and buy 45.66 units of manufactured goods in Great Britain for sale in the United States.

- Use $500 to buy 100 units of agricultural goods in the United States;
- Sell these agricultural goods in Great Britain for 100£;
- Use the 100£ to buy 45.66 units of manufactured goods in Great Britain;
- Sell these manufactured goods in the United States for $2,283.

Ignoring the cost of transportation and the time and risk involved, the trading company has turned a handsome profit. It has more than quadrupled its money, turning $500 into $2,283. Fundamentally, this profit is due to the price ratio in the United States (10:1) being more than four times the price ratio in Great Britain (2.14 to 1).

This kind of spectacular profit was obtained in ancient times, when international trade was very risky due to natural disasters, pirates, and so forth. In those days, merchants engaged in international trade made large profits, when their ships weren't lost because of the hazards of voyage. To spread the financial risk involved, merchants often traded shares in their ships for shares in the ships of fellow merchants, and also sold shares in their ships to investors. In addition, captains and members of the crews of merchant ships were often compensated in shares of the profits.[4]

To get an idea of how large were the profits that were obtained through international trade in ancient days, consider the teaching of Jesus known as The Parable of the Talents.

> For the kingdom of heaven is as a man travelling into a far country, who called his servants, and delivered to them his goods. And unto one he gave five talents[5], to another two, and to another one. . . . Then he that had received the

five talents went and traded with the same, and made them another five talents. And likewise he that had received two, he also gained another two. But he that had received one went and dug into the earth, and hid his lord's money. (Matthew 25:14–18)

According to Jesus the first two servants doubled their master's money. What kind of investment delivered a profit of 100 percent back in those days? Shares in merchant ships!

The transactions of only a few merchants engaged in international trade would not much affect supply and demand in the various countries of the world. Therefore, they would not much affect the prices of goods in those countries. But, as trade grows, it changes prices. In Great Britain, where manufactured goods are relatively cheap, the demand for manufactured goods by the British is supplemented by the demand for British manufactured goods by the Americans, raising the price of manufactured goods in the Great Britain. In the United States, where agricultural goods are relatively cheap, the demand for agricultural goods by Americans is supplemented by the demand for American agricultural goods by the British, raising the price of agricultural goods in the United States.

In equilibrium, continuing to assume the cost of transportation is zero and there are no tariffs or other interferences with trade, the ratio of the price of agricultural goods to the price of manufactured goods in each country will be equal. Taking into account that the cost of transportation is not zero, this is the implication of the law of one price: In the absence of tariffs and other interferences with trade, the price of goods in Great Britain that are imported from the United States is price in the United States plus the cost of transportation from the United States to Great Britain; and, the price of goods in the United States that are imported from Great Britain is the price in Great Britain plus the cost of transportation from Great Britain to the United States; in both cases, after adjusting for exchanges rates.

When the prices of goods in the countries of the world, after the exchange rates are taken into account, are within the cost of transportation of each other, then there is no longer any extraordinary profit to international trade. This condition is known as the law of one price. With free trade, prices in import markets will tend to equal prices in export markets plus the cost of transportation. The rate of return to the capital invested in international trading is, then, merely a fair rate of return.[6]

Recap of the Effects of Free Trade

This section demonstrates that free trade induces each country to specialize in the production of the goods and services in which it has a *comparative advantage*. These are not necessarily the goods and services in which it has an absolute advantage. Comparative advantage can only be determined by comparing the relative abilities of countries to transform resources into goods and services. Generally, the opportunity to gain through trade is indicated by different price ratios. For example, the prices of agricultural goods relative to the prices of manufactured goods. With free trade, price ratios will be brought into alignment other than the cost of transportation. The law of comparative advantage usually results in countries doing more of what they already do well. Each country involved in free trade improves its standard of living. This is called *mutual benefit*. Price ratios will tend to equalize. This is called *the law of one price*. The next section looks at the connection of unemployment with international trade; and, the patterns of trade in a world consisting of many countries, not just two.

EXTENSIONS AND APPLICATIONS

During the past two generations, continuing advances in transportation and communication and certain political agreements among nations have been causing enormous shifts in production. Low-wage manufacturing has been shrinking in countries like the United States and Japan, and expanding in countries like Mexico and Malaysia. Although all countries as a whole benefit from international trade, it can be shown under certain conditions that owners of factors of production specific to the shrinking sectors within each country are losing.[7] "Owners of factors of production specific to the shrinking sector" refers to the owners of land, physical capital, and human capital whose productivity is highest in the shrinking sector. Because of the loss of productivity, these factors cannot be transferred to the expanding sector without a loss.

The benefits of trade can be seen in Table 3.1, in the columns giving GDP per capita and GDP growth rate. The ten countries with the highest Trade Openness Index have an average GDP per capita ten times that of the ten countries with the lowest Trade Openness Index.[8] The ten countries with the highest Trade Openness Index are also growing on average twice as fast as the ten countries with the lowest Trade Openness Index. Countries heavily engaged in trade are much richer than those that are not much engaged in trade; and, they are becoming even more rich.

What about unemployment? Higher unemployment might be expected in the countries more engaged in trade. The idea is not unreasonable. There are, after all, shifts in production as countries become integrated into the global economy. In particular, there are shrinking sectors and it is not always easy for factors of production—land, physical capital, and labor—to move from the shrinking sector to the expanding sector. But Table 3.1 indicates that

Table 3.1   The Ten Most Open and The Ten Least Open Countries

	Trade Openness Index 2005	GDP per capita 2005 ($)	GDP Growth Rate 1980–2005 (avg. % per year)	Unemployment Rate 2005 (%) [1]
Hong Kong	10.0	30,989	3.9	6.7
Singapore	9.9	26.390	4.3	3.4
Bahrain	8.6	19,112	1.0	15.0
Belgium	8.6	28.575	1.7	12.0
Malaysia	8.6	9,681	3.6	3.0
Luxembourg	8.5	53,583	3.7	4.5
Netherlands	8.4	29,078	1.6	6.0
Taiwan	8.4	20,868	5.1	4.5
Ireland	8.1	34,256	4.5	4.3
Australia	7.9	29,981	1.9	5.1
Avg. top 10	*8.7*	*28,510*	*3.1*	*6.5*
India	4.3	3,072	4.0	9.2
Tanzania	4.1	662	2.3	12.7
Egypt	4.1	3,858	2.5	10.9
Pakistan	3.9	2,109	2.4	9.3
Syria	3.8	3,388	0.6	20.0
Algeria	3.4	6.283	0.5	25.4
Sierra Leone	3.4	717	−1.1	65.0
Burundi	3.0	622	−1.0	14.0
Iran	2.9	7,089	1.1	11.2
Bangladesh	2.5	1,827	2.2	40.0
Avg. bottom 10	*3.5*	*2,063*	*1.4*	*21.7*

[1] 2005 CIA World Factbook or an estimate found via a Google search.

unemployment is, on average, less than one-third in countries more engaged in trade than it is in countries less engaged in trade. How can this be?

Part of the answer for much lower rates of unemployment in trade-oriented countries is sociological. People who embrace change, to include its challenges as well as its rewards, will be more adaptable. When they suffer bad luck, instead of blaming others or "the system," they will try to discover what is now their best opportunity. The inability to deal constructively with change can be seen in the East Germans after reunification and in the Shia Muslims of Bahrain. Instead of embracing the opportunities offered by reunification of Germany or the liberalization of the economy of Bahrain, they resisted change and even became resentful of the success of their countrymen.

The other part of the answer is economic. While there are shrinking sectors in countries that integrate into the global economy, there are also expanding sectors. This means it is possible to move land, physical capital, and labor from the shrinking sector to the expanding sector. While the productivity specific to the shrinking sector is lost, not all productivity is lost. Workers, for example, can transfer their general human capital to the expanding sector, and can re-train. And, for workers who cannot re-train, possibly because they

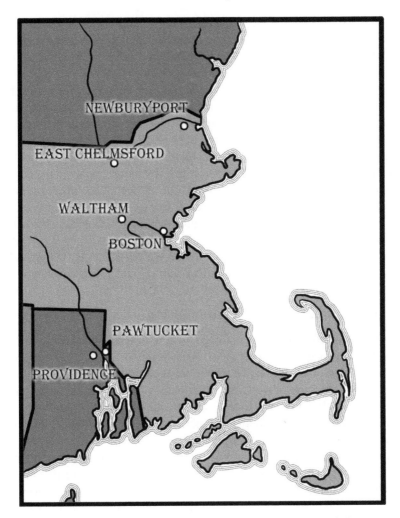

Figure 3.2   Location of New England's first textile mills. *Source*: Daniel Thies.

are older and could not recover the cost of re-training during their remaining years of work, they can try to hold on to the remaining jobs in the shrinking sector by accepting lower wages.

Case Study: The Textile Industry

During the early 19th century, textile mills were being opened in the states of Massachusetts and Rhode Island, reflecting the region's work ethic, spirit of enterprise, and accumulation of capital. The specific locations of the very first textile mills, shown in Figure 3.2, reflected the availability of waterpower to

run the mills. Throughout the 19th century, the textile industry was a significant part of the New England economy. But, by the late 19th century, the textile industry was shifting to the south (mostly to North and South Carolina),
because of the lower cost of labor in those states.

For about a hundred years, the textile industry thrived in the south. But,
toward the end of the 20th century, rising wages in the south in combination
with new, emerging economies, resulted in another relocation of the textile
industry. Textile manufacturing shifted once again, this time to places such as
China, Mexico, Malaysia, and Vietnam. Globalization proved very difficult for
the textile industry in the United States, which strenuously opposed the change.
Some companies, such as Burlington Industries of North Carolina, were forced
into bankruptcy. Others, such as Milliken & Company of South Carolina, survived and eventually embraced globalization. Milliken & Company has shifted
its low-cost textile manufacturing overseas and re-focused its textile manufacturing within the United States and other high-income countries on high value-
added production involving highly skilled workers and advanced technology.

Comparative Advantage in a World of Many Countries

The theory of comparative advantage was a tremendous advance in our
understanding of economic behavior. And, prior to recent times, when the
nations of the world could be characterized as either "rich" or "poor," it did
a reasonably good job of explaining the main patterns of trade in the world.
Specifically, rich countries exported manufactured goods and imported raw
materials and agricultural goods; and, poor countries imported manufactured
goods and exported raw materials and agricultural goods.

Because words like "rich" and poor" are not politically correct, the United
Nations prefers we say "developed nations" and "developing nations" (as
though every nation that is not developed is developing, which is not true).
Other terminology that, from time to time, has been popular is "First World"
and "Third World" countries (with the "Second World" referring to the
former communist bloc of nations), and the "North" versus the "South."
North-South Trade: Trade refers to trade between "developed countries" and
"developing countries."

Using membership in the Organization for Economic Cooperation and
Development (OECD) as a proxy for the rich nations of the world, prior to
1969, they were predominantly in the north (the only exceptions being Australia and New Zealand). They were also either European nations or nations
formed predominantly by transplanted Europeans (the only exceptions being
Turkey, which straddles Europe and Asia, and Japan).

The way economists used the theory of comparative advantage to explain
"North-South" trade was by reference to the ratio of physical capital to labor.

The higher this ratio within a particular country, the more production within that country would shift to manufacturing. Thus, the rich nations of the world—the North—exported manufactured goods; and, the poor nations of the world—the South—exported raw materials and agricultural goods.

Since the 1970s, trade patterns have become much more complicated than had previously been envisioned. At one level of analysis, the economies of high-income countries started to shift from a basis in physical capital and an orientation to manufacturing, to knowledge-based and service-oriented economies. In addition, middle-income countries started to emerge, and they seemed to supplant high-income economies in the area of manufacturing. These two changes required a re-thinking of how comparative advantage works.

The Emergence of Middle-Income Countries

During the late 20th century and thus far into the 21st century, many nations have transitioned from low-income to middle-income status, and some once low-income countries have made their way to high-income status. Today, there is a continuum of nations from rich to poor, with about half the people of the world in middle-income nations; and, it is no longer useful to characterize nations as either rich or poor.

Using OECD candidate status as a proxy, many people nowadays live in middle-income nations. Among these middle-income nations are six very large countries: Brazil, Russia, India, Indonesia, China, and South Africa, the so-called BRIICS. The emergence of middle-income countries combined with the shift of the economies in high-income countries to knowledge-based and service-oriented economies has brought about a complex pattern of trade that cannot be adequately explained in terms, merely, of the ratio of physical capital to labor. Instead, we have to deal with many factors of production. The following is, for the present purpose, an adequate list: (1) Unskilled labor, (2) Skilled labor, (3) Physical capital, and (4) Land.

With these several factors of production, we can explain the main patterns of trade among three types of countries:

- High-income countries—export the products of high-wage manufacturing and services;
- Middle-income countries—export the products of low-wage manufacturing;
- Low-income countries—export raw materials and agricultural products.

Notice that the more complex model involves two ways to transform savings into factors of production—through human capital as well as through physical capital. Accordingly, as countries develop, transitioning from low- to middle-income and from middle- to high-income, their economies go through a series of changes. With the first transition, nations become physical capital-based, and manufacturing-oriented; and, with the second transition, they become knowledge-based and service-oriented.

Even more complex models of international trade involve breaking land into (a) Arable land in a temperate climate; (b) Arable land in a tropical climate; and (c) Mineral deposits. It might be, for example, that a high-income country is also well endowed in arable land in a temperate climate and, so, exports certain agricultural products as well as the products of high-wage manufacturing and services. Think of the United States.

Table 3.2 shows the merchandise trade exports of several countries. Of these countries, Germany has a diversified economy with a standard of living comparable to that of the United States. Saudi Arabia is also a rich country, but its production is focused on the products that it exports. And, Ghana is an emerging economy, what the World Bank calls a "low middle-income country."

The table shows that the merchandise trade exports of Saudi Arabia are dominated by minerals, chemicals, and plastics. This is related to Saudi Arabia's wealth in crude oil. Saudi Arabia exports crude oil, refined oil, and various value-added products made from oil. Ghana exports gold (in the category of precious metals) and also oil (minerals) and the fruits of the tropics (foodstuffs). The exports of these two countries are clearly driven by their natural resources, geography, and climate.

Now compare the United States and Germany. Germany has big numbers in cars (transportation) and also machinery and chemicals. Germany is a manufacturing country. Compared with the United States, it's a much smaller country geographically. It has no oil and has practically run out of coal. Germany is and must be focused on adding value to raw materials imported from other countries, including energy. The United States, on the other hand, is a large country, rich in natural resources, arable land and a temperate climate. Accordingly, the United States has a much more complex array of exports. We have meaningful numbers in transportation (with the emphasis on trucks and planes rather than on cars), chemicals, and machinery, although these numbers are not as big as Germany's. We are exporters (as well as importers) of minerals. Basically, we export coal and import oil. And, we have real strength in agriculture, distributed over several categories in the table, including animal products, vegetable products, and half of what is described as textiles (the category includes raw cotton, we are the world's largest exporter of raw cotton).

But, doesn't the United States have a balance of trade deficit? Yes, the United States has a balance of trade deficit. Mostly we have a balance of trade deficit because we have a balance of services surplus. The real strength of the United States in the global economy isn't even shown in the table.

Table 3.2   Merchandise Exports (% of Total Merchandise Exports), 2012

	World	Germany	Ghana	Saudi Arabia	United States
Animal and Veg. Bi-Products	0.96	0.28	0.51	0.12	0.74
Animal Hides	0.71	0.04	0.03	0.11	0.55
Animal Products	2.59	1.38	0.16	0.05	4.24
Arts and Antiques	0.13	0.10	0.00	0.00	0.06
Chemical Products	9.72	12.63	0.75	31.84	16.83
Foodstuffs	4.30	2.82	19.33	0.04	4.33
Footwear and Headwear	0.93	0.00	0.04	0.00	0.00
Instruments	2.72	5.14	0.15	0.00	5.88
Machines	20.22	26.91	0.01	0.00	9.78
Metals	7.98	6.72	1.52	2.15	5.27
Mineral Products	18.20	0.47	20.18	32.64	9.17
Paper Goods	1.75	2.33	0.06	0.30	3.07
Plastics and Rubber	4.77	5.39	0.49	32.18	7.42
Precious Metals	3.03	0.68	50.85	0.40	3.29
Stone and Glass Products	1.01	0.96	0.00	0.14	0.61
Textiles	4.52	0.78	0.15	0.00	3.11
Transportation	9.65	31.93	0.00	0.00	10.36
Vegetable Products	4.49	0.47	3.40	0.00	14.40
Weapons	0.05	0.09	0.00	0.00	0.09
Wood Products	0.84	0.42	2.43	0.00	0.71
Miscellaneous	1.44	0.46	−0.06	0.03	0.09
Total ($billions)	14,287	1,320	14	260	1,230

Source: MIT Observatory of Economic Complexity.

Recap of Unemployment and Trade Complexity

While all countries benefit from trade, there are sectors within each country where the owners of factors of production whose productivity is specific to that sector lose. These sectors are the shrinking sectors of each country. Even though there are losers when countries become integrated into the global economy, unemployment rates are much lower in countries with more open economies. Possibly this is because of people in free economies are better able to deal with change.

Trade flows nowadays are much more complex than was imagined in the original development of the theory of comparative advantage. In David Ricardo's day, it was useful to think that trade involved rich countries exporting manufactured goods, and poor countries exporting raw materials and agricultural goods. Nowadays, there are two ways to invest savings: in human capital as well as in physical capital. It is useful to think: (1) High-income countries tend to be knowledge-based and service-oriented; (2) middle-income countries tend to be physical capital-based and manufacturing-oriented; and (3) low-income countries tend to have economies that are focused on mining and agriculture. In fact, the comparative advantages of countries often involve a mix of industries. The United States has comparative advantages in mining, agriculture, high-wage manufacturing, and services.

The next section looks at trade between developed nations using Paul Krugman's theory of international trade and Michael Porter's theory of competitive advantage.

FROM COMPARATIVE ADVANTAGE TO COMPETITIVE ADVANTAGE

International trade dates back to ancient times. The lure of adventure and the possibility of profit have always proven attractive. In the spice trade, Arabs sailed between west Asia and Africa and various places in central and east Asia, often in small boats built out of papyrus reeds. In the Mediterranean world, we associate trade, first, with the Phoenicians and, later, with the Italians. Marco Polo famously traveled to China along the overland trade route.

The Portuguese, seeking an alternate route to China, discovered how large was the continent of Africa. When, finally, they came to the southern tip of Africa, they named it Cape Hope. The English had another idea for an alternate route to China. They chartered a company, the Muscovy Company, to sail around Russia to China. But, the Little Ice Age put an end to that idea; and, the company turned its attention to whaling. The Spanish, also seeking an alternate route to China, financed an explorer named Christopher Columbus, who, based on a bad map, thought China was just over the horizon to the west of Europe.

Since the end of World War II, technological advances in transportation and communication as well as various political advances have, we can say, finally opened up the long sought "alternate route" to China, as well as opened up routes to just about every other place in the world. This section begins with a digression on triangle trade, and then proceeds to the theories of international trade developed by Paul Krugman and Michael Porter. These contemporary theories explain complex patterns of trade as when two countries both export to and import from the other, apparently similar products.

In a world of two countries, it might be supposed that the trade of pairs of countries tend toward balance. That is, that each country tends to buy and sell the same value of products from the other. Among the complications that arise in the real world is triangle trade. *Triangle trade* refers to a sequence of transactions such that country A exports to country B that in turn exports to country C that in turn exports to country A and thereby completes the triangle.

One of the more prominent examples of triangle trade today involves Saudi Arabia, China, and the United States. In this triangle, Saudi Arabia exports oil to China, which in turn exports the products of low-wage manufacturing to the United States, which in turn exports the products of high-wage manufacturing and services to Saudi Arabia. Each of the three countries involved in this triangle specializes in the production of goods and services where it has a comparative advantage. Saudi Arabia has an abundance of oil; China, an abundance of labor; and, the United States, an abundance of capital invested in human capital as well as in physical capital.

Saudi Arabia has major oil fields in its eastern regions. The oil is sent by pipe to cities on both coasts (the Red Sea and the Persian Gulf, called the Arabian Gulf in Arab countries). At the coastal cities, about 70 percent of the oil is exported. In 2012, crude oil accounted for 76 percent of Saudi Arabia's exports, and refined oil products another 9 percent.[9] Saudi Arabia's main export markets are China, Japan, South Korea, India, and Singapore. Altogether, 77 percent of Saudi Arabia's exports go to Asia.

China runs a trade deficit of $28 billion with Saudi Arabia and the Gulf States (and a larger trade deficit with oil-exporting countries in total). It earns the money to pay for its excess imports from oil-exporting countries by running a trade surplus with the United States. China has a huge trade surplus with the United States, $284 billion. Triangle trade explains only part of this surplus.[10] The United States, in turn, runs a balance of trade surplus with Saudi Arabia and the Gulf States of $25 billion.

Trade between High-Income Countries

While the theory of comparative advantage can be used to explain certain trade patterns in the world, it offers little insight into trade between high-income counties. Yet, trade between high-income countries constitutes a large majority of international of trade.

To a statistician, trade between high-income countries appears to involve the exchange of similar goods and services. An example is "vehicles and equipment" exported from Japan to the United States; and, "vehicles and equipment" exported from the United States to Japan. Another example is "Royalties" for entertainment products exported from Japan to the United States; and, "royalties" for entertainment products exported from the United States to Japan. To the statistician, there doesn't seem to be any reason for these exchanges.

But, to the consumer, these trade patterns make perfect sense. While Japan exports about $100 billion of vehicles to the United States, these are mainly small to mid-size automobiles. The United States, on the other hand, exports about $20 billion of large vehicles, airplanes, construction, agricultural and oil-producing equipment to Japan. Think of Toyota and Honda versus Boeing and Caterpillar. So, even though the statistician lumps all these products into the same category, they really are different products as far as consumers are concerned.

Among construction equipment manufacturers, Caterpillar of the United States is by far the world's largest, with $28 billion in sales in a recent year. Komatsu of Japan is solidly in the second place, with $17 billion. Rounding out the top ten are Sany and Zoomlion of China, Liebherr of Germany, Hitachi of Japan, Doosan of South Korea, Volvo of Sweden, and Deere and Terex of the United States, with sales ranging from $5 to 8 billion. These companies produce and sell construction equipment in many countries, competing with each other in terms of price, quality, financing, delivery, service, and in other ways.

With regard to entertainment products, Disney and Time-Warner—the two largest American companies in the entertainment industry—generate large fractions of their earnings from foreign markets. Sony, a Japanese firm, likewise generates a large fraction of its earnings internationally. But, regardless of how the statistician labels entertainment products, consumers like watching *different* movies and television shows, listening to *different* songs, and playing *different* video games.

Paul Krugman of Princeton University was awarded the Nobel Prize in Economics in 2008 for developing a theory of international trade that involves

- increasing economies of scale,
- cost of transportation, and
- consumer preference for variety.

With these conditions, production will tend, *on the one hand*, to be concentrated in only a few places in order to take advantage of economies of scale. But, *on the other hand*, production will also tend to be spread around the world, in order to minimize the cost of transportation. How these two opposite forces are resolved will continually change with changes in economies of scale in production and in the cost of transportation.

In former times, the cost of transportation was relatively high. For most goods, the distance over which trade occurred was short. Long-distance or international trade was restricted to the most precious commodities in terms of weight and volume. The high cost of transportation resulted in relatively little specialization. So, local economies were not much integrated with the global economy.

Advances in transportation can be seen in the evolution of boats. The first were made out of reeds, or papyrus, bundled and lashed together. The capacity of these boats was severely limited, and they had very little ability to travel against the current. But, with boats like these, the merchants of Sumer traded with the people in what is today western Iraq and eastern Turkey, traveling along the Tigris and Euphrates rivers.

With larger boats facilitated by the use of wood and with the development of sails, the Phoenicians and their counterparts on the Arabian Peninsula navigated the coastal waters of the Indian Ocean and turned the Mediterranean Sea into a lake of trade. But, wind power has its limitations. Winds are intermittent. And, so, large boats required a large crew of rowers for their primary source of power. The Roman galley that came to dominate the Mediterranean was sometimes referred to as a slave ship, as that was the status of the rowers. Even with slaves, the Roman galley was expensive to operate. In the case of a Viking boat, the large crew doubled as a fighting force.

The Spanish Galleon represented a breakthrough in shipping for the west, an all-sail boat.[11] Without the need for rowers, this type of boat could operate with a much smaller crew relative to its capacity. With an all-sail boat, the captain angles the sails in order travel in a desired direction regardless of the direction of the wind. Sailboats can even sail against the wind by "tacking" alternately to the left and to the right.

With knowledge of the prevailing winds, captains can chart courses so as to be mostly aided by the wind, taking advantage of the trade wind and the great swirls in the oceans. For example, to travel from Europe to the Americas by riding the Canary Current to the southwest, and then catching North Equatorial Current west. On the way back to Europe, the captain would veer to the north to catch the Gulf Stream. This is apparently what Christopher Columbus did on his voyage of 1492 to the Americas. On the way back, he was becalmed and he re-routed his boats to the north.[12]

During the 19th century, the age of all-sail boats was replaced by the age of (coal-powered) steamboats. And, during the 20th century, the age of steamboats was replaced by the age of diesel-powered boats. Today's bulk and containerized cargo ships operate with miniscule crews. They sail at an average speed of something like 24 knots per hour, and load and unload at docks very quickly. The cost of transportation has fallen so much, that most of the raw cotton produced in the United States is shipped overseas to be woven into cloth and then sewn into clothes. Many of the items of clothing are then returned to the United States for sale at retail. The reason for this circuitous supply chain is that the comparative advantage of other countries in low-wage manufacturing is greater than the cost of transportation.

Porter's Theory of Competitive Advantage

Krugman's model is well able to explain the *pattern of* trade observed between high-income countries. However, it does not speak much to *the specifics* of trade. Why do companies produce the particular varieties that they do? And, for that matter, how do these varieties come into existence? For matters such as these, we can refer to the theory of competitive advantage developed by Michel Porter of Harvard University.

> *Competitive Advantage*: A firm can have a *cost-advantage* (this is the traditional advantage) when it can produce a product or service for consumers at a lower unit cost than its competitors. A firm can have a *differentiation-advantage* when it can, at a profit, produce a product or service that results in greater value to its consumers than can its competitors.

How do firms gain a competitive advantage? One way is to have an advantage in resources; for example, (1) exclusive access to low-cost supplies or labor, (2) a patent, copyright, or some other proprietary advantage, or (3) the ability to produce at a large-enough volume to more fully utilize economies of scale. Another way is to better match the preferences of consumers through product differentiation; or, to use Porter's terminology, by "positioning" the product in the market. This refers to the entire process of product development, distribution, and promotion. Differentiated products and services have brand names, supported by a logo, perhaps also supported by advertising and packaging, so that consumers instantly recognize them. Among construction equipment manufacturers, Caterpillar paints its equipment yellow, Deere green and Massey-Ferguson red. To an engineer, the purpose of the paint is to prevent rust. To a businessman, it is also to communicate the brand. An economist, who entertains himself with abstract supply and demand curves, might not even know about rust.

Usually, firms gain a competitive advantage (as opposed to merely discovering that they have a competitive advantage) through a process of identifying (1) their natural or inherited advantages, and (2) investments that further develop their advantages until they are competitive at the level they need to be (local, regional or global). These investments can include investments in human capital, in infrastructure and physical capital, and in research and development. In theory, firms can gain a competitive advantage simply through investments, without any significant, initial advantage; but, in practice, they usually build on some natural or inherited strength.

In addition to firms discovering or gaining competitive advantages, so too do places. A city such as Philadelphia initially found itself in competition with other cities to become the financial capital of the newly organized United States. Then, by reason of the main office of the Bank of the United States being in Philadelphia, it emerged as the nation's first financial capital. Later, after the opening of the Erie Canal and the development of the economic potential of the Mohawk Valley of New York State, New York City became a rival to Philadelphia. When the Bank of the United States failed, New York City took over as the nation's financial capital. And, so, when the centralization of trading shares of corporate ownership was made possible by the telegraph, the stock market became centralized in New York City.

The competitive advantage of New York City in finance was strengthened by the reputation of its courts for fair treatment of the parties to financial contracts, by taxation and regulation that were sensitive to the interests of the industry, by the location decisions of commercial and investment banks, and by highly regarded schools of business. For a time, New York City displaced London as the most important financial center in the world.[13]

The advantages that come from the co-location of many firms in an area are known as economies of agglomeration. In the case of New York City, the original impetus for being a financial center (the trade associated with its port, especially after the Erie Canal opened up) is long gone. It is simply because it has been a financial center for so long that it remains one today.

Summary

- The theory of comparative advantage indicates that trade depends on relative differences in productivity. A country can be more productive in all industries and yet still have an incentive to specialize and trade if it has greater superiority in some industries relative to its superiority in other industries.
- There is mutual benefit to trade. All countries that engage in trade benefit.
- Large differences in prices, after adjustment for exchange, probably indicate potential gains from trade.
- While there may be extraordinary profits to the first companies that engage in trade, the tendency with trade is to eliminate extraordinary profits. While the first trading companies to take advantage of large differences in price make large profits, eventually trading companies only make a fair rate of return.
- The tendency, with trade, is for prices to reflect exchange rates and the cost of transportation.
- While all countries benefit from trade, there are sectors within each country where the owners of factors of production whose productivity is specific to that sector lose. These sectors are the shrinking sectors of each country.
- Even though there are losers, when countries become integrated into the global economy, unemployment rates are much lower in countries with more open economies.
- Because of triangle trade (among other reasons), trade does not have to balance between pairs of countries.
- Trade flows nowadays are much more complex than was imagined in the original development of the law of comparative advantage. In particular, there are now two ways to invest savings: human capital as well as physical capital, with high-income countries being knowledge-based and

service-oriented, and middle-income countries being physical capital-based and manufacturing-oriented.
- In addition, trade between high-income countries mostly consists of differentiated goods, meaning goods that are similar to each other but feature differences meaningful to consumers.
- Companies discover and/or make their competitive advantage.
- For some companies, their competitive advantage consists of producing at low cost.
- For other companies, their competitive advantage consists of better matching their products to the preferences of their customers.
- Not only companies, but places such as cities discover and/or make their competitive advantage.
- Although not developed in the chapter, this is also true of us as individuals.

NOTES

1. David Ricardo, *On the Principles of Political Economy and Taxation* (New York: Dent, 1973 [1817]).

2. ibid.

3. It is presumed that the exchange rate is fixed at 1£ equals $5.

4. Peter T. Leeson, "An-arrgh-chy: The Law and Economics of Pirate Organization," *Journal of Political Economy* 115 (2007): 1049–1094.

5. From an ancient Greek word for an amount of money. A talent of silver represented something like twenty years wages for a common worker.

6. Under certain conditions, free trade in goods can result in factor-price equalization. In particular, with free trade, wages (for comparable labor) and the rate of return on capital will also be governed by the law of one price. This result was independently proven by Paul A. Samuelson, "International Trade and the Equalization of Factor Prices," *Economic Journal* 58:230 (1948): 163–184; and, Abba P. Lerner, "Factor Prices and International Trade," *Economica* 19:73 (1952): 1–15.

7. This is called the Stopler-Samuelson Theorem. Wolfgang Stopler and Paul A. Samuelson, "Protection and Real Wages," *Review of Economic Studies* 9:1 (1941): 58–73.

8. Trade Openness is based on the ratio of imports and exports to GDP. While there are some problems with this index, its use is rather common.

9. All figures are from the MIT Observatory of Economic Complexity.

10. There are two other parts to a complete explanation: the United States surplus in balance of services and the desire of China to acquire international reserves.

11. The Chinese have had all-sail boats since the 2nd century, known as junk boats. The word "junk" refers to the type of sail.

12. William D. Phillips and Carla Rahn Phillips, *The Worlds of Christopher Columbus* (New York: Cambridge University Press, 1992), pp. 107–108.

13. London has recently regained the top spot.

Chapter 4

Trade Policy

Among the reasons for the American Revolution was the restriction on trade protested by the Boston Tea Party. The colonists objected to being forced to buy tea only from the British East India Tea Company. The colonists desired instead to buy tea from the Dutch East India Tea Company, or possibly to engage the tea-producing places of Asia directly in trade.

Opposition to the tea monopoly reached a climax in Boston. One thing led to another and, on December 13, 1773, something like a hundred people, thinly disguised as American Indians, boarded the three ships in the harbor containing tea. About 7,000 people looked on. With prior coordination with the ship captains, the Tea Partiers threw the boxes of tea overboard, taking care not to damage the ships or the ships' other cargo.

It was not long after this incident that thirteen of the colonies of British North America stretching from Massachusetts and New Hampshire in the north to Georgia in the south declared themselves independent states.

But, soon after independence was secured, individual states of the confederation were imposing tariffs and otherwise interfering with trade with each other. For this and other reasons, a convention was assembled to draft a constitution for a federal republic, one in which the powers of government were to be shared between the state and national governments, and in which certain rights were to be guaranteed to the people. In this new, federal arrangement, the states were forbidden from imposing a tariff or in any other way interfering with interstate or international trade, and only the federal government was given the power of regulating interstate and international trade.

This chapter examines the history of trade policy in the United States from the U.S. Constitution through the General Agreement on Tariffs and Trade (GATT) (the next chapter will examine the course of trade policy since GATT). This chapter also looks at the key issues involved in trade policy.

These issues include protectionism, tax revenue, economic efficiency, and the "game" involved in trade policy.

THE WHIG TARIFFS

While the American Revolution and the U.S. Constitution both were based, in part, on free trade, the truth is the United States was not committed to free trade until relatively recently. Until relatively recently, tariffs have usually been high, and sometimes very high. And, the consequences of the high tariffs have sometimes been disastrous.

Tariff: A tax on imported goods. (A tariff is not applied on similar domestically produced goods.)

A *moderate tariff* can *both* raise revenue (because some goods will be imported and the tariff will be levied on these goods) *and* provide a small advantage to domestic producers.

A *high tariff* will not raise revenue (because no goods will be imported) and will give domestic-producers a shared monopoly over domestic sales.

As can be seen in Figure 4.1, from the ratification of the U.S. Constitution to 1828, there was an upward trend to tariff rates. This trend culminated in

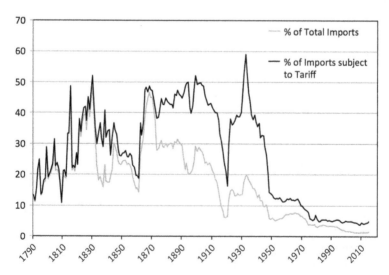

Figure 4.1   U.S. Tariff History. *Sources*: Created by author. 1790–1836—Douglas A. Irwin, "New Estimates of the Average Tariff of the United States, 1790–1820," *Journal of Economic History* 63 (2003): 506–513; 1837–1890—Historical Statistics of the United States, Millennial Edition, V. 5, Cambridge University Press, 2006; 1891–2015—U.S. International Trade Commission.

the Tariff of Abominations. By this time, the two issues that would eventually lead to the U.S. Civil War became clear: slavery and the tariff.

The manufacturers of the north sought to use the tariff to protect the emerging manufacturing industries of that region. The other people of the country were forced, by reason of the tariff, to buy the products of the northern manufacturers at high prices.

The planters of the south complained of the attempt of the north to exploit them; and, they became increasingly adamant in justifying slavery.

The tensions created within the country, due to slavery and the tariff, were seen by a number of observers of the new country. Foremost among them was the Frenchman Alexis de Tocqueville. De Tocqueville wrote a book, *Democracy in America,* following his tour of the country. "America is great," he famously said, "because America is good."

The country, de Tocqueville explained, was divided on the issues of slavery and the tariff. "Slavery," he said, "does not attack the American Union directly, in its interests, but indirectly, in its manners."[1] Specifically, the people of the north, not having slaves, developed the manners of men engaged in free enterprise. They were industrious, inclined to bargaining, and tolerant of others. The people of south, having slaves, were more interested in leisure, inclined to arguing, and arrogant.

The north, being oriented to capitalism, grew in wealth and population. While the states of the north and of the south started out about equal in wealth and population, by the time of the Civil War the northern states were much larger in both wealth and population. The people of the south, seeing the north grow in wealth and population, blamed the tariff. "If they discover a law of the Union which is not unequivocally favorable to their interests, they protest against it as an abuse of force . . . 'The Tariff,' said the inhabitants of Carolina in 1832, 'enriches the North and ruins the South.'"[2]

For the next thirty years, slavery and the tariff were two of the most important political issues. Most Democrats favored slavery and opposed the tariff. During these years, the Democrats tended to win the elections and, as Figure 4.1 shows, the tendency was for the tariff to be reduced. Most Whigs opposed slavery and favored the tariff. Politicians in both parties who aspired to national office, attempted to shade their positions so as to try to appeal to both northern and southern voters. But, by the 1850s, it was no longer possible to straddle the issue of slavery.

The Republican Tariffs

During the 1850s, a new political party was organized that immediately became one of the two major parties in the north. This was the Republican Party. The Republican Party clearly opposed slavery and—like the Whig Party—favored the tariff. When its second candidate for President, Abraham Lincoln, was elected in 1860, the states of the south seceded and the Civil War commenced. Lincoln is known as the Great Emancipator, and rightly so; but, as Figure 4.1 shows, the Republicans raised the tariff as well as freed the slaves.

For the next eighty years, the tariff was kept high on imports subject to tariff (even while the amount of goods not subject to tariff was increasing). In the pivotal election of 1896, the Republican speakers were told to "talk tariff, think tariff, dream tariff." The Republican candidate said of himself, "I am a tariff man, standing on a tariff platform."[3] Republicans appealed to working-men, arguing that their earnings, as well as the earnings of their employers, were protected by the tariff.

There was one exception to the trend of high tariffs. This exception was the eight-year period from 1913 to 1920 when the Democrats were in office. During this period, the country lowered the tariff and also added an amend-ment to the U.S. Constitution to prohibit the manufacture, sale or purchase of alcohol. To replace the tariff and the tax on alcohol, the federal government enacted an income tax.

The Smoot-Hawley Tariff

Following the election of 1920, the Republicans returned to office. As Figure 4.1 shows, they raised the tariff back up in two steps. The second increase was the Smoot-Hawley Tariff of 1930. This tariff, along with other policy blunders, pushed the country from a recession into the Great Depression. More than a thousand members of the economics profession signed a petition to ask the president to veto the bill. The petition claimed that the tariff would:

- Raise the cost of living;
- Hurt trade in general;
- Hurt farmers in particular;
- Result in retaliatory tariffs.

Nevertheless, the president signed the bill. He was, after all, a Republican.

For a short period of time, the high tariffs seemed to work. As Americans were forced to buy from domestic manufacturers, domestic manufacturers increased production and employment. But, other countries retaliated to the high tariffs on their exports to the United States by enacting similar high tariffs on the exports of the United States to their countries. This cut off our exports and hurt the farmers and ranchers of the country, as agricultural products were still our biggest export. The agricultural regions of the country were devastated. Marginal land was abandoned, and this contributed to "the Dust Bowl" of the 1930s.[4]

The Smoot-Hawley Tariff is considered by economists to be one of the great lessons provided by history of the importance of seeing the indirect effects of policy. An act designed to increase employment in domestic manufacturing had the result of reducing employment in agriculture, and of contributing to turning a recession into the Great Depression. This great lesson remains not much appreciated by most people, as is illustrated in a particular scene in the movie *Ferris Bueller's Day Off* in which Ben Stein plays a boring professor.

So, what exactly happened after Smoot-Hawley? First, as was expected in the legislation, imports fell. From a peak of $4.4 billion in 1929, imports fell to $1.3 billion in 1932. Second, as was foretold by the economists, exports also fell. Exports fell from $5.2 billion in 1929, to $1.6 billion in 1932. Exports fell hand-in-hand with the changes in imports, so that for every job protected by the Smoot-Hawley Tariff, approximately one job was destroyed.

Economists argue about the macroeconomic significance of the Smoot-Hawley Tariff. For some economists, the collapse of exports could not have been a major cause of the depression because, back in those days, trade was only a small part of U.S. GDP. For others, the collapse of trade was among the major causes of the depression not only because of its devastating impact on farmers, but because it weakened the rural banks of the country.

Reconstructing International Trade

In 1932, Franklin D. Roosevelt, a Democrat, was elected President. In keeping with the Democratic Party philosophy of that time, he sought to restore international trade. Because of the suspiciousness that ruled the world, due to the trade wars and also to the rise of fascism and communism in certain countries, Roosevelt did not seek to unilaterally reduce tariffs hoping that other nations would do likewise. Instead, he sought from Congress authority to negotiate tariff reductions with other countries on a reciprocal basis. With this authority, he began to restore trade.

Then, during World War II, the United States, the United Kingdom, and their allies began planning for the reconstruction of international trade and finance following the war. These negotiations led to two major agreements: the GATT and the Bretton Woods Agreement. The agreements will be covered in later chapters. The remainder of this chapter will develop a supply-and-demand type model to investigate the effects of tariffs and quotas.

TARIFFS

The first section of this chapter looked at the history of trade policy in the United States up to the Smoot-Hawley Tariff of 1930. The next chapter, Trade

Agreements, will examine trade policy from World War II until the present, taking a global, rather than an American perspective. This section examines the economic effects of a tariff, using a supply-and-demand approach.

Aside from causing depressions, wars, and slavery, tariffs have other, more mundane effects. These other effects involve price, production, consumption, consumer and producer surplus, revenue to the government, and economic efficiency. We can use standard supply and demand curves to identify these effects. We'll start with a country in autarky (i.e., with no international trade). In this case, supply is domestic supply and demand is domestic demand. Their intersection, given by the dot in Figure 4.2, gives the equilibrium quantity produced and consumed (necessarily equal, since the country is in autarky) and the equilibrium price. There is more.

Consumer surplus can be identified as the area between price and the demand curve; and, and producer surplus (or profit contribution) as the area between the supply curve and price. These areas are shown in light gray and dark gray in Figure 4.2. Consumer surplus plus producer surplus is equal to social surplus. It is the total gain from domestic trade. Why are the shaded areas consumer and producer surplus? Consider the last unit produced and consumed, unit number Qe. Its marginal utility is given by the height of the demand curve at Qe. But, this is also the price. So the consumer of Qe derives no increment to utility from its purchase. For the consumer, Qe is a break-even proposition.

The marginal cost of the last unit produced and consumed is given by the height of the supply curve at Qe. But, this is also the price. So, the producer of Qe also derives no increment to profit from its sale. For the producer as well as the consumer, Qe is a break-even proposition.

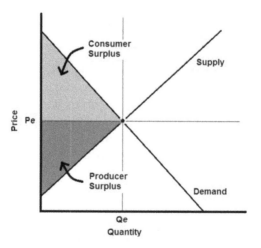

Figure 4.2   Consumer and Producer Surplus. *Source*: Created by author.

Now consider a unit produced and consumed somewhere between unit number 1 and unit number Qe. Its marginal utility is given by the height of the demand curve, which is higher than price. The difference is the increment to utility to the consumer of purchasing that unit. By similar reasoning, the increment to utility to the consumer of purchasing each unit from unit number 1 to unit number Qe is the sum of the heights of the demand curve above price. And, the total increment to utility to the consumer of purchasing all of these units is the area shaded in light gray.

Likewise, the total increment to profit contribution to the producer of selling all of these units is the area shaded in dark gray. With this standard model of supply and demand, we are in position to examine the effects of international trade.

To make the analysis as simple as possible, we'll assume that the good is available in the world market at price Pw (in economic jargon, that world supply is infinitely elastic at price Pw). In this case, domestic supply, Qf, is read off the supply curve at price Pw; and, domestic demand, Qg, is read off the demand curve, likewise at price Pw.

Notice that domestic consumption, Qg, is greater than domestic production, Qf. The difference is provided by imports. The country imports $Qg - Qf$ units of the good. Domestic production has decreased and consumption has increased, because the world price, Pw, is less than what had been the price in autarky. The gap that opened up has been filled by imports.

Consumer surplus with free trade has increased. This increase is due in part to consumers being able to buy the units they had been buying (from unit number 1 to unit number Qe) at the lower, world price. The increase is also due in part to the consumer surplus on the additional units being consumed.

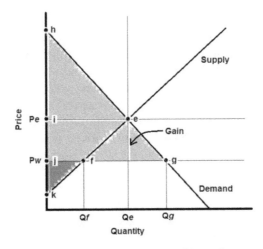

Figure 4.3 Equilibrium in Free Trade. *Source*: Created by author.

This part of the increase in consumer surplus is the light gray-shaded triangle above the quantities Qe and Qg.

While consumer surplus has increased, producer surplus has decreased. Producer surplus has decreased by the four-sided area denoted by the intersection of the lines associated with Pe and Pw with the vertical axis and the line associated with the supply curve.[5] This part of what was social surplus in autarky is transferred from producers to consumers.

Carefully comparing social surplus with free trade before and after free trade, the gain from international trade is the triangle indicated by the three dots e, f, and g, and is part of the new consumer surplus.

The above case involves the shrinking sector of a country's economy. Notice that even in this sector, there an increase in social surplus. Specifically, consumer surplus expands *by more* than producer surplus shrinks. In the expanding sector of a country's economy, there is another increase in social surplus. In that sector, the increase in producer surplus is more than the decrease in consumer surplus.

Economic Analysis of Tariffs

Having first developed the standard supply and demand model and then applying it to the case of free trade, the effects of a tariff are now examined. In this case, a moderate tariff—one that does not completely cut off international trade—will be analyzed.

Figure 4.4 features a tariff in the amount T. This tariff raises the domestic price from the world price, Pw to Pw + T. What makes this tariff a moderate tariff is that it is less than Pe – Pw. If the tariff were equal to or greater than Pe – Pw, the tariff would completely cut off international trade, and the country would return to autarky.

With price raised to Pw + T, domestic producers expand production to Qm. Also, quantity demanded falls to Qn. Necessarily, imports fall, to Qn – Qm.

Consumer surplus, the light gray-shaded area, shrinks relative to free trade. And, producer surplus, the dark gray-shaded area, expands.

Not all the consumer surplus that is lost is gained by producers. There are two areas associated with the loss of consumer surplus that are not gained by producers: the black rectangle and the two striped triangles. First, the black rectangle will be identified and, then, the striped triangles will be identified.

The black rectangle is gained by the government in revenue. On each unit that is imported, the tariff is collected. Since the quantity Qn – Qm is the number of units that are imported, and T is the amount of the tariff, revenue is equal to T times (Qn – Qm), which is reflected in the area of the black rectangle.

The striped triangles are the deadweight loss. They represent the loss of consumer surplus that is neither gained by producers nor by the government.

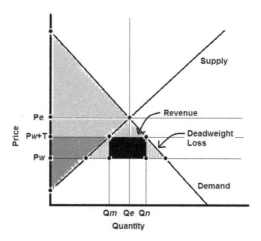

Figure 4.4 Economic Effects of a Tariff. *Source*: Created by author.

Negative Side Effects of Taxes

Most taxes have negative side effects. Income taxes reduce the incentive to work. Property taxes reduce the incentive to save. Sales taxes place a tax burden on the poor that, by most people's views, is inequitable.[6] So, just because tariffs have negative side effects (the deadweight loss), doesn't necessarily mean tariffs are bad. You would have to compare the negative side effects of tariffs to the negative side effects of other sources of the revenue needed by government.

In addition to the usual concern of economists to minimize the total negative side effects of taxes, some developing countries have administrative difficulties assessing income taxes. For them, tariffs and certain excise taxes (e.g., a tax on electricity) are the only practical sources of revenue.

Tariffs that are very high generate no revenue. The protection very high tariffs provide to domestic producers comes at a deadweight loss of the entire gain from international trade. Conceptually, a tariff of zero generates no revenue and a tariff of Pe – Pw also generates no revenue. Somewhere in between, T*, is the *revenue-maximizing tariff*. Where exactly is T* might not be known. But, it can be supposed T* is somewhere in the middle of (0, Pe – Pw). A tariff that is less than T* can be justified on the basis of the revenue it is generating for the government. A tariff that is greater than T* should, in the absence of some special consideration, be opposed since it generates less revenue and more deadweight loss than T*.

Case Study: Steel Tariffs of 2002

There was a time when steel production was a major part of the U.S. economy. In large part, this reflected a great natural advantage: (1) iron deposits in Minnesota and (2) coal deposits in West Virginia. The iron was mined, transported by railroad a short distance from the Missabe Range to Duluth, Minnesota, and then sent by ship via the Great Lakes to Cleveland, Ohio. From Cleveland, the iron would be sent by railroad or barge canal to Pittsburgh, Pennsylvania. The coal was mined in West Virginia, and then sent to Pittsburgh by railroad. When the railroad cars were loaded, they were basically going downhill from West Virginia to Pittsburgh. When they were sent back, from Pittsburgh to West Virginia, they were empty. The movement of the iron ore from Minnesota to Pittsburgh was mostly over water, and, therefore, inexpensive. The movement of the coal from West Virginia to Pittsburgh was mostly downhill, and, again, inexpensive. Although one might think that Pittsburgh is far from both the iron deposits in Minnesota and the coal deposits in West Virginia, it was actually in a strategic place relative to the two. Pittsburgh became a great steel-making town. But, as the iron deposits of the Missabe Range thinned out, so too did steel-making in Pittsburgh. The locus of steel-making today is in various coastal cities of the world where iron and coal from anyplace can be sent over water.

During the late 20th century, steel-making in the United States fell into decline. This proved difficult for the workers, capitalists, and communities involved in steel-making and its associated industries. Jobs and fortunes were lost, and property values declined. Relief was sought from government. In 2002, during the administration of President George W. Bush, relief was proposed in the form of a temporary increase in the tariffs on steel. Tariffs on steel products were to be increased from a range of 0 to 1 percent to a range of 8 to 30 percent for a period of three years. The tariff increases were proposed on March 5, 2002, and took effect on March 20. The tariff increases were, of course, supported by the steelworkers union and steel-making corporations. They were opposed by steel-using industries such as the National Association of Manufacturers. But, the tariff increases were not opposed by the public at large. In spite of the economic analysis presented in this section, showing that consumers are losers with tariffs, most people think "protecting American jobs" is a good idea.

The increased tariffs on steel were not unnoticed by foreign producers. Steel producers in Europe asked their government for relief, and the European Union filed a grievance with the World Trade Court. The stated reason for the tariffs was that American steel producers were suffering an emergency. The World Trade Court decided otherwise, and authorized the European Union to impose retaliatory tariff increases in proportion to the economic losses their steel producers suffered by reason of the U.S. steel tariff increases. The European Union then threated to raise its tariffs on cars from Michigan and oranges from Florida. On December 3, 2003, the U.S. president rescinded the tariff increases.

It is possible that the Bush administration was aware, all the while, that the World Trade Court was going to authorize retaliatory tariffs, effectively forcing it to return the tariffs on steel to their former levels. Nevertheless, the administration could "buy some time" for the industry. As it is, the higher steel tariffs were in place for about a year-and-a-half. This way, the Bush administration could say they tried to do something for the industry, but was prevented by the World Trade Court.

As things turned out, soon after the rescinding of the tariff increases, the global price of iron increased, and there was a return of prosperous times to iron mining in Minnesota. Iron mining today is much different from iron mining a hundred years ago. Today, iron mining is no longer labor intensive. Rather, enormous mechanical scoopers and trucks are used to haul ore from the iron pits. And, while most of the high-grade iron ore was hauled away long ago, with new technologies, it is economical to mine the low-grade ore that remains.

QUOTAS

The prior section developed a model for the analysis of a tariff. This section uses basically the same model to analyze the economic effects of a quota. This section also discusses *why* quotas are sometimes employed.

Quota: A quantitative restriction on imported goods. Quotas are often initially assigned to foreign producers based on their prior shares of the domestic market.

The effects of a quota are similar to the effects of a tariff with one important exception. With a quota, what would be revenue to the government with a tariff is, instead, a subsidy to the foreign producer. The prior figure, Figure 4.4, illustrates the effects of a quota in the amount $Qn - Qm$. A quota in the amount $Qn - Qm$ is the equivalent of a tariff in the amount T except that the area of the black rectangle should be relabeled as "foreign subsidy." With a quota, the domestic price is higher than the world price, but there is no revenue to the government. The foreign producers who are awarded the quotas simply receive the higher price. This higher price is an extra profit for them.

But, why would a government use quotas as part of its trade policy when the real beneficiaries of quotas are foreign producers? To answer this question, it is useful to first consider retaliatory tariffs. Do you remember the discussion in the first section of this chapter of the retaliatory tariffs enacted by countries in response to the Smoot-Hawley Tariff of 1930? Why did those countries enact the retaliatory tariffs? It was to do to the United States what the United States did to them. The United States used tariffs to restrict their products from entering our market, so they used tariffs to similarly restrict our products from entering their markets. The exact way that this happened is that the specific foreign manufacturers who were hurt by our tariff petitioned their governments for some form of relief. Their government, then, acted to provide this relief in the form of a retaliatory tariff.

To be sure, foreign producers are not the only people who are hurt by a tariff. Domestic consumers are also hurt. They are forced to buy products at the high price $Pw + T$ that, in free trade, would be available at the low price Pw. Consumer surplus is reduced by the tariff from the area of the light gray triangle shown on Figure 4.3 to the area of the light gray triangle shown in Figure 4.4. Possibly, if consumers were aware of how their interests were being affected, they would oppose the enactment of tariffs. But, few consumers understand economics. Many of them, in fact, actually favor protectionism. It saves jobs, they think.

So, there is only one effective check on tariffs, and that is the possibility of foreign producers petitioning their governments for some form of relief, which will probably mean a retaliatory tariff. This is where quotas come in.

Public Opinion Regarding Trade

Surveys indicate that, since 2011, Americans have been close to evenly divided regarding international trade. About as many favor trade as oppose it. And, by a wide margin, Americans are of the belief that trade destroys jobs.

Support or opposition to trade is indicated by questions in public opinion surveys such as (from the NBC News/*Wall Street Journal* poll): "In general, do you think that free trade between the United States and foreign countries has helped the United States, has hurt the United States, or has not made much of a difference either way?" And (from the Gallup Poll): "What do you think foreign trade means for America? Do you see foreign trade more as an opportunity for economic growth through increased U.S. exports or a threat to the economy from foreign imports?"

Public opinion regarding the effect of trade on jobs is indicated by questions such as (from the *Investor's Business Daily*/TIPP poll): "Do you believe that free trade between the U.S and other countries creates more jobs in the U.S, loses more jobs in the U.S, or do you think it makes no difference one way or the other?"

Since it started to be measured, American public opinion regarding trade has usually been moderately positive. It turned negative, however, during the tough times surrounding the Financial Crisis of 2008, and has since only rebounded to neutral.

By the way, the correct answers to the questions: (1) Trade offers mutual benefit. All countries (as a whole) engaged in trade benefit. (2) Trade both destroys jobs and creates jobs. It destroys jobs in the shrinking sector of the economy, in industries where other countries have a comparative advantage;

Table 4.1 American Public Opinion Regarding Trade, 1947–2017

	[1]	% Favoring Trade—Opposing Trade [2]	[1]	% Say Trade Creates Jobs—It Destroys Jobs
Avg. 1947–1989	5	20		
Avg. 1990–1992	8	−7		
Avg. 1993–1995	30	9		
Avg. 1996–1999	36	13	12	−19
Avg. 2000–2006	66	14	19	−20
Avg. 2007–2010	69	−12	7	−36
Avg. 2011–2017	28	3		

[1] number of polls; [2] excludes trade specifically with non-democratic countries.
Sources: Created by the author with data from PollingReport.com, American Enterprise Institute and Roper Center.

and, it creates jobs in the expanding sector of the economy, in industries where the United States has a comparative advantage.

The "Game" involved in Quotas

With a quota, the government can provide domestic producers with the same advantage of higher prices that can be provided with a tariff; and, can prevent foreign producers from petitioning their governments for relief, which will avoid a retaliatory tariff. Even though the foreign producers will be forced to reduce the quantity of their exports from the free trade amount to the quota amount, they will make a higher price on each unit they allowed to sell. This can result in increased profits for them.

With a quota, domestic producers get the high prices they want, foreign producers are bought off, and most consumers are either unaware of what is going on or support the policy because they believe it will save jobs. What could be better?

Aside from the problems that quotas are inefficient and unfair relative to tariffs, there are some practical problems with quotas in the long run:

- Foreign producers will open production facilities within the country to compete with domestic producers.
- Foreign producers not subject to the quota will fill the gap between what would be domestic demand and domestic production at the world price.
- The potential profits from the award of quotas will be spent on lobbying the government by the businesses seeking the award.

Quotas and certain other interferences with trade became popular during the 1970s, when average tariff rates had become quite low.[7] Quotas, often described as "export restraints," were adopted by many countries and covered many goods. Many countries continue to have quotas on agricultural goods and textiles, and attempts to restrict quotas on textiles and on agricultural goods have not been successful.

Quotas are popular mainly because they serve the interests of domestic producers, who are very much aware of their interests. Consumers, who are harmed by quotas, are generally unaware of or confused about their interests. Quotas, furthermore, avoid retaliation by buying off potential opposition from foreign producers. In the long run, the profits from quotas are largely spent on lobbying efforts to gain or retain the quotas. This lobbying effort, of course, serves the interests of politicians. Thus, everybody involved is taking advantage of the situation, other than consumers who are unaware what is going on.

Case Study: Japanese Automobiles

Ronald Reagan, who served as U.S. president from 1981 to 1988, had a mixed record on international trade. While he advanced international trade through certain multinational and regional agreements, he also engaged in protectionism.[8] In particular, Reagan persuaded the Japanese to impose a "Voluntary Export Restraint" on automobiles. The original agreement limited Japanese exports of cars to the United States to 1.68 million per year. The voluntary export restraint was subsequently extended several times, at higher numbers of cars.

In line with our model of quotas, the agreement increased the prices of cars and the profits of Japanese automobile manufacturers, as well as increased the prices of cars, the profit, the number of cars produced, and employment by American automobile manufacturers. The cost to the American consumer is estimated to have totaled $5.8 billion, or about $105,000 per job saved in the domestic industry. Furthermore, there was no real protest by consumers. In fact, the policy was politically popular.

Also in line with the discussion of the long-run consequences of quotas, other foreign manufacturers not subject to the voluntary export restraint entered the U.S. market; namely, Korean automobile manufacturers.

Also, in the long run, Japanese automobiles opened production facilities in the United States. Today, more cars are produced in the United States by foreign companies than are produced in the United States by American companies.

One more thing: In 2009, two of the three American automobile manufacturers went bankrupt and had to be bailed out by the U.S. government.

Embargos

A quota is a refusal to import. An embargo is a refusal to export. Examples include an embargo by the United States on trade with Cuba because of human rights violations, and an embargo by the United States on trade with South Africa prior to the end of apartheid, also because of human rights violations.

In the case of the U.S. embargo of Cuba, this policy may have made some sense when Fidel Castro first gained control of the country. By disrupting or threatening to disrupt existing trade patterns, the United States might have gotten the new government to make some small concessions (such as allowing the International Red Cross to visit political prisoners). But, as time passed, the new government was able to develop alternative trade patterns that made trade with the United States inconsequential. If anything, the continuing U.S. embargo of Cuba has proven to be counter-productive, as it provides the Cuban government with a convenient excuse for every shortcoming of the country.

In the case of the U.S. embargo of South Africa, the policy may have been somewhat effective because of its limited scope and objectives. For one thing, the United States never instituted a full-blown embargo, but only threatened to do so and, from time to time, instituted selective sanctions. For another thing, the United States remained heavily involved in the South African economy and society through trade, investment, and cultural exchange. It is fair to say that the United States played a constructive role in the eventual end of apartheid in South Africa but, of course, the lion's share of the credit must go to the South Africans.

The attempt to apply economic analysis to embargos seems to miss the point. Trade is mutually advantageous. Refusing to engage in trade, whether through quotas or embargos, means the nation is hurting itself. But, the embargo hurts the other country. The country imposing the embargo is willing to deny to itself a gain from trade in order to deny to the other country a gain from trade, in order to persuade the other country to change some aspect of its behavior. Yet, experience shows that embargos usually are not effective in persuading the other country to change. What is going on?

We should consider that at least part of what is happening, and perhaps all of what is happening is that the country imposing the embargo is making a statement of its values. In the case of human rights violations in Cuba or in South Africa prior to the end of apartheid, the United States' embargo was partly a statement of its values. But, wouldn't international trade, investment, and cultural exchange be more effective in promoting values? And, shouldn't we be concerned with the actual effectiveness of promoting our values, instead of being satisfied merely in making statements of our values?

Defense and Trade Policy

The final topic of this chapter concerns the connection between defense and trade policy. Following World War II, the world was divided into two great trading blocs: the United States and its allies and the Soviet Union and its allies. In Western Europe, the NATO (North Atlantic Treaty Alliance) military alliance was paralleled by the European Economic Community. In Eastern Europe, the Warsaw Pact military alliance was paralleled by the Council for Mutual Economic Assistance (COMECON). Throughout the world, relations were established with developing nations by one or the other trading bloc. Iraq, for example, was a client of the Soviet Union; and, Iran, a client of the United States. All of these things have dramatically changed. According to Joanne Gowa, the post–World War II connections between defense policy and trade policy were not unusual. "Because trade generates security externalities," she says, "free and non-discriminatory trade may not be optimal for states in an anarchic international system."[9]

Because of the concern of nations for their defense, they are inclined to become parts of great nations, if they are not large; or, to join into credible defense alliances, when faced with a military threat. Today, we see this principle in reverse in Europe. Because of a growing democratic spirit, the credibility of defense by alliance, and the reduction of military threats, there is a growth of nationalist movements in Europe. The people of regions such as the Dutch-speaking part of Belgium (the province of Flanders), the Basque region of Spain, and Scotland seek greater autonomy, if not complete independence.

For a nation or alliance of nations to feel secure, it must feel that it can sustain its industrial base as well as its military, in the event that a war disrupts its access to resources needed by its military. Therefore, the nation or alliance of nations may feel that it needs factories and raw materials, in order to defend itself during a war.

Japan, for example, feels it needs to maintain its domestic rice industry through high tariffs and strict quotas, so it could feed itself if necessary. During World War II, our submarines starved the people of Japan. Obviously, Japan could make a big gain from trade by importing rice, releasing its rice paddies for development. But, the memory of hunger is very long.

Nations whose economies become very specialized, to the point where these nations would lack certain abilities to defend themselves if trade were cut off, may indeed feel they need protectionist policies. But, there are some alternatives to protectionism that should be considered. One of these alternatives is a *strategic reserve*. Countries can invest in stockpiles of certain metals and other commodities that are usually imported, but which might be cut off during a war. Actually, stockpiles are not simply a concern of national defense. They are important for a variety of concerns for emergency preparedness, such as natural disasters and public health, as well as defense. Countries can also invest in reserve industrial capacity. These would be facilities normally in use for other purposes, or maintained in a dormant state ("mothballed") that could be called upon if necessary during a war or some other emergency.

In the case of rice cultivation in Japan, it might be better for that country to normally import the rice it consumes and invest in rice storage facilities sufficient for the expected period of a war or other emergency. In fairness, even though there may be a gain from trade, defense is a legitimate function of government, and the feeling of being secure is itself very important.

Summary

- The American Revolution and the U.S. Constitution were both based, in part, on free trade. Yet, the United States had a mixed record on trade until relatively recently.
- Soon after the formation of the United States, the political party that represented the manufacturers of the north sought to have high tariffs, while the political party that represented the farmers of the south, opposed high tariffs. Thus, the tariff led to sectional strife in the country and, along with slavery, was a cause of the Civil War.
- Following the Civil War, for about eighty years, the tariff remained one of the most important political issues. Then, in 1930, the Smoot-Hawley Tariff was enacted raising the tariff on goods subject to tariff to the highest level in the nation's history.
- For a short period of time, the Smoot-Hawley Tariff seemed to work, as domestic manufacturers enjoyed increased orders for their goods, and raised production and employment. Then, as foreign countries enacted retaliatory tariffs, demand for U.S. agricultural products fell. The rural economy collapsed and the nation fell from a recession into a depression.
- In general, there is a gain from trade even in the shrinking sector of the economy, as lower prices increase consumer surplus more than they decrease producer surplus.
- A moderate tariff reduces the gain from trade. It lowers consumer surplus. Part of the lost consumer surplus is transferred to producers, part is transferred to the government as revenue, and part is lost to all.
- The part that is lost to all is called the deadweight loss.
- The fact that there is a deadweight loss is not proof that moderate tariffs are bad. The inefficiency of this tax would have to be compared to the inefficiencies of other taxes.
- But, tariffs that are higher than the revenue-maximizing tariff are bad. From the standpoint of social surplus, they have a deadweight loss that is not justified by raising revenue for the government.
- Quotas are very similar to tariffs, except that what would be revenue to the government with a tariff is a transfer to foreign producers.
- As to why such an inefficient and unfair policy would ever be adopted, it is because consumers are usually unaware of what is going on. Domestic producers gain the advantage of protectionism and buy off the only group

with that might oppose them (the foreign producers). And, the politicians gain from the lobbying efforts of both domestic and foreign producers.

- In the long run, quotas are usually undermined by such things as the opening of production facilities within the country by foreign producers and by new foreign producers entering the market.
- Embargos are usually not very effective. Continued trade, investment, and cultural exchange may be more effective.
- It is not unusual for trade policy to be connected to defense policy.

NOTES

1. Alexis de Tocqueville, *Democracy in America*, vol. 1 (London: Longwood, Green & Co., 1875), p. 404.

2. Ibid, pp. 410–401.

3. R. Hal Williams, *Realigning America: McKinley, Bryan, and the Remarkable Election of 1896* (Lawrence, KS: University Press of Kansas, 2010), p. 139.

4. For many, the Dust Bowl was merely the result of unusually warm temperatures and drought. Yet, farmers and ranchers are always in a struggle with nature. When they are profitable, more land is brought into production; and, when they are not profitable, nature reclaims land.

5. In U.S. English, a four-sided figure with two parallel sides is called a trapezoid.

6. Prior to Karl Marx, most scholars said taxes should be proportional to wealth or income above the subsistence level. For example, in Christianity, there is the idea of the tithe, or 10 percent of the "increase" or change in wealth from one year to another. In Islam, there is the idea of zakat involving fixed-proportions of various kinds of wealth. Influenced by Marx, some scholars say that taxes should be of increasing percentages depending on one's total income or wealth. Still, there is the idea that the poor are to be fully or partially exempt from tax.

7. See Jagdish Bhagwati, *Protectionism* (Cambridge, MA: MIT Press, 1988); and, Jan Tumlir, *Protectionism: Trade Policy in Democratic Societies* (Washington, DC: American Enterprise Institute, 1985).

8. William Niskanan, *Reagonomics: An Insider's Account of the Policies and the People* (New York: Oxford University Press, 1988), who served on President Reagan's Council of Economic Advisors, has a surprisingly even-handed discussion of Reagan's trade policy.

9. Joanne Gowa, *Allies, Adversaries and International Trade* (Princeton, NJ: Princeton University Press, 1994), p. 7.

Chapter 5

Trade Agreements

The Grand Canal of China was constructed over a period of 1,000 years, from about 500 BC to about AD 500. The canal eventually connected Beijing in the north, which became the capital city of the country after it was unified, with Hangzhou in the south, a distance of 1,776 kilometers (1,104 miles). The canal is mostly a "lateral canal" (i.e., featuring only modest changes in elevation), between the two great rivers of China, the Yellow River in the north, and the Yangtze River in the south. The Grand Canal facilitated commerce between the north and south of China, as well as communication and troop movements.

The original parts of the canal, the standardization of the width of carts, the standardization of written language, and the development of a post office all helped to unite the several states from which China was formed. And with the unification of China came a time of rapid economic growth, scientific progress, expressiveness in the arts, and military power. It was a golden age. Then, over many years, because of corruption and war, this golden age came to an end.

Similarly, during the rise of the Roman Empire and during the rise of Islam, there were golden ages. The spread of the Roman Empire throughout the Mediterranean region and the Middle East allowed the people of diverse cultures and circumstances to interact with each other. The Roman army suppressed pirates and other criminals, enabling the people in the very large region to engage in trade and cultural exchange. The language of the Romans, Latin, became the language of business. Roman law governed contracts. The Roman silver denarius became the standard of value. The Romans borrowed from the knowledge and cultures of the many people with whom they came into contact, among these people were civilizations that had long predated Rome.

Corruption and war eventually led to the fall of Rome. During the period of decline, St. Augustine of North Africa commented on the moral decay he saw taking place. He distinguished the City of God from the City of Man. The City of God is holy, while the City of Man is corrupt. In concept, these are different cities. But, the cities that actually exist are partly one and partly the other. In his old age, barbarians from Germany were overrunning his province, as well as overrunning much of the western part of the Roman Empire. Augustine blamed the fall of the Roman Empire on moral decay and called for religious revival.

In parallel fashion, the spread of Islam was a golden age. During the first several hundred years following the death of the Prophet Mohammed, Islam spread from the Arabian Peninsula to Persia in the east and to North Africa in the west. Islam enabled the people in this very large region to interact with each other. The Arabic language became the shared language of the region. Islamic law governed contracts. The Islamic silver dirham became the standard of value. The Arabs borrowed from the knowledge and cultures of the many people with whom they came into contact, among these people civilizations that had long predated Islam.

Corruption and war eventually lead to the end of this golden age. The eminent scholar Ibn Taymiyyah of Turkey observed this decline. The wars in India, Spain, and the Balkans, and the invasions by the Mongols, proved a heavy burden on the Islamic community. He was highly critical of what he called blind adherence to tradition and advocated a return to the original meaning of the Quran in the context of present circumstances. He was repeatedly jailed and, during the last years of his life, when he was denied access to books, he devoted himself to memorizing the Quran and contemplating its teachings.

Through most of human history, opportunities for trade, investment, the sharing of scientific knowledge, and cultural exchange have been limited. The high cost of transportation, natural perils, legal uncertainties, and pirates kept trade from integrating the global economy. From time to time, empires facilitated trade, and so were initially characterized by vibrant economic growth and other forms of human flourishing. These times are correctly identified as golden ages. But, these times usually did not last for more than a few hundred years because of wars and corruption.

Today we find ourselves, we think, in a different age. In our age, trade, investment, the sharing of scientific knowledge, and cultural exchange can systematically occur among the people of sovereign nations. That is, these exchanges and relationships occur among people who are not part of an empire, but rather who are members of different countries which are open to trade and other international relations. In this new age, trade is based, initially, on self-interest. Then, over time, trade can also be supported by friendship. And always, the relationships are disciplined by reciprocity.

This new age is governed by certain agreements, some of which are multinational or global in scope, and others of which are regional or bilateral in scope. An example of the first is the World Trade Organization (WTO) (formerly, GATT); and, an example of the second is the North American Free Trade Agreement. This chapter examines these trade agreements: what they are today, how they have evolved, and how they might continue to evolve.

GENERAL AGREEMENT ON TRADE AND TARIFFS

As noted in section 1 of chapter 4, after being elected President of the United States in 1932, Franklin D. Roosevelt secured from Congress authority to negotiate tariff reductions with other countries on a reciprocal basis. With this authority, he began to restore trade. During World War II, the United States, the United Kingdom, and their allies began planning for the reconstruction of international trade and finance. These negotiations led to two major agreements: the GATT and the Bretton Woods Agreement. The Bretton Woods Agreement will be covered in later chapters.

The GATT was finalized in Geneva, Switzerland, in 1947. Twenty-three countries joined into the agreement, most of them highly developed, Western countries.[1] The agreement has subsequently expanded in its scope in several important ways, and in its number of members. During the 1990s, the GATT was succeeded by the WTO. As of 2015, there were 161 members of WTO, the majority of which are developing countries.

The GATT, now WTO, was to be a different approach to specialization and trade in the world. Instead of relying on empires and colonies, a framework was to be created for lowering tariffs and removing other obstacles to trade between sovereign nations. Key to this framework was fairness and transparency. Eventually, this framework included a process of adjudicating disputes and the authorization of proportional retaliation to subject countries to discipline while trying to avoid the outbreak of trade wars. According to the WTO, its mission includes:

- negotiating the reduction or elimination of obstacles to trade,
- monitoring the application of its rules by its members,
- reviewing the trade policies of its members, as well as regional and bilateral trade agreements,
- settling disputes among its members, and,
- building capacity of developing countries in international trade matters and assisting the process of accession of some thirty countries not yet members.

Lowering Tariffs

There is no question that the GATT/WTO has lowered tariffs. These reductions have been obtained through multinational agreements referred to as "Rounds," for example, the "Tokyo Round." Chad P. Brown and Douglas A. Irwin track the average tariff rate of the highly advanced economies of the world through these rounds. At Geneva, this average tariff rate was reduced from 22 to 16 percent. Subsequent rounds reduced this average tariff rate to 6 percent by the Tokyo Round, and then to 3 percent with the Uruguay Round.[2]

Most Favored Nation Status

In addition to lowering tariffs through multinational agreements, the GATT/WTO seeks to promote trust in trade relationships through fairness and transparency. Fairness means that the rules of the GATT/WTO are the same rules for all member countries, and these disputes that arise between member countries in the administration of these rules are decided by officials drawn from countries not on either side in the dispute. Transparency means that both the rules and the decisions made in administering them are published. In addition, trust is promoted by the rule of Most Favored Nation status (MFN). The MFN status means that, normally, a reduction in tariffs for any member country is a reduction for all member countries. With MFN status, countries need not be suspicious that other countries are receiving special deals. It is a nondiscrimination or equal rights rule. An important exception to this rule concerns preferential trade agreements. Preferential trade agreements will be discussed in the next two sections of this chapter.

Nontariff Barriers to Trade

In a sense, the GATT/WTO was too successful in reducing tariffs. The enormous changes that were occurring in the economies of the world due to tariff reduction put pressure on governments to find alternate ways to protect the workers and capital employed in their shrinking sectors. By the 1980s, the main obstacle to trade no longer was tariffs but had shifted to quotas. In 1986, 16 percent of trade among the highly advanced countries of the world was subject to quotas masquerading as voluntary export restraints. Other new restrictions on trade included antidumping laws and discriminatory regulations. The growth of protectionism through these loopholes called forth a new round of negotiations, the Uruguay Round.

Antidumping Agreement

The GATT/WTO allows countries to prevent foreigners from selling products at a price that is less than the price in the home country. To avoid getting too involved in the theory of dumping, it will simply be said that the view that selling in some places at a price less than the sales price in other places should be illegal is considered legitimate (which is not to say that this view is considered to be correct).

According to the theory of dumping, a company selling at a lower price in one place than the sales price in other places is said to be engaged in the unfair practice of predatory pricing. It is suspected that the purpose of selling at a low price is to drive rival firms out of business, monopolize the market, and then raise price. For example, in 2000, a German court found that Wal-Mart was selling consumer products such as milk, flour, butter, rice, and cooking oil below cost (as the court determined cost), and the company was ordered to raise its prices.[3]

Often in antidumping cases, there are problems with determining cost. For example, the product being exported might not be sold in the home market. There is also the case of determining the cost of products in nonmarket-oriented economies (i.e., when prices are heavily influenced by government regulation). In such cases, proxies might be used, such as prices in third countries.

The GATT/WTO allows antidumping measures, but requires the process of determining whether dumping has occurred to be transparent and limits retaliation to a special tariff equal to the difference between price and cost. In addition, national determinations may be appealed to the GATT/WTO.

Case Study: U.S. Antidumping Duties on Certain Products Made in China

In a case arising in 2007, the Appellate Body of the WTO in 2011 issued its definitive findings on the use of third country proxies to determine cost with respect to four products made in China and exported to the United States.[4] The finding mostly supported the position of the United States but, nevertheless, required the United States to make some changes in its process of determining cost. Notice how long this case took to wind its way, first, through the U.S. process and, then, through the WTO process.

Other Barriers to Trade

Governments regulate economic activity in many ways. There are consumer protection laws, laws to protect labor, and yet other laws to protect the environment. Laws set the minimum age for the purchase of some things, and require a prescription from a medical doctor for the purchase of other things. They require a license for certain professions and a permit for many construction projects. Laws prohibit the sale of meat from certain animals, require health inspections of food processing facilities, require over-time pay and mandate certain coverage in health insurance policies. The exercise of regulatory power is considered to be a "police power" of the state and is ubiquitous. The GATT/WTO does not attempt to oversee the exercise of regulatory power by governments. But, it will consider these regulations if they unfairly discriminate against foreign producers. Ideally, the GATT/WTO would like the regulations to be neutral with respect to the place where a good or service is produced.

Consider the following example: A 1965 law in the state of Florida required that beer be sold in certain size containers (specifically, eight, twelve, sixteen, and thirty-two-ounce containers). The effect of the law was to create a barrier to trade for beer in twenty-two-ounce containers (a popular size among microbreweries in the United States), and in metric containers, as are used by foreign breweries.[5] The GATT/WTO is not interested in the possible discrimination against U.S. microbreweries by Florida's regulation of the size of beer containers, as that would be a domestic issue for the United States. But, the GATT/WTO would be interested in the possibility of discrimination against foreign breweries.

In 2002, the state of Florida amended its regulation of the size of beer cans, so that beer could be sold in any size container as long it was at most thirty-two ounces. There followed a large increase in the variety of beers imported into the state from foreign breweries.

The fact that the prior regulation of the size of beer cans was a barrier to international trade would not have been sufficient to prove that the regulation violated the rules of the GATT/WTO against unfair discrimination. This is because the state of Florida might have had a good reason to regulate the size of beer cans (i.e., a reason other than creating a barrier to international trade). For example, the state of Florida might have asserted that allowing beer to be sold in both English and Metric measurements might have been a little confusing to beer drinkers. But, isn't becoming a little confused part of the reason people drink beer?

The Uruguay Round

The Uruguay Round started in 1986 and was only concluded seven years later, in 1993. For some time, it looked as though the round would end in failure. In the end, it turned out to be a spectacular success. Among the issues the Uruguay Round addressed were (1) tariff rates, (2) trade in agricultural goods, (3) trade in services, (4) intellectual property, (5) quotas in textiles, and (6) establishing a process of adjudicating disputes. These issues are summarized in Table 5.1.

One of the reasons for the comprehensiveness of this agreement was the increasing importance of developing countries in the GATT/WTO.

Table 5.1 Major Provisions of Uruguay Round

	Before Uruguay	Uruguay Agreement	Main Impact
Industrial goods	Tariffs on industrial goods averaged only 5% in rich countries.	Rich countries to cut tariffs on industrial goods by more than a third.	Easier access to world markets for exporters of industrial goods. Lower prices for consumers.
Agriculture	Farm subsidies in United States, E.C., and Japan lead to overproduction, quotas and dumping.	Subsidies cut by 20%. Barriers to trade to be converted to tariffs and cut by 36%.	Easier access to world markets for exports of agricultural goods. Lower prices for consumers.
Services	GATT did not cover services.	GATT extended to many services, though not to all.	Greater trade in services. Further liberalization likely.
Intellectual Property	Standards vary widely. Ineffective enforcement a source of friction.	International standards and agreements for effective enforcement established.	Benefits producers of intellectual property and will increase technology transfer.
Textiles	Rich countries had restricted imports through voluntary export restraints.	Quotas to be dismantled over ten years and tariffs reduced.	Benefit developing countries. Reduces prices for consumers.
World Trade Organization	GATT originally envisioned as part of an international trade organization. But, it was never ratified.	A common dispute resolution procedure.	More effective policing of the international trading system.

Agreements, therefore, had to reflect the interests of these countries (developing countries), as well as the interests of the highly advanced countries. Developing countries sought liberalization of trade in agriculture and textiles in return for accepting initiatives from the highly advanced countries in the areas of services and intellectual property.

The next section looks first at the challenges faced in the further extension of GATT/WTO, and then begins to examine the rise of preferential trade agreements such as free trade areas and customs unions, and (one-way) trade preferences with developing economies.

CUSTOMS UNIONS

By the 1990s, opinions regarding international trade in the developing countries of the world were changing. At the end of the colonial era, almost all intellectuals in the developing countries advocated "self-sufficiency." They emphasized import substitution through rapid industrialization, and deemphasized agriculture and other traditional industries. International trade was viewed as part of the colonial system, and these intellectuals were above all "anti-colonialists."

One example of the intellectuals in the developing countries of the world at the end of the colonial era is Julius Nyerere, the father of Tanzania.[6] Nyerere sought to make his country self-sufficient through import substitution, the nationalization of industry, and the collectivization of agriculture. The results were bankruptcy and famine. In 1985, when he retired as President, Nyerere supported his successor's policies of free-market reforms and trade liberalization. With these policies, the country made significant progress during the subsequent twenty years (although it is still one of the poorer countries of the world). As a result of the progress in developing countries such as Tanzania that have adopted free-market reforms, opinions in these countries (the developing countries) have shifted from viewing international trade as a new form of colonialism ("neo-colonialism") to viewing international trade as part of a strategy for economic development. Curiously, it appears that support for international trade is relatively low in the highly advanced economies of the world.

Table 5.2 gives the percent replying "yes" to the question "Is international trade a good thing?" in Pew Research Polls from 2007 to 2010. In the United States, during these four years, the percent endorsing international trade fluctuated in the 1950s and 1960s. In contrast, support for international trade in each of the BRIC countries has been higher. In particular, in China and India, support for international trade has been much higher.

Table 5.2   Percent Saying Trade is a Good Thing in Pew Research Polls, 2007–2010

	2007	2008	2009	2010
United States	59	53	65	66
Brazil	72	80	87	87
Russia	82	81	80	86
India	89	90	96	90
Indonesia	71	71	79	82
China	91	87	93	93

While these surveys show that a majority of the people of the United States support international trade, this is not a large majority. The history of trade policy in the United States, discussed in the prior chapter, can be interpreted as indicating that support for trade has never been very strong in this country. But, in conjunction with a lot of other information indicating that Americans are no longer confident about the future and have become inward and defensive in their thinking, it appears that support for trade fell during the first decade of this century.

The Doha Round

In 2001, in Doha, Qatar, another round of negotiation for promoting international trade got underway. The leaders of this round were Brazil, China, India, South Africa and South Korea. The overall goal for the round was to advance development in the world through further trade liberalization. Among the more contentious issues were subsidies and trade protections to agriculture. Contentions among these issues proved impossible to resolve.

According to the World Bank, in 1981, 52 percent of the people of the world lived in extreme poverty. In 2005, after twenty-five years, 26 percent lived in extreme poverty. These numbers highlight both the tremendous progress that has been made since the beginning of the trend of economic reform, and the significance of the remaining problem.

Today, about half of the people of the world live in countries that the World Bank classifies as middle-income countries. To be sure, "middle income" encompasses a wide range of income per capita, from about $2,000 to about $10,000. At the high end of "middle income" are countries such as Chile (which may soon be re-classified as "high income") and at the low end are countries such as India (which was formerly classified as "low income"). Since the beginning of the current trend of economic reform in the world, the tendency has been for countries to be re-classified upward, on average about one re-classification per year. At the top, what was first an anomaly (Japan joining the highly advanced economies of the west), is now normal (as a growing number of non-Western countries become highly advanced economies). In the middle, what had been a void is now a continuum. At the bottom, where the majority of the human race was a generation ago, there is today mostly an odd assortment of countries, many of them anarchic and totalitarian states.

With the expanded membership of the GATT/WTO, and with the success of economic reform in the developing countries of the world, it is understandable that the agenda of the rounds of negotiation for trade liberalization shifted. At the Uruguay Round of negotiations, a comprehensive package of agreements was negotiated. It included elements that were priorities for the highly advanced economies of the world (trade in services and intellectual property) and elements that were priorities for the developing economies of the world (trade in agriculture and textile quotas). At the Doha Round of negotiations, the package of agreements under discussion mostly involved priorities for developing countries.

Agriculture

On the issue of trade in agricultural products, the developing countries of the world (correctly) addressed the impact on international trade of subsidies to farmers. Subsidies to farmers result in chronic overproduction, the use of quotas and tariffs to protect domestic producers, and the dumping of farm products overseas. Highly advanced economies are inclined to provide foreign aid in the form of food products so as to reduce excess food stocks. This foreign aid depresses food prices in the world, reduces income to farmers in developing countries, and denies developing countries the opportunity to earn the funds that would be needed to acquire goods and services in the international market and to repay their country's foreign debts. Food is frequently used for "humanitarian relief" when people are starving, but has also had the effect of propping up dictators such as Mengistu Haile Mariamin of Ethiopia and Kim Jong Il of North Korea, whose economies were or are so dysfunctional that starvation is common.

The United States provides about $20 billion in direct subsidies to farmers, while the European Union provides about 40 billion euros. The U.S. system is strange in that some agricultural products are subsidized but others are not (grains are subsidized but fruits and vegetables are not, milk is subsidized but meat is not). The European system is much more comprehensive. In 1996, the United States enacted a law to phase out agricultural subsidies; but, in 2002, the former programs were restored before the phaseout was completed. In the Doha Round, the United States played the role of broker between it, the European Union and Japan, on the one hand, and the developing countries, on the other hand. While the United States appeared willing to embrace an end to agricultural subsidies, in the end, no deal could be finalized. Not helping the argument that the highly advanced economies should end subsidies was the argument by certain developing countries, most prominently India, that their farmers needed continuing protection.

While the focus of the developing countries of the world was to open up the markets of the highly advanced countries for their exports of agricultural products and, strategically, to diminish the production of agricultural products by the farmers of the highly advanced countries by ending agricultural subsidies, there was no appeal to the interests of the highly advanced countries. The negotiations, therefore, were about concessions rather than about mutual benefit. With the failure of the Doha Round, the focus of trade agreements shifted to preferential trade agreements.

Preferential Trade Agreements

Along with the World Trade Organization, there are, today, numerous preferential trade agreements. Among these are the North American Free Trade Area (NAFTA) and the European Union (EU). While there are similarities, NAFTA, as the name implies, is an example of a Free Trade Area; and, the European Union is an example of a customs union. There are also a number of (one-way) preferential agreements by highly advanced economies with developing countries.

Table 5.3 outlines the main characteristics of free trade areas and customs unions. In both cases, goods freely flow between the member countries. This is where the similarity ends. In the customs union, there is a *common external barrier* to trade with non-member countries. As a result of this common external barrier, a customs union can be more about *trade diversion* than

Table 5.3   Characteristics of Free Trade Areas and Customs Unions

	Free Trade Area	Customs Union
Goods—Internal	No tariffs or other barriers to trade	No tariffs of other barriers to trade
Goods—External	Each country has its own tariffs and other barriers to trade	All countries have the same tariffs and other barriers to trade
Weights and Measures	No agreement	Usually common set of weights and measures
Labor	No agreement	Usually free flow of labor
Capital	No agreement	Usually free flow of capital
Currency union	No agreement	Perhaps
Fiscal union	No agreement	Perhaps

about *trade expansion*. Trade diversion is the re-direction of trade from non-member countries, which may have a comparative advantage on a global basis, to member countries.

An historical example of a customs union is the United States following the adoption of the Constitution of 1789. As detailed below, the United States featured free trade internally and a common external barrier and most of the other characteristics of customs unions.

- Internal free trade—States were prohibited from interfering with interstate commerce.
- External common barrier—The U.S. Congress sets tariffs and otherwise regulates international commerce.
- Common weights and measures—The U.S. Congress sets weights and measures.
- Free flow of labor and capital—People and capital are free to flow between states. As a result, there is a tendency for wages for the same occupation and for the rates of return on capital to be brought into a kind of equality, just as the free flow of goods tended to bring prices into a kind of equality.
- Common currency—While each state had its own banking system, only gold and silver were to be the standard of value. Over time, the federal government gained control over the banking system.
- Fiscal union—While each of the states was and remains sovereign with respect to its debt, during the 1930s, the federal government began to share revenue with state and local governments.

While the United States began as a customs union, its tendency has been to become more of a unified nation than a federal republic. This is a general tendency. Economic integration tends, gradually, toward political union. A common language and mass communication has contributed to this transition in the United States.

The European Union

The most prominent customs union in the world today is the European Union. The European Union is more than a customs union, having extensive political as well as economic characteristics.

The European Union evolved out of a six-member customs union called the European Economic Council or simply "the Common Market." These nations were: Belgium, France, Italy, Luxembourg, the Netherlands and the Federal Republic of Germany. Following a series of steps, in 1993, a total of twelve countries, including the six already mentioned, formed the European Union.

The European Union today includes twenty-eight member nations. The most recent nations to be admitted were Bulgaria and Rumania in 2007 and Croatia in 2013. There are, at this time, five candidate nations, the most prominent one being Turkey. Iceland, Norway and Switzerland are not member nations but have extensive relationships with the European Union. The United Kingdom recently held a referendum on whether to remain in or to leave the European Union, with leave winning, and is currently in the process of withdrawing.

WEIGHTS AND MEASURES

In addition to free trade in goods internally and a common external barrier to trade, the European Union features many of the other characteristics of economic integration identified in Table 5.3. With respect to weights and measures, this includes the adoption of the metric system and much more.

The metric system was adopted in France in 1799, as part of the French Revolution. The metric system replaced the system of measurements based on custom. In the metric system, measurements are based on nature. For example, the foot, representing the length of a man's foot (possibly the length of the foot of the King at the time of the standardization of this measurement), was replaced by the meter (originally, one ten-millionth of the distance from the Earth's equator to the North Pole).

The metric system also replaced the use of fractions with the use of decimals. Fractions, such as twelve inches in a foot and sixty minutes in an hour, represent one of the original forms of counting, using the digits of the four fingers on one hand, with the thumb as a pointer, to count up to twelve or a dozen, and using the four fingers and thumb of the other hand to count the number of dozens, up to five, twelve times five equaling sixty. The coincidence of 12 and the approximate number of lunar cycles during one solar cycle must have fascinated man. This coincidence connected us to the universe. While we have mostly replaced fractions with decimals, we still use 12 and 60 in the measurement of time and in the radius of the circle.

Common weights and measures include many industrial standards, from the number of turns in a screw to the distance between the rails on railroad tracks. Industrial standards differ not merely because of different customs, but also for the purpose of creating barriers to trade. A screw may seem like an uncomplicated tool, but the precise number of turns of a screw over a given length may be important for the usefulness of the screw in certain applications, especially if the screw is to fit a pre-drilled hole. Through the promulgation of industrial standards, things such as screws become interchangeable regardless of place of origin. This kind of standardization increases competition and leads to greater productivity. The global counterpart to the process of standardization in Europe is the International Organization for Standardization (ISO).

An example where standardization would facilitate trade is standardization of the distance between the rails on railroad tracks, or gauge. In the United States, Canada and Mexico, in Europe and in China, standard gauge is 4' 10½" (or 1.435 meters). The historical origin for the standard was the width of the ruts in the old Roman roads of Great Britain, on which was based the width of carts (so their wheels would fit into the ruts). George Stephenson based the gauge of the first railroad in the world to use steam locomotives on this width.

For various reasons, this is not standard gauge throughout the world. In Russia and the other republics of the former Soviet Union, a wider gauge was adopted, which can be called broad gauge. As a result of differences in gauge, it is difficult to use railroads to transport passengers and cargo from Western Europe to Russia and from Russia to China.

In a partial solution to this problem, Deutsche Bahn, the German railroad company, recently initiated train service from China to Western Europe using containers placed on flatbed railroad cars. In this service, electronic equipment manufactured in China is placed in containers that are placed on flatbed, standard gauge railroad cars. These containers are transported to the border between China and Kazakhstan, where the containers are transferred to flatbed, broad gauge railroad cars. The containers are then transported to the border between Belarus and Poland, where they are again transferred, this time back to flatbed, standard gauge railroad cars. The cost of this service is greater than what would be cost if the entire route were of one gauge, but appears to be profitable for the transportation of high value manufactured goods. Transportation of bulk cargo, such as coal, grain or industrial chemicals, remains too costly because of differences in gauge along the route.

Free Movement of Labor and Capital

In addition to free flow of goods, the European Union features free flow of labor and capital. The movement of persons within the European Union has been significant. But, perhaps not as significant as might be expected. Internal migrants within the European Union (3 percent of the population, according to Eurostat) only represent a third of all foreign-born persons within the European Union (9 percent).

Getting into some of the details of migration within the European Union, the pattern is generally from east to west along the same latitude. Polish people have tended to relocate to Germany and the United Kingdom. Romanian people have tended to relocate to Italy and Spain. Further discussion of labor and capital flows, as well as discussion of currency union and fiscal union will be deferred to later chapters. The next section will discuss the North American Free Trade Agreement and the spread of Free Trade Agreements and customs unions in the world.

FREE TRADE AREAS

In 1994, NAFTA was formed by the United States, Canada and Mexico. It succeeded the U.S.-Canada Free Trade Agreement. The agreement provided for the phasing out of tariffs and other barriers to trade in industrial goods and services, although it allows certain tariffs and quotas on agricultural goods. By its inclusion of Mexico, it was the world's first "North-South" free trade area, that is, an agreement between one or more highly advanced economies and one or more developing countries.

NAFTA is today only one of many trade agreements into which the United States has joined. The countries with which the United States has negotiated FTA include: Canada, Mexico, Costa Rica, Guatemala, El Salvador, Honduras, Nicaragua, Dominican Republic, Panama, Colombia, Peru, Chile, Australia, Singapore, South Korea, Israel, Jordan, Bahrain, Qatar, Morocco, and Oman. Also, at various times, the United States has been in negotiations with Malaysia, Thailand, Taiwan, New Zealand, Kuwait, United Arab Emirates (UAE), Ghana, Kenya, Mozambique, Mauritius, and also with the Southern African Customs Union, European Union, and Trans-Pacific Partnership. In some cases, the negotiations could not overcome differences, for example, concerning intellectual property. Several negotiations were succeeded by shifts in trade policy from bilateral to multilateral agreements. Some were ended by political changes in one or more of the countries involved.

The United States had been part of the Free Trade Area of the Americas (FTAA) and continues to be part of the Asia-Pacific Economic Cooperation (APEC) (alternately, the Pacific Rim Initiative). The FTAA was to include all the nations of the Western Hemisphere except Cuba.[7] However, with the breakdown of the Doha Round and the ascendency of "Bolivarian" politicians in Venezuela and elsewhere in Latin America, this project has been dormant since 2003.

The APEC currently consists of twenty-one members on the east and west coasts of the Pacific Ocean. At this time, the members of this group agree to cooperate with each other in matters of trade and economic development; and, to encourage the negotiation of FTA among members with no timetable. The brilliant idea to not have a timetable (so that the Pacific Rim Initiative could never fail) was due to President Suharto of Indonesia. He suggested it at a meeting of APEC in Jakarta, in 1994. Prior to his suggestion, it looked as though negotiations would fail because of difficulty in gaining agreement on a timetable for progress toward a region-wide free trade agreement. At this time, with the breakdown of the Doha Round, the Pacific Rim Initiative is the greatest North-South trade liberalization initiative in the world.

Trans-Pacific Partnership

In recent years, the United States was involved in negotiations of two major FTA: (1) the Trans-Pacific Partnership, with Pacific Rim countries, and (2) the Trans-Atlantic Partnership, with the European Union. In both cases, the Congress gave the president "fast-track authority" to negotiate an agreement, meaning that the Congress is committed to approving or disapproving an agreement without amendment in an "up or down" vote. The Trans-Pacific Partnership was to include up to twelve Pacific Rim countries, many of which already are free trade partners of the United States.

Some problems emerged during negotiations leading up to the proposed Trans-Pacific Partnership. Among these problems were that Japan would like to retain its quotas on the importation of food; and, the United States would like to retain its quotas on the importation of automobiles and light trucks from Japan. While the final agreement gradually expanded the quotas, it stopped short of ever eliminating them. As a result of the quotas and other provisions worked into the proposal, it became something of a managed trade agreement, not a pure free trade agreement. President Barack Obama, when he endorsed the proposal, said, "I know that if you take a look at what's actually in the TPP, you will see that this is, in fact, a new type of trade deal." A chapter-by-chapter analysis by scholars at the Cato Institute indicated that the proposal was, in net, pro-free trade. They rated fifteen chapters of the agreement positively, five chapters negatively, two chapters neutral, and considered the remaining eighteen chapters not quantifiable.[8]

During the Presidential campaign of 2016, both major party candidates said they opposed the Trans-Pacific Partnership.[9] Then, following his election, President Donald Trump withdrew the United States from the agreement.[10]

Negotiations for a Trans-Atlantic Partnership were never as far along as those for the Trans-Pacific Partnership. Possibly, a final agreement would have involved Canada and Mexico as well as the United States, and the European countries in the EU common market not members of the European Union as well as those that are. Trade between the United States and the countries of the European Union account for 30 percent of the world's international trade, so there are potentially enormous consequences. The European Commission estimates that an agreement could improve average family annual income by something like $500.[11] However, a pure free trade agreement would have threatened jobs in many vulnerable industries. In particular, heavily subsidized farmers in France and elsewhere in Europe opposed free trade with the United States. If the prior administration had been able to negotiate a proposal, it might have looked like the "new type of trade deal" achieved with the Trans-Pacific Partnership; that is, something of a managed trade agreement.

Other Trade Agreements in the World

In addition to the European Union and NAFTA (and other U.S. trade agreements), there are quite a few other trade agreements in the world. These include regional trade agreements, bilateral trade agreements, and trade preferences given to developing countries by certain highly advanced economies. The member nations of most of the regional trade agreements of the world are presented in Table 5.4. These regional trade agreements are difficult to summarize. Some feature a dominant member, such as Russia within the Eurasian Economic Union and India within the South Asia Free Trade Agreement. Other regional trade agreements feature countries that vary in size without any one of them dominating.

Some regional trade agreements are relatively homogenous with respect to language and culture, such as the Greater Arab Free Trade Agreement and the Central and West Africa Unions. Others are quite diverse, such as the countries of the Association of South East Asian Nations. Some are customs unions, with coordination of external tariffs and other barriers to trade, the development of common weights and measures, and so forth. Others are merely FTA. A few have opened the possibility of political union. Some countries are members of multiple regional trade agreements.

The motivation for organizing regional trade agreements vary. With NAFTA—the first north-south regional trade agreement—a huge common market was opened to the very different production capabilities of the member nations. The motivation clearly was greater specialization and trade in keeping with the classical theory of international theory. With the European Union, mostly highly advanced economies were joined together. In this case, the economic motivation was to increase competition via economies of scale and variety along the lines of Paul Krugman's new theory of international trade and Michael Porter's model of competitive advantage.

In addition to gaining the classical and new advantages of trade, some of the trade agreements have additional motivations:

- Facilitating *the flow of* goods, especially important for landlocked countries such as Botswana in the Southern African Customs Union and Nepal in the South Asia Free Trade Agreement.

Table 5.4   Regional Trade Agreements

Regional Trade Agreement	When Formed	Original Members, (Additional Members), [Candidates]
Andean Community	1969	Bolivia, Colombia, Ecuador, Peru[c]
Mercosur	1991	Argentina, Bolivia, Brazil, Paraguay, Venezuela, Uruguay
Association of South East Asian Nations	1992	Brunei, Indonesia, Malaysia, Philippines, Singapore, Thailand, (Burma, Cambodia, Laos, Viet Nam)
Gulf Cooperation Council	1981	Bahrain, Kuwait, Oman, Qatar, *Saudi Arabia*, United Arab Emirates
Greater Arab Free Trade Area	1997	Above six plus: Egypt, Iraq, Lebanon, Libya, Morocco, Sudan, Syria, Tunisia, (Algeria, Jordan, Palestine, Yemen), [Comoros, Djibouti, Mauritania, Somalia]
South Asia Free Trade Agreement	2004	Bangladesh, Bhutan, *India*, Maldives, Nepal, Pakistan, Sri Lanka
East African Community	2000[a]	Burundi, Kenya, Rwanda, Tanzania, Uganda
Southern African Customs Union	1970[b]	Botswana, Lesotho, Namibia, *South Africa*, Swaziland
Southern African Development Community	1980	Above five plus: Angola, Madagascar, Malawi, Mozambique, Tanzania, Zambia, Zimbabwe, (Dem. Rep. of Congo, Mauritius, Seychelles)
West African Community	1975	Benin, Burkina Faso, Cape Verde, Gambia, Ghana, Guinea, Guinea-Bissau, Ivory Coast, Liberia, Mali, Niger, Nigeria, Senegal, Sierra Leone, Togo[d]
Central African Community	1966	Cameroon, Central African Rep., Chad, Rep. of Congo, Gabon, (Angola, Burundi, Dem. Rep. of Congo, Equatorial Guinea, São Tomé and Príncipe)
Eurasian Economic Union	2015	Armenia, Belarus, Kazakhstan, Kyrgyzstan, *Russia*
Black Sea Economic Cooperation	1992	Albania, Armenia, Azerbaijan, Bulgaria, Georgia, Greece, Moldova, Romania, Russia, *Turkey*, Ukraine, (Serbia)

[a]Reorganized. [b]Originally organized in 1910, making this the oldest Customs union in the world. [c]Chile was formerly a member. [d]Mauritania was formerly a member. Dominant member, if one, in italics.

- Joining into trade blocs so as to gain bargaining power relative to large nations and other trade blocs.
- Developing shared culture and language as in the Greater Arab Free Trade Agreement and the East African Community (which nations share the Swahili language).

Bilateral Free Trade Agreements

Bilateral FTA include country-to-country agreements, country-to-bloc agreements, and bloc-to-bloc agreements. An example of a country-to-country free trade agreement is the U.S.-Chile FTA; and, an example of a country-to-bloc free trade agreement is the China-to-ASEAN FTA. Bilateral trade agreements are the most dynamic part of trade promotion in the world at this time.

China and India are large countries that are actively negotiating bilateral trade agreements. Both of these countries are emerging economies, but there are significant differences. China is a high-middle income country that is mostly socialist and not democratic. China mostly imports natural resources and exports manufactured goods. Its objectives in trade agreements are relatively clear: to better secure the supply of natural resources. India is a low middle income country that is mostly free-market and is democratic. Its economy is more diverse, and its objectives in trade agreements harder to describe. In addition, being a democracy, trade agreements are complicated by the interests of domestic industries threatened by exposure to outside competition. In particular, India seeks to protect its agricultural sector.

Trade Concessions

In addition to allowing preferential trade agreements on a reciprocal basis, including customs unions and FTA, the WTO allows developed countries to offer (one way) trade concessions to developing countries. Historically, these trade concessions have been extended by European countries to former colonies.[12] More recently, they have been extended by the United States to a variety of developing countries as part of the Millennium Challenge, established in 2004.

The Millennium Challenge conditions foreign aid, trade concessions and other assistance with meeting certain thresholds for policies that we believe will lead to sustained economic development and poverty reduction. These policies include establishing the rule of law, fighting corruption, and delivering basic human services such as immunizations against communicable disease and primary school. The idea is to focus assistance to those countries where it will do the most good; namely, to the countries whose governments are doing their job (as we, the donor country, judge). Various countries have been fully or partially qualified for assistance under this program, and a few have been de-listed because of backsliding.

Summary

- The nations of the world are today engaged in a great experiment: to determine the extent to which the advantages of international trade can be gained by sovereign nations through trade agreements, as opposed to gaining these advantages through empires and colonies.
- Trade Agreements include both those that are global (the GATT/WTO) and those that are "regional" (NAFTA and the EU).
- The (WTO) today has more than 150 members, covers trade in many goods and services along with intellectual property, and has a process of adjudicating differences among its members.
- The WTO began as the GATT in 1947. This was an agreement by twenty-three countries, covering a relatively limited range of goods in international trade. It has grown in size and scope mainly because of its success.
- Through numerous rounds of negotiation, tariffs have been greatly reduced.
- But, possibly because of the significant reduction of tariffs, the use of nontariff barriers to trade has grown. The WTO has attempted to address the problem of nontariff barriers to trade, with only limited success.
- The most recent round of negotiation, the Doha Round, began in 2001. It was focused on extending free international trade to agricultural products. The round did not have a successful conclusion.
- One type of a regional or preferential trade agreement is a FTA of which the NAFTA may be the most prominent example. FTA's involve (only) free internal trade. Each of the members of an FTA is free to determine its tariffs and trade policies with respect to countries that are not members of the FTA.
- The other type of regional or preferential trade agreement is a customs union of which the European Union (EU) may be the most prominent example. Customs unions involve free internal trade and a common external tariff and trade policy.
- In addition, customs unions often involve the free flow of labor and capital as well as the free flow of goods, and the standardization of weights and measures. Customs unions sometimes also involve currency unions and fiscal unions.
- In addition to NAFTA, the United States has entered into bilateral and multilateral FTA with about two dozen countries. Mostly, these agreements have been with democratic countries in east Asia, Latin America and the Middle East.
- The United States had been in negotiation for several years with the EU and with several Pacific Rim countries concerning a Trans-Atlantic Trade and Investment Partnership and a Trans-Pacific Trade and Investment Partnership. Negotiations have been complicated by desires by the countries

involved, including by the United States, to maintain certain protectionist policies, and have not reached a successful conclusion.

- During the past twenty years, and especially since the failure of the Doha Round, the nations of the world has been expanding existing multilateral preferential trade agreements, and adding new ones.
- Among the more significant preferential trade agreements are the ASEAN Free Trade Agreement (southeast Asia) and the South Asia Free Trade Agreements.
- Customs unions are in various stages of development among the Arab nations, Russia and several "near Republics," the countries of east, south and west Africa, and South America.
- Some developed nations extend (one-way) trade concessions to certain developing nations. The United States offers trade concessions, development loans and grants and other assistance to developing countries that take steps to adopt policies such as the rule of law that we think will bring about sustainable economic development and reduction of poverty.

NOTES

1. Many of today's countries in Africa and Asia were then part of certain European colonial empires.

2. Douglas A. Irwin, "The GATT Starting Point: Tariff Levels Circa 1947," Center for Economic Policy Research, Discussion Paper No. 10979, 2015.

3. "Germany Says Wal-Mart Must Raise Prices," *New York Times*, September 9, 2000.

4. World Trade Court Appellate Body, "United States-Definitive Anti-Dumping and Countervailing duties on certain products from China," March 11, 2011. The products were circular welded carbon quality steel pipe; light-walled rectangular pipe and tube; laminated woven sacks; and, certain new pneumatic off-the-road tires.

5. "New Law A Boon For Beer Drinkers," *Orlando Sun-Sentinel*, April 5, 2002.

6. Another example is Barack Obama, Sr., the father of President Barack Obama.

7. Brazil and Mexico had been trying to coax Cuba into joining.

8. Daniel Ikenson, et al. "Should Free Traders Support the Trans-Pacific Partnership? An Assessment of America's Largest Preferential Trade Agreement," Cato Institute, September 12, 2016.

9. Eric Brander, "Clinton's TPP controversy: What you need to know," *CNN*, July 27, 2016.

10. Peter Baker, "Trump Abandons Trans-Pacific Partnership, Obama's Signature Trade Deal," *New York Times*, January 23, 2017.

11. Joseph Francois, *Reducing Transatlantic Barriers to Trade and Investment: An Economic Assessment* (London: Centre for Economic Policy Research, 2013).

12. Raymond J. Ahearn, "Europe's Preferential Trade Agreements: Status, Content, and Implications," Congressional Research Service, 2011.

Chapter 6

International Capital Flows

If capital were mobile, it would flow from the places in which it was relatively abundant to the places in which it was relatively scarce. This would tend to equalize the rate of return on capital across the world. It would also tend to equalize wage rates across the world. This kind of capital flow would quickly end mass poverty in the world.

Capital flow based on its relative abundance and scarcity is illustrated in the early history of the United States. As the United States gained the confidence of investors in Europe, Europeans invested in the development of the United States. These investments included the purchase of stocks and bonds of many banks, railroads and industrial corporations, as well as the bonds issued by the state and federal governments. These investments in the United States offered higher rates of return than could be obtained with investments in the already well-developed economies of Europe. Plus, with the commitment of the United States to the rule of law, there was not much concern for risks such as expropriation, excessive taxation, or regulation or interference in contracts. As a result of these capital flows, the savings of the Americans were augmented by capital flows from Europe, and rapidly developed the economic potential of a vast country.

Even prior to the United States, capital flow based on its relative abundance and scarcity is illustrated in the Dutch Republic of 1581 to 1795. The Dutch Republic was greatly influenced by the Christian reformer John Calvin (1509–1564). In the Dutch Republic, the Calvinist doctrine of "predestination" was debated. This doctrine is that God predestines each individual to accept or reject salvation. Yes, it was conceded in these debates, God predestines the salvation of each person, in the sense that He knows and wills all things from the beginning of time. But, predestination does not deny that each person makes a choice in the matter of his salvation.[1] Therefore, our nature as human beings, as moral creatures, capable of accepting or rejecting salvation, requires that we be free.

With acceptance of religious freedom, social tolerance, and the protection of property, the Dutch Republic began a golden age. This golden age encompassed art and science, exploration, commerce and finance, as well as philosophy and law. And, the Dutch people became enormously wealthy. Capital became so abundant, and the rate of return on capital within the Dutch Republic became so low, that capital flowed from the Dutch Republic to other places, primarily to Great Britain. Thus, the capitalist revolution that began in the Dutch Republic spread elsewhere.

Unfortunately for the Dutch Republic, debts that accumulated over several wars and the rise of Napoleon put an end to its golden age. Subjugated by France, the place lost its economic vitality. It would only rebound following the formation of the Kingdom of the Netherlands.

This chapter first examines the balance of payments, which includes all financial flows, not merely those related to international trade. These financial flows include, in the current account, flows of trade and services, international earnings of labor and capital, foreign aid by governments and international private charity. These financial flows also include, in the capital accounts, flows of financial assets such as monetary reserves, government debt, private-sector loans, stocks and bonds, and equity claims on real assets. By construction, any imbalance in the current account is offset by an opposite imbalance in the capital account. Given the discussion above concerning the Dutch Republic, it might be supposed that capital flows primarily from highly advanced economies to developing countries. But, actual capital flows differ considerably from this pattern.

After covering the balance of payments, the chapter examines the issue of sovereign debt risk. Sovereign debt risk is the risk of nonpayment of debt. The broader concept of country risk includes the risk of nonpayment of debt. Country risk includes, in addition, the risk of unfair or discriminatory regulation of business and taxation, the risk of disruption of business and financial transactions, and the possibility of the injury to personnel and destruction of property due to civil disorder and insurrection. The truth is many of the poorer countries of the world suffer from underlying problems such as anarchy and violence, political instability, corruption, and authoritarian governments. In countries with these problems, foreign debt is frequently not used to foster development, but to favor the members of the ruling class. As a result, foreign debt does not increase the supply of capital in the country and does not raise wage rates in the country. Instead of enriching the people of the country, it only burdens them with future repayment obligations.

A similar problem with foreign debt pertains to modern democratic countries. In these countries, foreign debt is often used to finance continuing deficit spending by government. If the foreign debt were used to finance productive investments, the investments would generate the income needed to retire the debt in the future. But, when the foreign debt is used to finance continuing deficit spending, it merely burdens the future taxpayers of the country. At some point, the credibility of these governments for repaying their foreign debt becomes suspect. At this point, the government has to reduce spending and/or increase taxes sufficient not only to balance its budget but also to meet its foreign debt obligations.

After examining sovereign debt risk, the chapter examines international rates of return. It looks at the relationship between government bond yields and credit ratings, and discusses the dynamic and somewhat subjective aspect of sovereign debt risk.

THE BALANCE OF PAYMENTS

The balance of payments is a record of a country's financial dealings with the rest of the world. It is conveniently divided into two parts: (1) the current account and (2) the capital account. In theory, these two accounts always sum to zero; however, because of secret, illegal, and difficult to estimate transactions, a nontrivial balancing sum referred to as "statistical discrepancy" is used to make the balance of payments add up to zero.

THE CURRENT ACCOUNT

The current account includes four major items. These are: (1) the balance of trade, (2) the balance of services, (3) the income account, and (4) the transfer account. Sometimes the balance of trade and the balance of services are combined into a single category, the balance of trade and services:

1. Exports of goods (a positive entry);
2. Imports of goods (a negative entry) [1 plus 2 = balance of trade];
3. Exports of services (a positive entry); and
4. Imports of services (a negative entry) [3 plus 4 = balance of services].

It should be pointed out that trade in services includes transportation services and financial services such as banking and insurance. It also includes what is called "travel and tourism." This category includes vacation travel, but it also includes spending on medical and educational services of foreigners when they are here, and of nationals when they are there.

The income account includes the following four items:

1. Earnings on foreign investments by nationals (a positive entry);
2. Earnings on investments in this country by foreigners (a negative entry);
3. Foreign labor earnings of nationals remitted home (a positive entry); and
4. Labor earnings in this country of foreigners remitted home (a negative entry) [1 plus 2 plus 3 plus 4 = Balance of Income].

Remittances are a major source of foreign exchanges for many low- and middle-income countries. For Mexico, remittances—mostly from the United States—amount to about 2 percent of the GDP of Mexico, and are the tenth largest sources of foreign exchange for the country. Western Union, originally a telegraph company, has revived itself as a major company by facilitating remittances through its money transfer business.

The transfer account (sometimes referred to as the unilateral transfer account or the secondary income account) includes foreign aid by governments and international charity. With regard to unilateral transfers by the United States, about two-thirds of the foreign aid provided by the government is in the form of military assistance and about one-third is in the form of developmental assistance. While the U.S. government gives more money in developmental assistance than any other country, it gives a smaller percentage than the governments of many other highly advanced economies.

But, foreign aid by the U.S. government is only about half of the unilateral transfers from the United States to the rest of the world. According to the Hudson Institute, during 2014, the United States distributed $33 billion in development assistance, and $44 billion in international private charity.[2]

Because funds contributed to private charity are susceptible to diversion, some organizations have emerged that help to qualify charities for donors. Let's say you are a Muslim American, and in celebration of the Holy Month of Ramadan and in the American tradition of Thanksgiving, you would like to make a contribution to bless others. Perhaps, you have heard of Islamic Relief USA or have just come across it through a search of the internet. One thing you can do to qualify the charity is to look it up in the Charity Navigator (this is simply a mention of Charity Navigator, not an endorsement).

For some of the poorest countries of the world, foreign aid and international charity amount to a significant percentage of GDP. But, foreign aid has often been used to maintain those who are in power. And, international food relief has often undermined the local agricultural sector. The track record in terms of actually promoting development has been mixed. Even so, foreign aid and international charity, in combination with remittances from workers abroad and private investment, can be part of an overall strategy of development.

To recap: The current account balance is equal to the balance of trade plus the balance of services plus the balance of income plus the balance of transfers. In 2016, the United States had a huge deficit in the balance of

Figure 6.1 U.S. Current Account Balance, percent of GDP, 1960–2016. *Source*: Created by author. Data from FRED (Federal Reserve Economic Data), Economic Research Division of the Federal Reserve Bank of St. Louis.

trade ($753 billion), partially offset by surpluses in the balances of services and of income ($248 and 173 billion). With a deficit of $120 billion in the transfer account, this left the United States with a current account deficit of $452 billion. Figure 6.1 tracks the U.S. current account from 1960 to 2016, as a percent of GDP. Going into the 1960s, the U.S. current account featured a small surplus. Since the 1970s, the U.S. current account has trended down and has featured two periods of massive deficits.

THE CAPITAL ACCOUNT

If the current account were in balance, then the capital account would also be in balance. But, if the current account were in deficit, the capital account would have an equal surplus (if there were no statistical discrepancy). For example, if a country is importing more goods and services than it is exporting, and if the income account and unilateral transfers sum to zero, then foreigners would be accumulating financial claims against the country.

Foreigners can accumulate financial claims against a country by accumulating the currency of the country, bonds issued by the government of the country, stocks and bonds issued by the private corporations of the country, and other financial obligations of the people of the country. Foreigners can also acquire equity in real assets such as land and unincorporated businesses.

Connections and Causes

The capital account necessarily mirrors the current account (ignoring statistical discrepancy). When one is up, the other is down. But, this connection does not tell us which is the cause and which is the effect. In fact, the underlying cause might be a third variable.

During the 1980s, there was a strong stock market in the United States. This strong U.S. stock market was probably the underlying cause of both the current account deficit and the capital account surplus of that time. That is, foreigners were seeking U.S. dollars in order to participate in this bull market. To obtain these dollars, foreigners had sell more goods and services to Americans than they bought from Americans. Thus, the bull market induced foreign accumulation of U.S. assets and a deficit in the current account.

During the 1990s, there was another strong stock market in the United States. This one was known as the Dot.com Bubble. Again, foreigners acquired U.S. dollars by selling more goods and services to Americans than they bought from Americans. They used these dollars to acquire U.S. assets during the bubble. Again, the U.S. current account was driven into deficit and the U.S. capital account was driven into surplus.

During the first decade of the 2000s, there was another bubble. This time, it was the housing bubble. Among the causes of the bubble were the lowering of interest rates by the U.S. Federal Reserve; and, the lowering of down payments on homes to zero, encouragement of the use of nonconventional mortgages, and the loosening of paperwork requirements by the U.S. Department of Housing and Urban Development (HUD) and by Fannie Mae and Freddie Mac. Again, downward pressure was put on the U.S. current account and upward pressure on the U.S. capital account.

But, by the end of the first decade of the new century, another new combination of underlying causes started to kick in: a combination of massive U.S. government deficits and the financial crisis associated with the bursting of the U.S. Housing Bubble. These developments contributed to a further deterioration of the current account deficit and increase in the capital account surplus.

Recap of the Section

The balance of payments summarizes all the financial transactions of a nation with the rest of the world. These include the transactions dealing with trade and services, but they also income and transfer transactions, and they also include the corresponding transactions in financial claims.

For many years now, the United States has been running a current account deficit and, necessarily, has been exporting financial claims. In part, these current account deficits reflect the desire of the American people to consume more than they produce, financing the excess of their consumption by borrowing. In part, these current account deficits reflect a willingness of foreigners to lend to the governments, corporations, and people of the United States.

Notice that this flow of capital to the United States is the reverse of what economic theory says should happen. Economic theory says capital should flow from the wealthy countries to the poor countries of the world, promoting the economic development of the poor countries. The continuing deficits of wealthy countries have been identified by the World Bank as one of the two greatest impediments to the economic development.[3] The next section examines risk and return in international investments.

RISK AND RETURN IN INTERNATIONAL INVESTMENTS

As stated in the prior section, capital tends to flow from advanced economies to emerging economies. This was seen first in the Dutch Republic during the commercial revolution. With the new "Protestant Ethic" emphasizing work and thrift, capital accumulated and rates of return on capital fell. Because of the low rate of return in the Dutch Republic, there were brighter opportunities for investment in other places, not as well developed, where the rule of law was being established, at first England and then the new United States. So, the commercial revolution in the Dutch Republic was followed first by the Industrial Revolution in England and later by a similar industrial revolution in the United States.

For more than two hundred years, international capital flow has usually been, in net, from the advanced economies to the emerging economies where the rule of law was being established. But, from time to time, when emerging economies suffered financial crises, the flow of capital was disrupted and possibly there was reverse capital flow (the flow of capital from emerging economies to advanced economies) or even capital flight (an exaggerated form of capital flowing out of a country).

Periods of strong capital flow to developing economies include the United States and Latin America during the 19th century. Capital flow to the United States was disrupted for a time by the debt crisis of the 1840s. Capital flow to Latin America during the late 19th century was ended by the debt crisis of the 1890s.

For the country receiving a capital flow, there is a combination of a current account deficit and a capital account surplus. That is, more goods and services are flowing into the country than are flowing out; and, the excess of imports over exports is financed by the "export" of financial claims. The financial claims include bank loans, long-term bonds, corporate stock, and titles to real estate. Hopefully, the capital that is flowing into a country is enabling the country to increase its rate of investment. This way, when it comes time to make payments on the financial claims of foreigners, the increase in productivity makes the payments easy.

For example, during the early 19th century, when the United States was an emerging economy, capital flowed from Great Britain to the United States. This meant we ran a balance of trade deficit with Great Britain, and financed the surplus by exporting bonds. These bonds enabled the states of the country to do such things as finance banks and construct canals. The idea was that the banks and canals would increase future productivity and make payments on the bonds easy. Unfortunately, things didn't always work out as hoped. During the 1840s, several of the states of the United States defaulted on the bonds they had issued to finance development. While most of these states soon reconciled with their foreign creditors, some did not.

More recently, capital has been flowing to the emerging economies in Asia and Latin America and to the countries in transition from centrally planned to market-oriented economies in Eastern Europe.[4] The amount of net capital flow has been volatile, with large swings associated with times of financial crisis. In 2016, net capital flow to emerging economies turned negative (i.e., there was reverse capital flow).

Necessarily, net capital flow to the emerging economies of the world is a function of national savings and investment in both developed and the developed countries and, so, is buffeted by many shocks. Even during normal times, gross capital flows are enormous, with investors in developed countries seeking the higher returns by investing in developing countries, and investors in developing countries seeking lower risk by investing in developed countries.[5] The amount of net capital flow also varies significantly from one developing country to another, depending on factors such as the degree of financial liberalization in particular countries.[6]

International Diversification: A Simple Approach

In addition to the tendency of capital to flow from advanced economies to emerging economies in response to higher rates of return, capital will flow internationally in order to lower risk through more effective diversification. Even for an economy as large as the United States, taking advantage of the opportunity to diversify internationally can lower portfolio risk.

If the risks in investments were independent, then portfolio risk could be reduced to zero by including a very large number of different investments in the portfolio. This is what insurance companies do. They insure a very large number of risks that are independent of each other in order to eliminate portfolio risk. But, because the risks in stocks tend to be imperfectly positively correlated, portfolio risk in stocks cannot be completely eliminated through diversification. Portfolio risk in stocks can only be reduced to an asymptotic level.

Restricting a portfolio to U.S. investments, that asymptotic level is a small fraction of the risk in individual stocks. By including international investments in the portfolio, portfolio risk can be reduced to an even lower level. Such a reduction in portfolio risk indicates that there is some independence in the risks of investments from one country to another, as well as some shared risks. This analysis of the effect of international diversification is simple and should only be treated as a step in the direction of the correct analysis.

International Diversification: The Correct Approach

Because risk is non-linear, to a limited extent it is possible to lower risk while achieving a higher expected rate of return. This makes a degree of international diversification optimal even for the most risk averse investors in stocks. Figure 6.2 shows that a portfolio consisting only of U.S. stocks has lower risk and lower return than a portfolio consisting only of emerging market stocks. Choosing between these two portfolios, the rule of risk and return applies (higher return can only be achieved with higher risk). But, investors are not restricted to an all-or-nothing decision with regard to international diversification.

If U.S. stocks and emerging market stocks were perfectly positively correlated, the risk and return of portfolios consisting of various percentages of the two would fall along the thin continuous straight line connecting them. If, on the other hand, the two sets of stocks were perfectly negatively correlated, one would be a hedge of the other, and a portfolio consisting of 50 percent of

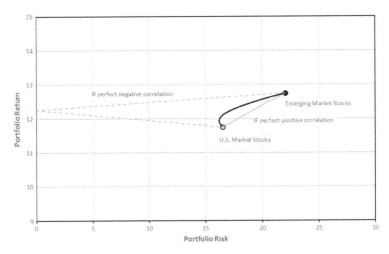

Figure 6.2 Portfolio Risk and Return with International Diversification. *Source:* Created by author.

each would be risk-free. With perfect negative correlation, the risk and return of portfolios consisting of various percentages of U.S. stocks and emerging market stocks would fall on the two dashed straight lines connecting the two via the risk-free, 50-50 portfolio.

In fact, because U.S. stocks and emerging market stocks are imperfectly positively correlated, the risk and return of portfolios consisting of various percentages of the two fall on the thick curved line. A portfolio consisting of something like 80 percent U.S. stocks and 20 percent emerging market stocks will have lower risk and higher return than a portfolio consisting only of U.S. stocks. Clearly, such a portfolio is superior to a portfolio consisting only of U.S. stocks. The fundamental reason for this seemingly illogical result (adding a small percentage of risky emerging market stocks to a portfolio of U.S. stocks lowers risk) is that risk is non-linear. Because of non-linearity, some of this and some of that are not on the straight line connecting this and that.[7]

Spotlight: John Templeton

John Templeton (1912–2008) was born into a poor family in Tennessee and "worked" his way through college by playing poker. After he accumulated a small fortune in stocks, he opened a mutual fund specializing in international investment. By outperforming the U.S. stock market by an average of 2 percentage points a year for fifty years, he turned his small fortune into one of the largest fortunes in the world. In retirement, he turned his attention to philanthropy. Today, the John Templeton Foundation finances research in: science, genetics, genius and creativity, individual freedom and free markets, and the development of virtuous character.

Foreign Direct Investment

International investments sometimes take the form of acquiring government debt, sometimes stocks and bonds in private corporations, bank loans, and other private financial obligations. Sometimes, international investment involves foreign direct investment. Foreign direct investment is defined as the acquisition of an ownership interest in excess of 10 percent in a business in a foreign country. Examples include a 100 percent owned subsidiary, and 50 percent ownership in a joint venture with a company from the host country.

Reasons for foreign direct investment (in addition to the usual financial considerations of risk and return) include:

- Access to resources;
- Access to markets; and
- Strategic presence.

Spotlight: The Evolution of Business Organizations

International—The key word "inter" meaning in-between. The company views itself as operating between countries. For example, producing in its home country and opening international sales offices.

Multinational—The company views itself as a part of the economy of more than one country. For example, producing in several countries and selling its products in these and yet other countries.

Global—The company views itself as a part of the emerging global economy, with managers and other key employees drawn from the entire world, design and production facilities in many countries, and with ownership dispersed throughout the world.

From the standpoint of entering emerging markets where the rule of law is not established, foreign direct investment offers some real advantages relative to portfolio investments (stocks, bonds, loans, etc.). Specifically, foreign direct investment extends the social institution of the corporation into the country. Key employees, for example, can be citizens of other countries; Key technology kept secret or even overseas. While the physical capital invested in the host country is placed at risk, the foreign corporation retains significant bargaining power with the government of the host country relative to a domestic company. In any case, it can minimize its loss in the event of an adverse development such as a nationalization or civil disorder.

Country Risk

This section concludes with a few comments on two other risk considerations in international investments: country risk and sovereign debt risk. Country risk includes the risk of nonpayment of debt. In addition, it includes the risk of unfair or discriminatory taxation and regulation of business, the risk of disruption of business and financial transactions, and the possibility of physical harm to and kidnaping of personnel, extortion in general, and destruction of property due to civil disorder and insurrection.

Many of the poorer countries of the world suffer from underlying problems such as anarchy and violence, political instability, corruption, and authoritarian governments. In countries with these problems, foreign debt is frequently used to favor the members of the ruling class. Instead of increasing the supply of capital, and raising wages, it enriches the ruling class, curropts them, and entrenches them in power. As far as the people of the country are concerned, foreign debt only burdens them with future repayment obligations.

An analogous problem with foreign debt pertains to modern democratic countries. In these countries, foreign debt is often used to finance continuing deficit spending by the government. If the foreign debt were used to finance productive investments, then the investments would generate the income needed to retire the debt in the future. But, when the foreign debt is used to finance continuing deficit spending, it merely burdens the future taxpayers of the country.

At some point, the credibility of government for repaying foreign debt becomes suspect, at which point the government has to reduce spending and/ or increase tax revenue to balance its budget including meeting its foreign debt obligations. This issue will be explored in detail in the next section.

SOVEREIGN DEBT RISK

In 1840, the state of Mississippi defaulted on $7 million of bonds. At about the same time, seven other states and a territory later granted statehood defaulted on their debts, as did the Republic of Texas (later annexed as a state). Most of these places later reconciled with their creditors. Not Mississippi. Mississippi proceeded to repudiate its bonds.

Until 1928, nations that defaulted on their debts put themselves at the risk of invasion. Such invasions, and threats to invade, were called gunboat diplomacy. In an 1843 debate between a pro-bond Mississippian and an anti-bond Mississippian, the anti-bond Mississippian spoke of British warships off the state's shore. At this point, a member of the audience spoke:

> Sir, in that event I join my countryman who opposes the payment of the bonds. My sword . . . sir, the last drop of my blood, shall be spent in resisting the demand. My state, sir, may she be always right, but, right or wrong, the state, sacred, intangible and profane, forever.[8]

In the United States, states are sovereign with respect to debt. They are the final authority when it comes to debt repayment. Furthermore, states seem to be immune to invasion for nonpayment, since the U.S. Constitution requires the federal government to defend the states. Great Britain, were it to invade Mississippi for nonpayment, would have to fight the entire United States, not merely the state of Mississippi. But, in 1843, John Quincy Adams, a former president who was serving in the U.S. Congress, offered a resolution that would deny Mississippi the protection of the federal government.

> In the event of such a war, the State involving herself therein will cease thereby to be a State of this Union, and will have no right to aid in her defense from the United States, or any one of them.[9]

In the Congress, some advocated a federal assumption of state debts, either to preserve the peace, or to maintain the credit of the United States. Others thought that if other states were to reconcile with their creditors, the state of

Mississippi might become a pariah within an otherwise creditworthy United States; but it would not be invaded.

In the end, there was no federal assumption of state debts, neither was Mississippi invaded. But, it did become a pariah. The state became increasingly estranged from the world of commerce and finance. The chief spokesman for repudiation as part of the doctrine of states' rights was none other than Jefferson Davis of Mississippi, the man who would become President of the Confederate States of America.

Through the early part of the 20th century, there were many invasions of countries in default of their debts. Among the more prominent examples were the invasion of Mexico by France in 1862 and the invasion of Egypt by Great Britain in 1875. Many of these invasions were followed by the colonization of the country.

In the case of Mexico, the French attempted to re-colonize the country during the U.S. Civil War, when we were unable to come to Mexico's aid. At the time, by reason of the (President James) Monroe Doctrine, any invasion of an American republic was viewed as a threat against the United States. The Mexicans achieved a great military victory over the invaders on May 5, 1862.[10] The French did not give up and sent a larger military force to subdue the country. Only after our Civil War were we able to aid the Mexicans. We made it increasingly clear that we opposed the occupation of Mexico and demanded that the French withdaw, which they did. That was the last time a European country invaded an American republic.

Roosevelt Corollary

As the United States grew as a military power, President Theodore Roosevelt declared that if any American republic were in default of its debts, *we* would invade the country, not the Europeans. We would then reorganize the government so it could resume its debt payments, and then restore independence to the country. It would not be made into a colony. Of course, none of the countries we invaded by reason of that declaration has thanked us for keeping them from being re-colonized by the Europeans. Nobody likes debt collectors.

The Kellogg-Briand Pact

The time of gunboat diplomacy and invasion for nonpayment of debts came to an end in 1928. The United States and France were instrumental in negotiating a very radical treaty, one that renounced of use of war as an instrument of national policy. The only justification of war was defense. This treaty was signed by almost every nation in the world. It was almost entirely a failure.

Within a generation, the world was engulfed in a new world war. But, the treaty was not a complete failure, because it put an end to gunboat diplomacy. Since 1928, it has no longer been acceptable to invade a country for default on its debt. Therefore, the only reason countries repay their debts nowadays is because they choose to repay. They can no longer be forced to repay.

Why Do Nations Repay?

Without the threat of invasion, why do nations repay? The answer appears to be complex.[11] First, nations do not always repay. Second, when they do repay, it appears that reputation (and continued or renewed access to capital) more than sanction is the motivating factor. One economist, examining three centuries of sovereign debt repayment, finds that reputation as opposed to sanction better explains why nations repay.[12]

The amount of the debt probably plays a role. An examination of the experience of the American states that defaulted during the 1840s indicates that those with the lowest per capita debt tended to resume debt payments.[13] Those with intermediate debt burdens tended to settle with creditors at less than the face value of their debt. These findings might be taken to indicate that reputation alone can be sufficient to induce sovereign debt repayment if the debt burden is relatively small.

Carmen M. Reinhart and Kenneth S. Rogoff, in a highly acclaimed book,[14] examine sixty-six episodes of debt crises, covering countries on five continents and over eight centuries. They identify what is now called the Reinhart-Rogoff line, a ratio of 90 percent debt to GDP. After a country crosses this line, it is rare for the country to repay its debt. Instead, they resort to devaluation or inflation, or to partial or complete repudiation. The United States had a ratio of debt to GDP of about 60 percent from 2003 to 2007. We crossed over the Reinhart-Rogoff line in 2010.[15] Among the things that tend to happen during times of debt accumulation is that the people who are involved say "This time it's different." The old rules do not apply. No, things are not different. The creditors of the United States should consider themselves warned.

Sovereign Debt Credit Ratings

The above discussion suggests that the probability of repayment is related to the burden of repayment and the benefits from continued access to capital. This suggests that variables such as the ratio of debt to GDP and the level and rate of growth of GDP per capita can be useful in predicting problems with meeting debt payments. Contemporary credit rating agencies consider these variables and many others when assessing the creditworthiness of sovereign debtors. In addition, they take a variety of qualitative information into account. No simple formula is used. Although a lot of quantitative information is taken into account, in the end, the assigned ratings involve professional judgment.

The first credit ratings were issued by Moody's in 1909, and were for railroad bonds. Soon, its main competitor—Poor's—who started to issue an annual manual of investments in railroad securities in 1872 was also issuing credit ratings. Poor's later merged with Standard Statistics to form Standard & Poor's (S&P).

Today, credit ratings are published by several well-known rating agencies as well as by many lesser-known agencies. Among the well-known agencies are Moody's, S&P and Fitch (the "big three"), Dun & Bradstreet, and A.M. Best. All of these companies are American. Fitch is both American and European. Dagong Global Credit Rating is a Chinese credit rating company that recently gained some attention for downgrading the United States.

The highest possible rating is "AAA" for S&P and "Aaa" for Moody's, pronounced "triple A." Bonds with such a high rating are expected to pay as promised even in a great depression. As a practical matter, they are considered free of risk. Countries that are rated Triple A by both S&P and Moody's include Australia, Canada, Germany, Singapore, Sweden, and Switzerland.

The next three categories, Double A, Single A, and Triple B, are considered, along with Tripe A, to be "investment grade." These bonds are considered to be relatively safe and, in the unlikely event of a default, it is expected that they will still be worth most of their stated value. China, France, Kuwait, South Korea, and the United Kingdom, among other countries, are rated Double A. Botswana, Israel, and Saudi Arabia are Single A. Whereas Colombia, India, Italy, and Japan are Triple B. The United States is rated Aaa by Moody's and AA+ by S&P.

Bonds rated less than Triple B are considered to be speculative grade. These bonds involve a significant risk of default or are already in default.

The categories from Double A to Double C often involve qualifiers. S&P uses a "+" and "−" scheme. Moody's uses a "1," "2," "3" scheme. A bond rated AA+ or Aa1 is considered to be slightly better than a bond rated AA or Aa2. Analogously, a bond rated AA− or Aa3 is considered to be a slightly worse than a bond rated AA or Aa2.

Credit Ratings and Interest Rates

The lower is a bond's rating, the greater is its risk of default. It is expected that the yield on lower rated bonds is higher to compensate investors, on average, for this risk. During 2016, triple A-rated government bonds were paying less than 1 percent interest. But, with every downgrade, the tendency was for the yield to increase by fifty-nine basis points (or, 0.59 of 1 percentage point).

Some countries with speculative grade bonds had to pay 10 percent or more to borrow money.

Interest Rates and Deficits

Just as government deficit spending can affect the yield on government bonds, so too can the yield on government bonds affect government deficits. This happens when the following dynamic is triggered:

- Growth of government deficits threatens the ability of the government to repay its debt.
- The risk of default raises the interest rate the government is required to pay.
- The higher interest rate the government is required to pay raises the deficit even more.
- Return to the top and repeat.

To be sure, there is some indeterminacy to this spiral. It depends on the perception of the risk of default that sets off the spiral. This perception is something that hasn't happened in the case of the United States. It did happen in the case of Greece.

In 2011, Thomas Sargent and Christopher Sims[16] were awarded the Nobel Prize in Economics for developing what is called the "fiscal theory of the price level." Although their theories are quite abstract, and involve expectations that cannot be directly observed, they make the point that fiscal policy ultimately determines the price level of countries that issue debt denominated in their own paper money. An implication of the fiscal theory of the price level is that as long as interest rates remain low, it can be inferred that the market maintains confidence in the ability of the government to make the promised payments on its debt.

Summary

- The Balance of Payments reflects all transactions of one country with the outside world. These include the current account (imports and exports of goods and service, earnings abroad both of labor and capital, and unilateral transfers) and the capital account (international flows of financial claims). The Balance of Payments sums to zero (except for a balancing entry called "statistical discrepancy"). Any deficit or surplus on the current account must have an equal and opposite sum on the capital account.
- Sometimes when there is a deficit in the current account and a surplus in the capital account (meaning a country is importing more goods and services than it is exporting, and is "exporting" more financial claims than it

is "importing"), it is because the country is investing more than it is saving. That is, it is augmenting its own saving with capital supplied by foreigners to more rapidly develop its economic potential. This can be called an investment-oriented trade deficit.

- When there is an investment-oriented trade deficit, it can be anticipated that the foreign capital will pay for itself (i.e., out of the profits of the investments). Furthermore, the additional capital provided by an investment-oriented trade deficit will increase the marginal productivity of labor, and therefore increase wages and the standard of living.

- At other times when there is a deficit in the current account, it is to enable the people of the country to consume at a higher rate than the country produces. The most prominent example of this is the financing of large government deficits. This kind of trade deficit will be burdensome to the people of the country in the future, when the financial claims of foreigners must be repaid, or else result in some form of repudiation of those claims.

- Normally, capital flows from the developed world to the developing world. The main reason attracting capital to the developing world is the higher rate of return there, due to the relative scarcity of capital. The main impediment to the flow of capital to the developing world is higher risk due to the lack of the rule of law. As developing countries establish the rule of law, domestic savings plus international capital flow transforms the country into a developed country.

- When considered one by one, investments in emerging economies tend to involve greater risk and greater reward than investments in highly advanced economies. However, in the context of a well-diversified portfolio, combining investments in both emerging economies and highly advanced economies can, to a limited extent, both increase return and lower risk.

- Normally, a lesser amount of capital flows from developing to developed countries. This is called reverse capital flow. Reverse capital flow is usually motivated by safety. During civil wars and other times of civil disturbance, reverse capital flow turns into capital flight.

- Prior to 1928, repayment of sovereign debt was motivated in part by gunboat diplomacy. That is, the invasion of countries in default on their debt by the military forces of creditor nations in order to obtain repayment. Examples of gunboat diplomacy include the invasion of Mexico by France during the U.S. Civil War (when we were temporarily unable to defend our fellow American republics), and the invasion of Egypt by Great Britain in 1875.

- Since 1928, the use of gunboat diplomacy to motivate repayment of national debts has been unacceptable. Nowadays, reputation and continued access to international markets for trade and finance are the reasons countries repay their national debts when they do. Accordingly, when the value of reputation and continued access to international markets is high relative to the cost of repayment, we expect countries to repay; and, when the cost of repayment is high relative to the value of reputation and continued access to international markets, we expect them to repudiate.

- The risk of default of sovereign debts is reflected by the ratings of credit rating companies including Moody's and Standard & Poor's. During 2011, S&P downgraded the United States from AAA to AA+.
- Country risk is a broader measure of risk. It includes the risk of default and also includes risks such as the expropriation of wealth, high and discriminatory taxation and regulation, and the impact on personal safety as well as on property of crime and civil disorder.
- Multinational corporations offer some protections against country risk. This is because they can employ key personnel from outside the country and better secure their proprietary knowledge. Accordingly, while their physical capital within a country is at risk, they are in a better bargaining position with national governments than local businesses.
- International charities can avoid much of the misdirection of funds and other forms of corruption often associated with government-to-government foreign aid. In addition, by creating networks of people that cross national borders, they offer the possibilities of strengthening democracy and civil liberty, support for openness, and acceptance of diversity. International charity suffers its own form of misdirection of funds due to fraud.

NOTES

1. The belief that each person is judged *individually* on Judgment Day for his or her own sins is found in many religions.

2. "The Index of Global Philanthropy and Remittances," 2017.

3. The second is corruption and lack of the rule of law (considered to be two parts of the same thing) in developing countries.

4. Graciela L. Kaminsky, "Internal Capital Flows, Financial Stability and Growth," United Nations Department of Economic and Social Affairs, Working Paper No. 10, December 2005.

5. Ben S. Bernanke, Carol Bertaut, Laurie Pounder DeMarco, and Steven Kamin, "International Capital Flows and the Returns to Safe Assets in the United States, 2003–2007," Board of Governors of the Federal Reserve System, International Finance Discussion Paper 1014, February 2011.

6. Tashin Saadi Sedik and Tao Sun, "The Effects of Capital Flow Liberalization—What is the Evidence from Recent Experiences of Emerging Market Economies?" IMF Working Paper 12/275, November 2012.

7. Just to be sure, from the risk-minimizing point on the thick curved line to the point representing a portfolio consisting only of emerging market stocks, the rule of risk and return holds true.

8. J. F. H. Claiborne, *Life and Correspondence of John A. Quitman*, vol. I (New York: Harper & Row, 1960), p. 208.

9. William A. Scott, *The Repudiation of State Debts* (New York: Crowell, 1893), pp. 243–244.

10. Cinco de Mayo is celebrated more in the United States than in Mexico.

11. Ugo Panizza, Federico Sturzenegger, and Jeromin Zettelmeyer, "The Economics and Law of Sovereign Debt and Default," *Journal of Economic Literature* 47 (2009): 651–698.

12. Michael Tomz, *Reputation and International Cooperation: Sovereign Debt Across Three Centuries* (Princeton, NJ: Princeton University Press, 2007).

13. William B. English, "Understanding the Costs of Sovereign Default: American State Debts in the 1840s," *American Economic Review* 86 (1996): 256–275.

14. Carmen M. Reinhart and Kenneth S. Rogoff, *This Time is Different: Eight Centuries of Financial Folly* (Princeton, NJ: Princeton University Press, 2009).

15. Considering national debt held by the U.S. Treasury in trust funds and that held by the Federal Reserve, the United States might not be across the Reinhart-Rogoff line.

16. See: Thomas J. Sargent and Neil Wallace, "Some Unpleasant Monetarist Arithmetic," *Federal Reserve Bank of Minneapolis Quarterly Review* 5:3 (1981): 1–17; and, Christopher A. Sims, "A Simple Model for Study of the Determination of the Price Level and the Interaction of Monetary and Fiscal Policy," *Economic Theory* 4 (1994): 381–399.

Chapter 7

International Labor Flow

Give me your tired, your poor,
Your huddled masses yearning to breathe free,
The wretched refuse of your teeming shore.
Send these, the homeless, tempest-tost to me,
I lift my lamp beside the golden door![1]

When I was a boy, my maternal grandfather was already an old man. He came here at the turn of the 19th into the 20th century. He left his wife and their first child in Italy, and regularly sent money to his family for their support. Then he decided this would be his home and called for them to join him here. My grandmother, with their son in her arms, crossed over. At the same time her sister left for Argentina. They would never see each other again. My grandfather told me it was true what they said about this country. Here, he said, the streets really are paved in gold as long as you are willing to work. But, he continued, if tomorrow there were a better country, he would go there.

I couldn't believe him. How could you say that, grandpa, when your sons served in the army during World War II—one in Third Army and another in the 82nd Airborne Division; and, when my father's older brother served in the 8th Army Air Force and my father served in the army during the Korean War? I didn't realize until later what my grandfather was telling me. He was telling me that every day he stayed here was an affirmation that he continued to believe that America was the greatest country in the world.

The United States is predominantly an immigrant country. At the founding, there were already significant minorities of Germans and Dutch, Africans free and slave, and American Indians both among the citizens of this country and not. Through the 19th century, there were large numbers of immigrants from various parts of Europe. The first two great waves of immigrants during the

115

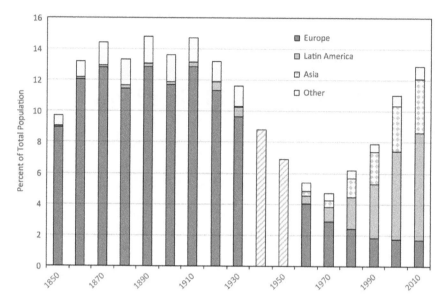

Figure 7.1 Composition of foreign-born population of the U.S., 1850–2010. *Source:* Created by author. Data from U.S. Census, place of origin not available for 1940 or 1950.

19th century involved Irish following the Potato Famine of the 1840s and Germans following the failed Revolution of 1848.

Early during the 19th century, it was not unusual for immigrants from Europe to "pay" for their voyage across the ocean by agreeing to be sold into indentured service upon arrival, with the proceeds going to the ship captain. Ethnic-based fraternal societies were organized to bid for their countrymen at these auctions. Later in the century, as the cost of the voyage fell, immigrants were able to pay in advance. Many of them traveled in mostly empty cargo hulls. Ships that had been fully loaded with agricultural goods on the way to Europe from America, returned with manufactured goods taking up much less space.

Then, early during the 20th century, Congress enacted the first laws restricting immigration. For a time, the flow of immigrants fell. By the late 20th century, immigration picked back up in large part because of illegal immigration. Also, the origins of recent immigrants became very different from those of prior times. As Figure 7.1 shows, these new immigrants were mostly from Latin America and Asia.

DEPENDENCY

In each generation, complaints arose concerning immigrants. They were said to be filthy, did not work regularly, were prone to crime, street gangs and alcohol abuse, and were heavily dependent on private charity and public relief.

Poverty, crime and pauperism there are in Boston, but for the most part they may be regarded not as chronic nor as epidemic, but as, to a large extent, importations from without, or abnormal and exceptional.[2]

There appears to be some truth to these complaints. During the early part of the 19th century, Boston was a destination for many Irish immigrants. At the time, the city was predominantly a Protestant one, bustling with business, commerce and finance, and growing in wealth. The Irish immigrants, almost all Catholic, crowded into certain neighborhoods. They took what jobs they could find and seemed to have many broken families and children who could not be supported. Immigrants in total constituted 34 percent of the population of Boston according to the Census of 1850. They averaged 56 percent of the dependent population from 1847 to 1856, according to Annual Reports of the House of Industry (the city's poorhouse).

In New York City, immigrants amounted to 40 percent of the population according to the Census of 1880. They averaged 68 percent of the dependent population from 1888 to 1894, according to Annual Reports of the Association for Improving the Conditions of the Poor of New York. In Baltimore, a time series can be pieced together from the Annual Reports of the Trustees of the Poor and those of the Association for Improving the Conditions of the Poor of Baltimore. From 1850 to 1910, immigrants were overrepresented among the dependent poor.

While a review of the country's experience with immigrants during the 19th century verifies that they were a greater burden on private charity and public relief than the native-born population, the differences were not extreme. Considering the circumstances of immigrants, it should not be surprising that they were economically vulnerable.

Much the same can be said about recent immigrants. Recent immigrants are likewise more dependent on welfare programs than the native-born population. The differences, however, remain modest. In 1999, 21 percent of immigrant households received some form of noncash assistance (food stamps, housing or housing subsidies, and Medicaid), as compared to 15 percent of native-born households. Eight percent of immigrant households received some form of cash assistance (Temporary Aid to Needy Families, general relief, and Supplemental Security Income), as compared to six percent of native-born households.[3]

Wages

Another recurring complaint has been that immigrants take jobs from native-born workers and depress wages. There is also some truth to this, although less than many suppose.[4]

The argument that there is no impact: According to Say's Law,[5] supply creates its own demand. The way Say's Law works is that the earnings of a worker will be spent one way or another. The money that is spent creates demands for employment in other industries. For example, a $2 purchase of a tube of toothpaste creates demand for many tiny fractions of jobs. One tiny fraction of a job is in the aluminum industry, to make the toothpaste tube. Another is in the plastic industry, to make the cap for the tube. Yet another is in the industry that makes the stuff that's inside the tube, whatever that stuff is. Then there is the tiny demand for a truck driver to transport the toothpaste from the factory to the store and the tiny demand for a clerk at the store to ring up the sale. When all of these tiny demands are added up—from the purchase of toothpaste and from all the other purchases by the immigrant worker—a new job is demanded.

The argument that there is an impact: Immigrant labor is mostly unskilled labor. Therefore, without any contradiction of Say's Law, immigration impacts wages. It actually has two impacts on wages: it lowers wages among native-born workers who are unskilled and raises wages among native-born workers who are skilled.

The first of the pair of charts shown in Figure 7.2 pertains to the market for unskilled workers. For simplicity, all immigrant workers are presumed to be unskilled. Their influx increases the supply of unskilled workers. As above, this is not all that happens. The immigrant workers spend their earnings. They spend their earnings on a mix of things. Therefore, there are increases

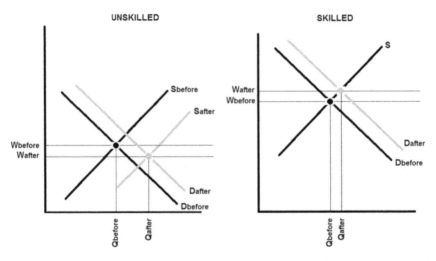

Figure 7.2   Impact on wages when immigrants are unskilled workers. *Source*: Created by author.

in the demands for unskilled and skilled workers totaling the earnings of the immigrant workers.

Because of the split in the increase in demand for workers, the increase specifically for unskilled workers is not sufficient to offset the increase in the supply of unskilled workers. As a result, wages for unskilled workers fall. With regard to skilled workers, there is no change in supply, only an increase in demand. As a result, wages for skilled workers rise.

The resumption of immigration during the late 20th century has been one of the factors contributing to the increase in inequality in the United States. Without attempting a complete analysis of inequality, immigration has lowered the income of Americans below the median and has increased the income of Americans above the median. Necessarily, the resumption of immigration has increased inequality.

The feeling of many low-income native-born workers that immigrants are depressing their wages is valid, although exaggerated. The feeling by many high-income native-born workers that there is no substantial problem with immigration may reflect that they benefit by the resumption of immigration. The next section examines the flow of labor elsewhere in the world.

THE GLOBAL EXPERIENCE

The experience of the United States has been one of rapid assimilation of immigrants. The earnings of immigrants start off low relative to the earnings of the native-born population. Their earnings and the earnings of their children then rise relative to the native-born population with years of residency and from one generation to the next. The average income of subsequent generations approximates that of the general population. The following contribute to the rise of earnings: mastering the language, formal education, and intermarriage.[6] A mix of social and economic factors is indicated. In addition, the size of the gap between initial earnings and those of the native-born population generally reflects the human capital of the immigrant at the time of arrival.

Intelligence

As the 19th century came to a close, nativists in both major parties agitated for an end to the country's open immigration policy. One of the leading voices for this movement was Richard T. Ely, a founder of the American Economic Association and a leader of the Social Gospel Movement and the Progressive movement.

"Transportation has become so cheap that even an industrially inferior class is able to secure means to come to our shores."[7]

"The problem is to keep the most unfit from reproduction, and to encourage the reproduction of those who are really the superior members of society."[8]

The progressives entertained themselves with pseudoscientific theories of race and genetics. In particular, they considered Poles, Italians and other non-WASP (White Anglo-Saxon Protestants) Europeans to be inferior, along with Africans and Asians. In a path-breaking work, Thomas Sowell showed that the intelligence of an entire population could change over time.[9] Sowell looked at the scores on an IQ-like test of the men inducted into the armed forces during World War I and World War II. During the first, the members of white immigrant groups looked inferior in intelligence, as was argued by the progressives. During the second, the next generation of the white immigrants scored similarly as the WASPs, questioning the genetic-based theories of the progressives.

Recent experience in Europe shows the same thing. At the time of the fall of the Berlin Wall, the average IQ in East Germany was about 1 standard deviation lower than the average IQ in West Germany. Today, there is little difference.[10] The Estonians and the Poles, once thought to be inferior, today score the same on IQ tests as the Germans and the Swedes.

There is even more profound evidence of the malleability of IQ for entire populations. Richard Flynn has shown that intelligence as measured by the IQ test has been rising in the advanced nations for the past hundred years. This rise has been masked by the periodic "re-norming" of the test to keep the average score equal to 100. While his work has been replicated many times, the causes and implications of these rising scores are subjects of debate.

There are strong correlations between intelligence (as measured by IQ tests and internationally standardized school achievement tests) and GDP per capita among the countries of the world. These correlations probably reflect both cause and effect. That is, intelligence rises with, or is caused by, high GDP per capita. And, that a more intelligent population is more productive. Intelligence can rise because of better nutrition when young, or better schooling, or the more invigorating challenges and opportunities that people face in a vibrant economy.

Immigration in Other Countries

While the United States is an immigrant nation, foreign-born persons no longer constitute a particularly large fraction of its population. Of the countries with at least 5 million foreign-born persons, UAE is extraordinary. UAE, Saudi Arabia, and the other Gulf States host many "guest workers." *Guest workers* are foreign persons granted temporary visas (such as one year) and allowed to work in a country. There is no right or expectation of permanent residence or citizenship.

Because of internal growth, naturalization, and guest workers, the population of Saudi Arabia increased from 3 million in 1950 to 32 million in 2015. Citizenship can be obtained through naturalization and usually involves wives and children. Guest workers are mostly unskilled workers and almost all of them are Muslim. UAE and the other Gulf States are more liberal with respect to guest workers. They have many non-Muslims among their guest workers. While there is no right to religious freedom, in keeping with the Arab and Muslim culture of welcoming guests, the practice of religion by the non-Muslim guest workers of these countries is condoned and, in certain ways, facilitated.

Australia and Canada are, like the United States, immigrant nations. Foreign-born persons comprise considerably larger percentages of their populations than ours. The United States, today, is merely in a range defined by the countries of Western Europe, and many of the foreign-born persons in the United States are here illegally. Germany actually has a higher percentage of foreign-born persons as a fraction of its population than does United States, and almost all of their foreign-born persons have legal status.

During the 1950s, Germany started a guest worker program. Mostly southern Europeans and Turks were allowed to come to Germany to work. In addition, Germany extended a right of return to ethnic Germans from all over the world. Invoking this right required proof of German ancestry, if possible, and proficiency in the German language. Over time, guest workers and others gained a right to citizenship. Today, about half of the foreign-born population of Germany is from elsewhere in Europe (mostly Poland and Russia) and about a quarter is from Turkey and elsewhere in the Middle East. Increasingly, Germans think of "German" as a language and a culture, as distinct from an ancestry. Many foreign-born Germans serve in public office. In 2013, the first two Germans of African ancestry were elected to the Bundestag, one a Christian Democrat and the other a Social Democrat.

Emigration

Every immigrant is simultaneously an emigrant. For each country that is a destination, there is a country of origin. Sometimes in migration studies, a distinction is made between "push factors" and "pull factors," or between refugees and "economic migrants." *Push factors* are conditions within a country that cause people to leave. Examples include ethnic and religious persecution, war and other forms of civil violence, famines, and other natural disasters. *Pull factors* are conditions within a country that cause people to arrive. Examples include a vibrant economy, civil liberty, personal security, and availability of welfare benefits. An integrated model of migration would consider conditions in countries relative to each other, as well as geographic proximity, natural and man-made barriers, and social acceptance.

Among the countries of the world with significant numbers of emigrants (leavers) in both absolute numbers and as a percent of the population, Syria and Afghanistan have the most. The push-factor of war is obviously at work in these two countries.

Diversity

Many countries have significant diversity within their native-born populations. Elements of this diversity include the original people of places that came to be dominated by transplanted populations, the progeny of slaves and indentured servants brought from distant places, and the incorporation of different peoples into countries upon the drawing of borders. Countries deal with diversity in many ways.

Queen Isabella of Spain came to be known as Isabella the Catholic (meaning, all-embracing) because she did not distinguish among her subjects whether on the Iberian Peninsula or in the New World. Great Britain, on the other hand, was reluctant to incorporate the peoples of its empire as subjects, which would have endowed to them the substantial rights of Englishmen. Eventually, as the lands of these original people came to be enveloped, a reservation system emerged.

In Russia, the language and culture of many of the diverse peoples of that vast country are preserved in the organization of republics (as distinct from other federal entities such as oblasts). An example is the Komi Republic in the north mid-west of the Russian Federation, the Komi people being a distinct ethnic group. In Malaysia, a majority Muslim country, the ethnic Chinese and other minorities are recognized in various ways. According to some, Malaysia is a secular state in which Islam is the official religion; but, according to others, to be fully Malay, one must be a Muslim. The population of Trinidad & Tobago consists mostly of two distinct ethnic groups: Indo-Caribbean people (descendants of indentured servants from India) and Afro-Caribbean people (descendants of slaves from Africa). Trinidad & Tobago is a democratic country. Its two main political parties are mostly organized along ethnic lines.

In the United States, the struggle to—as Martin Luther King put it—"redeem the promise" in the Declaration of Independence continues to this day. While the focus is usually on the remaining gap in earnings between black and white Americans, it is good to recognize the tremendous progress the country has achieved in this struggle. From emancipation to today, the earnings of black men working full-time has grown from 30 to 85 percent of that of white men. To be sure, there have also been intervals of stagnation and retrogression.[11] On the positive side, in recent years, there has been progress in black educational attainment relative to white; and, on the negative side, the collapse of the black family relative to white.

MORAL TRANSFORMATION

Adam Smith begins *The Theory of Moral Sentiments*,[12] "However selfish man may be supposed, there are evidently some principles in his nature which interest him in the fortunes of others." This opening sentence makes it tempting to think that Smith's two great works—*The Wealth of Nations* and *The Theory of Moral Sentiments*—are disconnected, one concerned with the implications of self-interest and the other with the implications of benevolence. Certainly the focuses of these two works differ. One is focused on transactions in a marketplace and the other on personal relationships. But, to say they are disconnected would be a misreading. Smith continued to revise *The Theory of Moral Sentiments* while writing and later revising *The Wealth of Nations*. At least to him, the two works were parts of a larger view of society.

According to Smith, free societies enable most of their members to achieve at least a measure of success (1) through work, the accumulation of property, and by entering into free associations with others through family life and civil society, (2) by securing the persons, property and liberties of individuals through the administration of law, and (3) by developing social institutions and customs that evince in most people an appreciation of the moral foundations of a free society. A free society encourages virtue, directs people to productive pursuits, develops in people a sense of dignity from being productive, and engages people with each other on the basis of free association.

Smith's version of sympathy involves projection of one's own feelings to others. It is how the viewer would feel if in the situation of the other. Thus, for Smith, sympathy involves judgment and moral approbation.

Just as Smith's sense of sympathy involves projection of one's own feelings to others, people sense that they, too, are being observed, ultimately, by the "impartial spectator." It is this sense of being observed that induces "self-command" in individuals, tempering selfishness, ambition, and so forth, and exciting what Smith calls the "amiable" virtues such as kindness, tenderness, and humanity. As members of society, individuals find themselves in a web of exchanges and relations in which it is difficult to say where exchanges in the marketplace end and social relationships begin.

In *Centesimus Annus*, Pope John Paul II said that by being able to own something, buy and sell in the marketplace, and join in free associations with others, a person could see how wonderful a creature he is, and come to love himself, and also come to love others as himself. "The fundamental error of socialism," said Pope John Paul II, "is anthropological in nature." Ayn Rand, an avowed atheist, affirmed the teaching that we should love others as ourselves. She said self-love is the proper foundation of love of others.[13]

On the matter of justice, Adam Smith is exact. Society absolutely must protect the innocent from injury, and may rightfully punish those who harm others. But, with regard to such things as decency, charity and other duties that ought to be performed, these are only inexact. Civilized society may require that enough individuals with enough means embrace the amiable virtues, but it cannot compel the same. Instead, it develops this embrace in people through upbringing, schooling, customs, religion, and social institutions. There is, in addition, the discipline of continuous dealings in the marketplace. Business people, in particular, learn that they should be honest in their dealings with others in order to develop a good reputation and loyalty from their customers, employees, suppliers, and others.

> Govern the people by regulations, keep order among them by chastisements, and they will flee from you, and lose all self-respect. Govern them by moral force, keep order among them by ritual and they will keep their self-respect and come to you of their own accord.[14]

The idea that customs and social institutions arise in a free society to modulate relations among individuals might seem to be a "third way" position relative to capitalism and socialism. Yet, to proponents of a free society, defining capitalism as radical individualism, devoid of relationships and social institutions, while perhaps useful for some purposes, is a straw man construction.

Aristotle talked of "households," within which there are individuals with many shared values (these households could include business associations as well as families), joining into a political order (the polis) on the basis of relatively few shared values (most probably, defense). Conservative thinkers have long talked about the importance of the "little platoons" of society (Edmund Burke) and "eleemosynary institutions" (John Marshall). Alexis de Tocqueville famously commented upon the formation of social institutions in *Democracy in America*.

Following Smith, social reformers sprang up in both Great Britain and the United States. Foremost among these social reformers were Thomas Chalmers of Scotland and Joseph Tuckerman of Massachusetts. Through their efforts, private charity came to supply much of the material relief provided to those in need, with a concerted effort to envelop those aided in a web of community through "visiting." The idea was that poverty was not simply a lack of income, but a lack of moral character that could only be learned socially.

St. Vincent de Paul, a Catholic priest of France, preceded the social reformers of the Protestant world. To St. Paul's dictum, "If a man will not work, he shall not eat" (2 Thessalonians 3:10), St. Vincent de Paul added the following rules: that those who could not work at all—children, the sick and the aged—be given full support, while those who could earn half their needs, only be given half. The religious order he founded—the Daughters of Charity—*invented* visiting.

Lawfulness

As demonstrated in the prior section, the people of the more advanced countries of the world tend to be more intelligent. This makes sense merely from the fact that children in these countries have good nutrition when young and, so, can more fully develop their potential. Schooling and the stimulus provided by the opportunities and challenges of life in a vibrant economy also contribute to intelligence. This section examines two issues concerning the moral transformation that accompanies a free society. The first of these is whether people in a free society are more law-abiding. This is a particularly interesting issue since free societies tend to respect civil liberty including the rights of the accused and restrain the punishment of those who are found guilty.

There are problems with the reliability of statistics concerning crime. People are often reluctant to report crime to the police. Indeed, with regard to sexual assault, it is thought that an increase in reporting may be a good thing, a sign of greater trust in the police. In addition, in many countries, the police are suspected of manipulating crime statistics. Recently, the Gallup Organization has incorporated a short "victim survey" into its World Poll. By "victim survey" it is meant that people are asked directly if they have recently been victims of crime. The survey indicates that there is a positive correlation between economic freedom and freedom from crime (or, a negative correlation between economic freedom and crime). But, the correlation isn't strong. In a multiple regression, civil liberty and several other variables are found to also be significant in determining the level of crime.[15]

The Gallup World Poll shows Singapore and Hong Kong to be practically free of crime. These two places are #1 and #2 in economic freedom. The United States and Canada, though high in economic freedom, are a little lower than other highly advanced countries in terms of crime. Chile is also high in economic freedom, but it is more like its fellow Latin American republics in crime than it is like the highly advanced countries. Since the moral transformation that accompanies a free society takes time, the position of Chile should not be too surprising. Let's see the level of crime in Chile a generation from now.

Generosity

The second way that free societies morally transform people is with respect to what Adam Smith calls the "amiable virtues," to include decency and generosity. A free society, by generating wealth, gives people *the capacity to be* generous, but do the people of a free society *actually give* of their wealth to charitable causes? The same Gallup World Poll used in the prior section to explore lawfulness can be used to explore generosity. Included in the Gallup World Poll are three questions from which the Charities Aid Foundation of the United Kingdom has constructed a World Giving Index.

The relationship between charitable giving and economic freedom is flat until countries reach a certain level of economic freedom. Then, the relationship is increasing. It appears that there is an important threshold effect or crossover point in this relationship. Perhaps this is true of individuals as well. A person has to crossover from being selfish to being generous.

As I started this chapter recalling my childhood, I will so conclude it. When I was a boy, I felt put off by the line "Land where my fathers died," in the song "My Country, 'Tis of Thee." My fathers did not die here. They died in Germany on my paternal side, and in Italy on my maternal side. Did this song mean I was not truly an American? Yet I, like my father and my uncles, served in the army—as has my son. Things have changed since I was a boy. Today, with the passing of my parents and grandparents, this is the land where my fathers died.

Summary

- In the first great migration, humans departed Africa and made their way along the southern coastline of Asia, eventually, to Australia. In the second, following the last Ice Age, humans made their way to Europe, Asia, and the Americas.
- Migrations have continued ever since, sometimes through conquest, sometimes through infiltration and colonization. In addition, millions of people were forcibly relocated upon being enslaved.
- Contemporary migrations are characterized as due to "push factors" and "pull factors." Push factors include being displaced by war and fleeing religious persecution, and pull factors include the greater opportunities found in highly advanced economies.
- Today, many countries feature significant percentages of foreign-born persons among their populations. These include citizens and permanent residents, tourists and students, and guest workers.
- Saudi Arabia and the Gulf States have the highest percentages of foreign-born persons among their populations. Most of these foreign-born persons are guest workers.

- The United States has a moderate percentage of foreign-born persons within its population. But, so do other English-tradition countries (the United Kingdom, Canada, Australia, and New Zealand), and so do most of the countries of Western Europe. Germany, in particular, has a larger percentage of foreign-born citizens and permanent residents, while the United States has a large percentage of illegal aliens.
- Because immigrants tend to be unskilled, they tend to depress the earnings of low-skilled native-born workers while increasing the earnings of high-skilled native-born workers.
- Immigrants present certain challenges to the host country, being low-income, prone to depending on public and private charity, facing problems of language and discrimination, and having criminals among them.
- Speed of assimilation as measured, for example, by earnings, greatly differs by immigrant group.
- In addition to immigrants, many countries feature significant diversity within their native-born populations.
- Countries deal with diversity in very different ways.
- The people of free societies tend to be more law-abiding and more generous. These virtues are induced through upbringing, schooling, customs, social institutions, and the ability of most people to achieve at least a degree of success in life.

NOTES

1. Emma Lazarus, "The New Colossus."

2. Joseph Tuckerman, *On the Elevation of the Poor: A Selection of His Reports as Minister at Large in Boston*, ed. E. E. Hale (Boston, MA: Robert Brothers, 1874), p. 7.

3. U.S. Census Bureau, "Profile of the Foreign-born Population in the United States, 2000," 2001. p. 49.

4. Robert J. LaLonde and Robert H. Topel, "Immigrants in the American Labor Market: Quality, Assimilation and Distributional Effects," *American Economic Review* 81 (1991): 297–302.

5. Say's Law is the counterpart to Keynes's Law (that demand creates its own supply). The two can be reconciled by supposing that Say is presuming that the economy at or near full employment, while Keynes is presuming that the economy features massive unemployment.

6. Xin Meng and Robert G. Gregory, "Intermarriage and the Economic Assimilation of Immigrants," *Journal of Labor Economics* 23 (2005): 135–174.

7. Richard T. Ely, "Thoughts on Immigration, No. II," *The Congregationalist*, June 28, 1894.

8. Richard T. Ely, *Studies in the Evolution of Industrial Society* (Chautauqua Press, 1903), p. 139.

9. "New Light on Black IQ," *New York Times Magazine*, March 27, 1977, p. 15 ff.

10. Eka Roivainen, "Intelligence, Educational and IQ Gains in Eastern Germany," *Intelligence* 40 (2012): 571–575.

11. Robert Higgs, *Competition and Coercion: Blacks in the American Economy, 1865-1914* (New York: Cambridge University Press, 1977). Updated by the author based on the decennial census.

12. Adam Smith, *The Theory of Moral Sentiments*, ed. D. D. Raphael and A. L. Macfie (Indianapolis, IN: Liberty Fund, 1982 [1759]).

13. Both Christianity and Buddhism embrace self-denial on the part of, for example, monks in service to the greater community. With regard to martyrs, to die in testimony of the truth is not, for believers, a sacrifice. In fairness, it should also be said that no society could long survive without people willing to defend the community against criminals, invaders, and the destructive forces of nature at the risk of their own lives.

14. *The Analects of Confucius* (London: George Allen & Unwin, 1949), p. 88.

15. Clifford F. Thies, "Economic Freedom and Crime: An Examination of the Gallup World Poll's Embedded Victim Survey," *Virginia Economic Journal* 18 (2013): 21–29.

Chapter 8

Exchange Rates

Among the earliest forms of money were cattle. Cattle were useful as money since they were in wide demand, more or less maintained themselves, and could be transported from one place to another (if the distance was not vast and if there were opportunities for the cattle to graze and water along the way). In many languages, words for money come from words for cattle.

Pecuniary (having to do with money) can be traced to the Latin word *pecu* meaning cattle or flock. *Pecu* is clearly related to the Sanskrit word for cattle, *paśu*. The first sound of pecuniary *pec* seems related to the Arabic word *baqara* and the Hebrew word *baqar*, which two words mean cow.

While cattle were useful as money, their usefulness as money for international trade was limited. As was intimated above, it was difficult to transport cattle across vast distances, especially when oceans or deserts intervened. Another form of money, more durable and more concentrated in weight and volume, would be better.

Eventually, metal coins emerged as money, both for domestic trade as well as for international trade. This section traces the evolution of the international monetary system from the time that coins served as money to modern fixed exchange rates. This history begins when units of metal became standardized in various shapes, including small disks. It continues with the impressing of symbols of national sovereignty onto the small disks, along with symbols of their value in domestic trade. This history then examines the attempt to get both gold and silver coins to simultaneously serve as money, a policy known as bimetallism. This section concludes with the classical gold standard and its breakdown. The next section looks at the attempt to restore a kind of gold standard (the Bretton Woods fixed exchange rate system).

EMERGENCE OF COINS

One of the early trading people of the Mediterranean region was the Phoenicians. The Phoenicians might be thought as living in modern day Lebanon because of the reputation of the overseas Lebanese for business, like the reputations of the overseas Chinese and overseas Indians. But, the Phoenicians lived in several places in the eastern Mediterranean. One of these places was the island of Crete, as part of the Minoan Civilization. The Minoans worshiped the bull, the symbol of male fertility. Their boats, which were large for that time, carried cattle across the Mediterranean, to offer the cattle in trade for local products.

About 1500 BC, the Phoenicians invented a new form of money that proved to be more efficient than cattle in international trade. This form of money involved curved metal rods evocative of a bull's horns. The rods contained a standardized measure of weight and the original rods were made of iron. The metal in the rods could be melted and recast into other forms, such as tools. After some time, the Phoenicians used other metals, such as copper, silver and gold, cast in standardized units that we would recognize as coins; that is, small disks.

Following the invention of coins, governments began to affix onto coins symbols of their sovereignty and of the coin's value in domestic trade. These markings might be viewed as attesting to the weight and fineness of the coins. The truth is that government-minted coins had the tendency to suffer from debasement, combined with the attempt to use the force of the state to maintain the value stated on the coin. *Debasement* is defined as the substitution of base metal for more valuable metal in coins; for example, the substitution of copper for silver in the Roman denarius.

The practice of debasement goes back to ancient times. The prophet Isaiah wrote, "Your silver has become dross, your wine diluted with water." Dross refers to base metal. The prophet Isaiah told us that the silver coins that had formerly circulated had come to be replaced by coins of base metal.

Similarly, the Islamic scholar Ibn Taymiyyah wrote, "If the ruler cancels the use of a certain coin and mints another kind of money for the people, he will spoil the riches which they possess." In both cases, these men severely criticized the rulers of their day for betraying the people through the practice of debasement, and called for religious revival.

The first recorded instance we have of the effects of debasement combined with the attempt to use the force of the state to maintain the value stated on coins is in the play "The Frogs," by Aristophanes of Greece, in the 5th century BC.

You know what I often think:
We treat our best men
The way we treat our mint
The silver and the golden
We were proud to invent
These unalloyed
Genuine coins, no less,
Ringing true and tested
Both abroad and [in] Greece
And now they're not employed
As if we were disgusted
And want to use instead
These shoddy coppers minted
Only yesterday
Or the day before
(as if that matters).[1]

In "The Frogs," a delegation from Athens descends into Hades for the purpose of resurrecting two well-respected politicians of the past to save the city-state from its current rulers. The current rulers are said to be like the base-metal coins in circulation, corrupt; while the rulers of the past are like the full-bodied, precious-metal coins that formerly circulated.

The full-bodied coins "rang true," that is, when flipped onto a solid wooden table, they gave out a distinctive ring. Think of Edgar Allen Poe's poem "The Bells." The heft, feel, and tone of the coins were sufficient, for most purposes, to distinguish a counterfeit from the genuine article. And these coins circulated abroad as well as at home because they had intrinsic value. In contrast, the debased coins were impossible to distinguish from any counterfeit, since they had no distinctive qualities, and were repugnant to foreigners and anyone else not compelled by law to accept them, just like the current politicians.

The passage does not actually say how the base-metal coins came to replace the full-bodied coins. Nevertheless, it can be inferred that the audience knew what had happened, since the play was a comedy, not an economics lesson. From historical sources, we know that Athens had been involved in a series of wars against Sparta and other Greek city-states, and that it was threatened by Persia.

The continuing expenses of these wars depleted Athens's treasury. Even the gold and silver objects at the temple were melted and recast as money. Then the city resorted to debasement and to legal-tender laws compelling acceptance of the debased coins at the values of precious-metal coins.

In the Roman Empire, the process of debasement was perfected. Gradually, the standard coin of the empire, the denarius, turned from the color of silver to the color of copper, as the government called in the outstanding coins, recast them with increasing proportions of copper, returning one new, further debased coin for each old coin turned in. Then, from time to time, the debased coins were called in, silver coins were distributed for multiple numbers of old copper coins, and the process re-commenced.

China developed a new form of debasement, replacing metal coins first with leather money and then with paper money. Marco Polo brought the news of the paper money to the Europeans. He wrote in his travelogue, "nor does anyone, at the peril of his life, refuse to accept it in payment." During the later years of Kublai Khan's reign, the issues of paper currency became excessive, and an inflationary cycle got underway.

During the reign of his successor, the fourth Mongol emperor, the world's first "currency reform" was undertaken. This currency reform involved a forced conversion of the old currency for new currency at the rate of five to one. The former prosperity was also replaced by corruption and decline.

As Europe began to emerge from its Dark Age, a new problem developed with coins: the circulation of a variety of coins with values other than the value of the metal of which they were made.[2] If a coin were greatly over-issued relative to the need of its country of origin for money, its value tended to equal the value of the metal of which it was made. That is, the over-issue of coins would tend to result in inflation to the point where the value of the coin reflected the value of its metal. But, if a coin were *not* over-issued, its value domestically tended to equal the value affixed to it by the government, even though the metal in these coins might not have been worth as much.

To illustrate this principle, let's say that a country needs 10,000 one-ounce silver coins to serve as its money. Let's also say that the country issues 5,000 one-ounce copper coins, engraved with the mark of the government that they were worth the same as one-ounce silver coins; and, that these coins were impossible to counterfeit. Then, the copper coins would not cause inflation but only displace an equal number of silver coins in domestic circulation.

With the emergence of many new nation-states in Europe, many of which issued coins whose stated values were greater than the value of the metal of which they were composed, there was a confusion of coins. To resolve this confusion, and to get both gold and silver coins simultaneously into circulation in Great Britain, King James II commissioned Sir Isaac Newton to determine the correct ratio of the value of silver to gold.

In 1703, after a careful study of the values of the various coins in circulation in Europe, Sir Isaac issued his report. But, Sir Isaac did not know that, in economics, what falls down might also rise up (or, that prices fluctuate). See Figure 8.1. And, he set the price of gold too high relative to the price of silver. As a result, full-bodied silver coins, being worth more as silver than as coins, were recast as silverware or shipped overseas to be recast as foreign coins.

Only worn, and therefore underweight, silver coins remained in circulation. Great Britain, in a botched attempt to establish a bimetallic standard, merely shifted the country from a silver standard to a gold standard.

Bimetallism

A century later, in 1803, the French succeeded in developing a working bimetallic standard. France decreed the price of gold to be 15½ times the price of silver. Several other countries did likewise. For about the next seventy years, this ratio set the worldwide ratio of the value of silver to the value of gold.

When the true value of gold was less than 15½ times the value of silver, France saw the coins in circulation and in bank reserves shift to gold coins. When the true value of gold was greater than 15½ times the value of silver, France saw the coins in circulation and in bank reserves shift to silver coins. For seventy years, France and the countries that joined with it in setting the official value of gold at 15½ times the value of silver were large enough to absorb whichever metal was overvalued by this ratio. Therefore, the ratio 15½ to 1 ruled throughout the world.[3]

The ratio 15½ to 1 was not only the price of gold relative to the price of silver, it also established a fixed exchange rate system for the world. For example, the exchange rate between the money of Great Britain (the pound),

Figure 8.1 Sir Isaac Newton fails to see that what falls down might bounce up. *Source:* Daniel Thies.

a gold standard country, and the money of India (the rupee), a silver standard country, was determined by the 15½ to 1 ratio.

Let's say that an Indian rupee was 11.66 grams of silver; and, that a British Crown (a gold coin worth 1 pound) 7.32 grams of an alloy consisting of 11 parts gold and 1 part silver.[4] Then, a British pound would tend to be worth 8.97 Indian rupees.

7.32 grams in a British pound * (11/12 gold) * 15.5 + 7.32 grams * (1/12 silver) = 104.62 grams of silver in a British pound

104.62 grams of silver / 11.66 grams of silver in an Indian rupee = 8.97 Indian rupees

The French bimetallic standard worked well enough in bringing stability to the value of money domestically (i.e., in terms of inflation) and internationally (i.e., in terms of exchange rates). But, this standard broke down during the 1870s because of a rise of the value of gold relative to the value of silver, beyond the ability of France to absorb the excess supply of silver.[5] The bimetallic standard was then replaced by the British gold standard for most of the world.

Gold Standard

It cannot be definitively said when the gold standard began (or, when the prior bimetallic standard ended), but it can be definitively said when the gold standard ended. The gold standard began during the 1870s, as one after another country shifted from silver or bimetallic standards to gold, and it ended in 1914, with the suspension of the gold standard associated with the outbreak of World War I.

The gold standard was, for most of the world, a system of fixed exchange rates.[6] Among the gold standard countries of the world, exchange rates were determined by the weight of coins.

Let's say that a U.S. Half Eagle (a $5 gold coin) consisted of 8.75 grams of the same gold-silver alloy as in a British Crown. Then, a British pound would tend to be worth 4.12 U.S. dollars.

7.32 grams in a British pound / [8.75 grams in a U.S. Half Eagle / 5] = 4.12

A Digression on Coins

In gold standard countries, silver performed what was called a subsidiary role. Specifically, silver coins served as small denomination currency at a stated value a bit in excess of their metallic value.

In the United States, from 1834 (when the United States shifted from a silver standard to a gold standard) to 1850, the country suffered from periodic shortages of small denomination currency (as happened in Great Britain following its adoption of the gold standard). This problem was solved by the issue of lightweight silver coins; that is, coins that have a stated value slightly in excess of their metallic value. During the time of the gold standard, the amount of these lightweight silver coins was kept limited, and they circulated at their stated value.

Eventually, the inflationary policies of the United States made the originally lightweight silver coins worth more as silver than their stated value. Therefore, in 1965, the federal government replaced silver coins with coins made mostly of copper and clad with a nickel-copper alloy polished so as to look like silver.[7]

Copper Coins

In China, the first coins were cast in the general shape of tools. This particular type of coin is called "knife money." By the 6th century, Chinese coins known as "cash" coins were standardized in the form a disk with a hole in the center. Because of the hole, these coins could be put onto strings. Chinese cash coins served the people of China and of certain neighboring countries into the early 20th century. During these times, China was officially on a silver standard, and the cash coins served as the money of the people at an exchange rate to silver that was sometimes set by custom and was sometimes at a floating exchange rate.

In the West, copper coins primarily served the purpose of small change in retail transactions. Private enterprise as well as governments issued copper coins.[8] In Great Britain, copper coins were typically issued as half-pennies and farthings (quarter-pennies). In the United States, copper coins (or, trade tokens if issued by private enterprise) were typically issued as pennies and half-pennies. Taking exchange rates into account, the British and American copper coins were roughly equal in value.[9]

Because of the continuing effect of inflation, the penny is no longer made of copper. Rather, since 1982, the penny is made out of zinc and electroplated with copper. Since inflation never stops with paper money, and because of the extra cost involved in electroplating, pennies now cost about two cents apiece to produce.

Other metals that have been used for coins include iron, nickel, zinc, lead, and aluminum. Nickel is a relatively soft metal and, to preserve the detail of any engraving, it should be cast in an alloy. The problem with nickel coins can be seen in the Buffalo Nickels that were in circulation in the United States during the early 20th century, which are badly worn.[10]

During World War II, the Jefferson Nickels that replaced the Buffalo Nickels were hardened with silver, to conserve on nickel. Because of inflation, the metal content of the early Jefferson Nickels is today worth about $3. Nowadays, Jefferson Nickels are cast with an alloy of nickel and copper. While this alloy serves to sufficiently harden the coin at a lower cost than the nickel-silver alloy, because of the continuing effect of inflation, the metal content of today's Jefferson Nickel is now worth about seven cents.

Contemporary Coins

Because of the continuing effect of inflation, an increasing number of countries have stopped trying to imitate the appearance of the coins that circulated when money had intrinsic value. For these countries, the purpose of coins is simply to serve the purpose of small denomination currency. Instead of coins establishing the standard of value for paper money, the paper money establishes the standard of value for coins. More will be said about *how* the standard of value of paper money is established in the next chapter. An increasing number of countries issue coins whose only relationship to value, other than their stated value, is their relative size. With these coins, the larger denomination coins are physically larger than the smaller denomination coins, but not necessarily in proportion to stated value.

FIXED EXCHANGE RATES

For thousands of years, silver was money. Then, following a series of attempts to have both silver and gold serve simultaneously as money, the Western nations wound up with a gold standard. The gold standard began during the 1870s, as one after another country shifted from silver or bimetallic standards to gold, and it ended in 1914, with the suspension of the gold standard associated with the outbreak of World War I.

The gold standard was, for most of the world, a system of fixed exchange rates. Among the gold standard countries of the world, exchange rates were determined by the weight of coins. This was discussed in the prior section. This section describes the system of fixed exchange rates established at the end of World War II that lasted until 1971, when the current floating exchange rate regime began. A *Fixed Exchange Rate* is when a currency's value is fixed against either the value of another currency, or to another measure of value such as gold. A *Floating Exchange Rate* is when a currency's value is allowed to fluctuate in response to the forces of supply and demand in the foreign exchange market. The next section talks about floating exchange rates.

The Bretton Woods Agreement

At the turn of the 19th into the 20th century, people in the highly advanced economies of that time looked forward with anticipation. Since the Napoleonic Wars, most countries had not had a major war. There was almost a hundred years of relative stability in prices and exchange rates. There was a stream of inventions including the automobile, the flying machine, a practical electric light bulb, the typewriter, and the adding machine. With rising standards of living, and the growth of democracy and free enterprise in the world, the future appeared to be very promising.

But, looking back, we know how things turned out: the rise of totalitarianism, world wars and genocide, the Great Depression, and the atomic bomb. Pope John Paul II described the 20th century as "the Century of Sorrows."

For many people during the early 20th century, a particular tragic event captured the disappointment. In 1912, a luxury passenger ship named the *Titanic*, the largest in the world, on its maiden voyage from England to New York, hit an iceberg and sunk. Of its 2,223 passengers and crew members, 1,517 perished. Most of those who died were men because of the rule "women and children first." Two years later, the world was engulfed in war.

The war that began in 1914 was originally known as "The Great War" until another came in 1939, "greater" than it. Then, the war that began in 1914 became known as World War I, and the war that began in 1939 as World War II. With the outbreak of World War I, the gold standard was suspended. During the years between World War I and World War II, there was an attempt to re-establish the gold standard, but the attempt failed. The details of the attempt and its failure are not important to this chapter. Rather, it is sufficient to say that during World War II, the United States, United Kingdom, and certain of their allies began to plan for the reconstruction of international trade and finance.

A prior chapter examined the attempt to reconstruct international trade that culminated in the GATT in Geneva, Switzerland, in 1947. This section examines the attempt to reconstruct international finance that culminated in an agreement at Bretton Woods, New Hampshire, in 1944. The Bretton Woods Agreement consisted of three parts:

- A system of fixed exchange rates;
- The International Monetary Fund (IMF); and
- The World Bank (originally, the International Bank for Reconstruction and Development).

The Bretton Woods System of Fixed Exchange Rates

Technically, the Bretton Woods system was a gold standard. But, instead of relying on currencies each being directly convertible into gold, it relied on currencies being fixed in their exchange rate to a reference currency (the U.S. dollar) that was convertible into gold for international settlements.[11] The purpose of this indirect gold standard was to enable the world's supply of gold to support a greatly increased world money supply. This would enable the countries of the world to avoid deflation.

During World War II, as during many other wars, countries suspended the gold standard and proceeded to largely finance the war with paper currency. The result this time, as during other wars, was inflation. After prior wars, there were deflations and associated recessions, to return prices to the former level and allow resumption of the gold or silver standard at the prewar parity. After the War of 1812, there was a sudden deflation that resulted in the Panic of 1819 and a long period of depressed economic conditions in many places south and west of Philadelphia. After the Civil War, there was a protracted gradual deflation along with a series of panics and recessions. After World War I, there was a two-part deflation, with the second part being devastating.

The Bretton Woods Agreement was to concentrate the world supply of gold in the United States, to "back" a multiplied amount of U.S. dollars. With the U.S. dollar "as good as gold," it could "back" an even larger multiple of the other currencies of the world. With this arrangement, there was no deflation after World War II and the postwar recession was relatively modest.

To be sure, from time to time, certain countries had difficulty maintaining their fixed exchange rates. One of the countries that had difficulties was Great Britain. In 1949 and again in 1967, Great Britain devalued the pound. In 1949, burdened by an enormous war debt, the pound was devalued from $4.03 to $2.80. In 1967, with a trade deficit, a budget deficit and a weak economy, the pound was again devalued from $2.80 to $2.40. This period of weakness in the British economy and finances continued into the 1970s.

Eventually, the United States was unable to maintain the value of the dollar relative to gold. In theory, the United States could have then devalued the dollar relative to gold; but, in fact, the United States, in 1971, floated the dollar.[12] The next section examines floating exchange rates.

FLOATING EXCHANGE RATES

In theory, it is easy to implement fixed exchange rates. One way is simply to define a currency as a weight of silver and only mint full-weight coins. This approach worked well for the United States for the first several decades of our country's existence. During that time, the dollar was defined as a certain weight of silver.

Coinage Act of 1791 defined the U.S. dollar as 416 mills of silver (this was the abstract money of the country). The dollar was approximately equal to four British shillings (but there weren't many of these). And, it was approximately equal to one Spanish dollar (in practice, this was the actual money of the country). The U.S. Mint in Philadelphia produced U.S. silver coins for a small fee.

Accounting books were kept in the abstract measure of value of the U.S. dollar. Bank notes and other evidences of debt were expressed in this abstract measure of value. While the U.S. Mint issued coins, most of the silver coins in circulation were Spanish, with the Spanish dollar usually passing at $1, but sometimes passing at a value based on weight.

Today, several countries use the U.S. dollar as their currency, most prominently, Panama. Since independence, Panama has used the U.S. dollar, supplemented by small denomination local currency. Panama has never suffered anything like the inflation certain other Latin American countries have suffered, and the country is known within its region for its strong private banks.

Breakdown of the Bretton Woods Agreement

If a government issues currency in the form of paper money, would it be able to maintain a fixed exchange rate? As was mentioned in the first section of this chapter, if the government issues *only a limited amount* of paper money, it can peg or maintain a fixed exchange rate of its currency to a reference currency. But, history is littered with failed attempts to maintain a peg. Among these failures was the failure of the United States to maintain the peg of the U.S. dollar to gold so as to maintain the fixed exchange rate system agreed to at Bretton Woods. Our failure ushered in the present system of floating exchange rates.

In some cases, the failure to maintain a pegged or fixed exchange rate has been so spectacular that it caused a financial crisis; for example, the East Asian Currency Crisis of 1997. Financial crises will be investigated in a later chapter.

Why do governments fail to maintain the pegged or fixed exchange rate of their paper money? In part, it is because of money illusion. Money illusion is the false appearance that a mere representation of value has value; or, that pieces of paper can be made valuable merely by printing numbers on them. Actually, there is some truth to this magic. But, who has the discipline to use this magic well?

Governments start deficit spending and covering their deficit with newly printed paper money.[13] The new money seems to be valuable, but as it circulates in the economy it eventually results in rising prices. In effect, the new money gains value at the expense of the mass of old money that becomes less valuable because of rising prices. The time between the issue of the new money and the rise of prices is variable, and this variable delay in the rise of prices contributes to the money illusion.

During the 1960s, the United States started deficit spending. Before then, deficits were episodic, associated with war and bad recessions, following which surpluses were run to gradually retire the debt. But, since the 1960s, the federal government has been deficit spending almost all the time. And, the deficits have tended to get larger and larger.

As prices began rising in the United States, it became increasingly clear that the country would not be able to maintain the peg of the U.S. dollar to gold at $35 per ounce. Although Americans were prohibited by law from owning gold bullion, foreign governments could demand that the U.S. Treasury redeem dollars in gold. After several requests were made to the United States to exchange gold for dollars, the president of the United States ended the gold standard.

Today, the major currencies of the world float against each other according to supply and demand in the foreign exchange market. The foreign exchange market exists almost everywhere. It exists wherever one currency is exchanged for another. Transactions in this market range from transactions between banks conducted electronically in million-dollar amounts, to transactions between retailers and their customers conducted with hand-to-hand currency in the amount of a few dollars.

The Interbank Market in Foreign Exchange

Nowadays, the backbone of the exchange market is an interbank market. This market consists of electronically connected market makers and their customers. *Market makers* set buy and sell prices for financial assets such as shares of stock (in the NASDAQ market) and currencies (in the foreign exchange market). The price at which a market maker is willing to buy is called the "bid;" and, the price at which a market maker is willing to sell is called the "ask." The ask price is high enough above the bid price so that on a "round trip" (a purchase by the market maker offset by a sale) the market maker makes a profit sufficient to cover the cost and risk involved in being a market maker. All transactions pass through the market maker (or one of the market makers if there is more than one).

Specialists are similar to market makers, but transactions can be made directly from a broker representing the seller to a broker representing the buyer. That is, transactions can bypass the specialist, at a price within the bid and ask agreeable to the two parties. This describes the trading of shares of stock in the New York Stock Exchange.

Among the very largest market makers in currencies are Deutsche Bank, UBS, and Citibank. These banks are market makers for each of the major currencies in the world, and continuously update their quotations of bid and ask prices so as to maintain their exposure to unexpected changes in foreign exchange rates within acceptable limits. These banks operate in very large volumes and with very small margins. Their customers are mostly other banks, governments, and large corporations.

In addition to the very largest market-making banks, there are several hundred other banks that engage in foreign exchange operations. These banks mainly provide foreign exchange services to nonbank customers.

The daily volume of foreign exchange transactions is about $3 trillion. This compares to about $1 trillion a day in stock market transactions.

To illustrate a market-maker transaction, a market maker might quote the Swiss franc at "1.4585-90" or just "85-90," if it can be assumed that the "big figure" (i.e., 1.45) is understood. In any case, it means that the market maker is willing to buy $10 million at the rate of 1.4585 Swiss francs for 1 U.S. dollar, and sell $10 million at the rate of 1.4590 Swiss francs for 1 U.S. dollar.

To illustrate what is typically involved in updating quotations, let's say that a very large market marker receives a series of orders to buy Swiss francs. In real time, the bank assesses its exposure to unexpected changes in each of the currencies in which it deals. In the case where the bank has a series of sales of Swiss francs, unless these sales are offset by other transactions, the bank may need to hedge its newly developed exposure to a possible loss if the Swiss franc were to suddenly strengthen in value. For example, it could buy Swiss francs from another bank. But, if other banks also find that they too have been selling Swiss francs, they too would be looking to buy, not sell Swiss francs.

The first market maker to figure out that the Swiss franc is in worldwide short supply would then raise both its bid and ask price so as to limit its risk. This change in price will be imitated by other banks and will bring about a new equilibrium in the worldwide supply of and demand for this particular currency.

Scenario A. To further expound on this example, let's say the market maker has a series of five sales of Swiss francs for U.S. dollars. And, during the same time, the market maker has a series of five sales of U.S. dollars for Swiss francs. Then, the market maker has maintained its holdings of Swiss francs and need not take any further action.

Scenario B. Now let's say the market maker has a series of five sales of Swiss francs for U.S. dollars. And, at the same time, *some other* market maker has a series of five sales of U.S. dollars for Swiss francs. In this case, each of the market makers has an imbalance. One has too few Swiss francs and the other too many Swiss francs. Then, each market maker will seek to rebalance its holdings of Swiss francs—the first by buying, and the second by selling Swiss francs. Since the change in the demand for Swiss francs in the interbank foreign exchange market is equal to the change in supply, the sale of Swiss francs from the surplus market maker and purchase by the deficit market marker will occur at the current exchange rate.

Scenario C. Now let's say the market maker has a series of five sales of Swiss francs for U.S. dollars. And, at the same time, some other market maker *also has* a series of five sales of Swiss francs for U.S. dollars. In this case, each of the market makers will seek to re-balance its holdings by buying Swiss francs. The demand for Swiss francs in the interbank foreign exchange market goes up without a corresponding change in the supply, and this increase in demand will cause the Swiss franc to appreciate or rise in value relative to the U.S. dollar.

The Retail Market in Foreign Exchange

For centuries, one of the functions of banks has been money changing. Money changing includes exchanging the mix of denominations received during the course of a day's business by merchants for the mix of denominations they need to open their shops the next day.

Money changing can have religious significance. Today, in the state of Kelantan in Malaysia, some Muslims prefer using gold and silver coins to using the paper money issued by their national government. In the days of Jesus, money changers outside the Temple of Solomon exchanged the coins of the Roman Empire, depicting the image of Caesar as though he were a god, for traditional Jewish coins, as it was forbidden to bring the Roman coins into the temple.

Money changing is offered by bankers, international hotels, cab drivers, and merchants in tourist locations as a service. These money changers deal in small amounts, and at fees that are relatively large. For example, while the fee implicit in the bid-ask spread for the very largest market makers is 0.03 of 1 percent (referred to as 3 basis points), the fee charged at a bank kiosk at the airport might be 3 percent and the fee charged by an international hotel 7 percent. The next chapter considers the underlying factors involved in the determination of exchange rates.

The International Monetary Fund (IMF)

The IMF was created to assist countries in maintaining their fixed exchange rates or, upon a devaluation, to establish and maintain a new fixed exchange rate. The main tool available to the IMF to provide this assistance was the money it received from its member nations. The IMF can use this money to make loans to governments having difficulty maintaining their exchange rates, presuming that the difficulty is only temporary.

With the end of the Bretton Woods fixed exchange rate system, the purpose of the IMF has changed. Today, its concern is to help countries maintain their balance of payments. Problems with balance of payments typically arise when a country has become dependent on foreign credit to finance government deficit spending.

The main tool of the IMF remains the money it has received from its member nations. It will use this money to make loans to governments with debt problems that have adopted plans considered by the IMF to be credible for restoring balance to the government's budget. The IMF might also "restructure" debt so as to bring the restructured debt payments in line with the country's ability to pay. The IMF will usually do this by stretching out loan repayment periods and lowering the average interest rate on the debt.

The governors of the IMF are named by its member nations. These governors have votes in proportion to the contribution of their member nations. The governor appointed by the United States, which provides 17.7 percent of the capital of the IMF, has the largest vote, followed by the governors appointed by Japan (6.6 percent) and Germany (6.1 percent). The current managing director of the IMF is Christine Lagarde of France.

The World Bank

In a sense, the mission of the World Bank is the opposite of the mission of the IMF. The IMF was created to deal with problems. The World Bank was created to deal with opportunities. The IMF deals with the problems associated with deficit spending. The World Bank deals with the opportunities associated with investment spending. The World Bank uses the money it receives from its member nations to finance development projects in the poorer countries of the world. Examples of these projects include roads, dams, irrigation projects, education, and health services. Assistance is given either in the form of loans or grants.

Some of these development projects directly produce revenue with which loans can be repaid. For example, an electricity-generating plant can sell the electricity it generates. Some other projects indirectly develop revenue. For example, improved roads can develop additional revenue from excise taxes on increased sales of gasoline and diesel fuel. These two kinds of projects can be easily financed by loans. The repayment of these loans serves to replenish the fund out of which the World Bank can finance new projects in the future. In addition, the proof that these projects are actually facilitating economic development is that these loans are repaid.

There is a third kind of project that does not lead to easy-to-identify revenue, but which can be justified based on a fair estimate of the costs and benefits involved. An example of such a project is inoculations against contagious diseases, where the benefit consists of enabling more children to reach working age. If we can presume that the country is progressing as a whole in terms of establishing the rule of law, developing its infrastructure, providing basic education, and fighting corruption, then we can project a future in which these children, upon reaching working age, will be able to find employment. It cannot be over-emphasized that the mission of the World Bank is to eradicate poverty. It is not to maintain people in poverty. The World Bank is not interested in enabling more children to survive to working age so they will be poor. It is interested in enabling more children to survive to working age so they will find work. Projects of this third kind—where it is difficult to identify revenue—are sometimes financed by loans (to be repaid from general revenue) and sometimes financed by grants.

The World Bank says "the vicious cycle of poverty" continues, where it does, for two reasons:

- The lack of the rule of law and corruption, which prevents investors from financing economic development in countries that should be attractive places to invest in terms of their economic potential; and,
- The lack of capital in the world, primarily because of the deficits being run by the governments of many of advanced economies.

In theory, there should be no systematic poverty in the world; although, of course, there will always be poor individuals. In practice, some countries are geographically isolated, or closed to international relations, or suspicious of foreign investment; and, some countries have so many fundamental problems as to make the potential benefits of foreign investment problematic.

As with the IMF, voting within the World Bank is proportional to capital contributed. The United States has the largest vote (15.9 percent), followed by Japan (6.8 percent), China (4.4 percent), and Germany (4.0 percent). The current president of the World Bank is Jim Yong Kim of the United States.

There are several multinational and national development banks, organized similar to the World Bank. Most prominent among these other development banks are the African Development Bank and the Asian Development Bank.

Today's Pegged Exchange Rates

While most major currencies today float relative to each other, many currencies are fixed or "pegged" to reference currencies. The most significant reference currencies are the U.S. dollar and the euro. Among the currencies that are pegged to the U.S. dollar are several Caribbean Basin and Latin American currencies, several Arab currencies, and several East Asian currencies. The forms of these pegs vary widely, from dollarization to a managed float. Among those pegged to the euro are the West Africa CFA franc and the Central Africa CFA franc. Reasons for pegs include: fixing the exchange rate of a country to its main partner in international trade and investment and ending the consequences of ruinous inflation.

Pegged Exchange Rate: While some people consider a pegged exchange rate to be the same thing as a fixed exchange rate, a pegged exchange rate can be defined as a fixed exchange within an overall floating exchange rate regime.

Dollarization: Since independence in 1904, Panama's currency has been the U.S. dollar (except that the country issues its own small denomination currency). In recent years, several other countries dollarized in order to end ruinous inflations. These include Ecuador in 2000, El Salvador in 2001, and Zimbabwe in 2009. In Zimbabwe, total inflation had reduced the Zimbabwe dollar to a very small fraction of its original value.[14]

1 Zimbabwe dollar at beginning = 10 septillion or 10^{25} Zimbabwe dollars at end

Currencies with 1-to-1 exchange rates: Several countries peg their currency to the U.S. dollar at a 1-to-1 exchange rate and, domestically, dollars and the domestic currency both circulate. Among these countries are: The Bahamas, Bermuda, Brunei, Liberia, and Argentina from 1991 to 2002. In the case of The Bahamas and Bermuda, the 1-to-1 exchange rate reflects the interests of the country in tourism.

Currencies with exchange rates different from 1-to-1: Several countries peg their currency to the U.S. dollar at a ratio different from 1-to-1. The fact that the exchange rate is not 1-to-1 makes it a little awkward for dollars and the domestic currency to circulate together.

- *Belize*: US$1 = 2 Belize $
- *Hong Kong*: US$1 = 7.75 to 7.85 HK$
- *Saudi Arabia*: US$1 = 3.75 Saudi riyals
- *Taiwan*: US$1 = 30 New Taiwan $
- *Venezuela*: US$1 = 4.3 Venezuela bolivars (*2011-2012*)[15]

To say that a currency is pegged to the U.S. dollar does not necessarily mean that it is never devalued (or, revalued, that is, increased in its exchange rate relative to the U.S. dollar). Since the 1990s, the New Taiwan dollar has been devalued twice, from 25-to-1 to 28-to-1, and again to 30-to-1.

Also, to say that a currency is pegged to the U.S. dollar does not necessarily mean the peg is exact. In 1983, Hong Kong pegged the Hong Kong dollar to the U.S. dollar at 7.80 HK$ to US$1. Today, Hong Kong allows small fluctuations about this peg.

Currencies with a Managed Floating Exchange Rate

Several countries have a managed floating exchange rate against the U.S. dollar. Most prominent among these countries is China. China has a "managed floating exchange rate" because its currency is not fully convertible. That is, there are restrictions on the conversion of renminbi (meaning, units of Chinese yuan) for foreign currency, and of foreign currency for renminbi.

According to the United States, China is using exchange controls to maintain an undervalued currency. According to China, it is still in the process of moving from a closed, centrally planned economy to an open, market-oriented economy.

Currencies with a Dirty Floating Exchange Rate

While some people consider a managed float and a dirty float to mean the same thing, these can be distinguished in the following way:

Managed Floating Exchange Rate: The monetary authority attempts to influence the exchange rate by quantitative controls on conversion of domestic for foreign currency.

Dirty Floating Exchange Rate: The monetary authority attempts to influence the exchange rate by buying and selling international reserves.

Summary

- Soon after the invention of coins, the process of minting coins was taken over by the government. In theory, the stamp of the government could assure the weight and fineness of coins. In fact, the stamp of the government often involved the special form of inflation known as debasement.
- During the early modern age, Western governments attempted to get both gold and silver coins into side-by-side circulation. They attempted to do this by fixing the value of gold in terms of silver. The most famous attempt was that of Sir Isaac Newton. The failure of this attempt shifted Great Britain to a gold standard.
- A subsequent attempt by France to fix the value of gold in terms of silver worked well for about seventy years. As a result, for most of the 19th century, almost all of the currencies of the world, whether gold or silver, were fixed in their exchange rates to each other.

- During the 1870s, the French bimetallic standard broke down, and was replaced by the British gold standard. The British gold standard lasted until the start of World War I.
- From the end of World War I, there was a failed attempted to re-establish the former British gold standard.
- At the end of World War II, there was an attempt to establish a new gold standard called the Bretton Woods Agreement. With this new system, all the currencies of the world were to be fixed in their value to the U.S. dollar. The U.S. dollar was, in turn, to be convertible into gold for the purpose of international settlements. This system lasted until 1971.
- Today, the major currencies of the world float against each other. Their exchange rates are determined by the forces of supply and demand. (The next chapter examines the underlying causes of the supply and demand for currencies.)
- While the major currencies of the world float against each other, a number of currencies are pegged to the U.S. dollar and to the euro.
- Two financial institutions that were part of the Bretton Woods Agreement survive to this day.
- One of these financial institutions is the IMF. The original purpose of the IMF was to help countries maintain or re-establish their fixed exchange rates. Today, the purpose is to help countries with their balance of payments. Usually, the IMF helps countries make their payments in return for the adoption of reforms that will increase the capacity of the country to make its payments on its own in the future.
- The other financial institution is the World Bank. The World Bank provides loans and grants to assist the economic development of low- and middle-income countries.

NOTES

1. *Aristophanes: The Complete Plays*, trans. Paul Roche, (New York: New American Library, 2005), p. 573.

2. Thomas J. Sargent and François R. Velde, *The Big Problem with Small Change* (Princeton, NJ: Princeton University Press, 2002).

3. Lleland B. Yeager, *International Monetary Relations*, 2nd ed. (New York: Harper & Row, 1976), p. 296.

4. Because gold is a relatively soft metal, it is usually made into coins as part of an alloy.

5. At the time, this was called the fall of silver, not the rise of gold. Among the factors contributing to the fall of silver and the rise of gold was the reduced demand for silver as money in countries switching to the gold standard, so that as some countries switched to the gold standard other countries felt that they, too, had to switch to the gold standard.

6. It was also a system of floating exchange rates between the gold standard countries (such as Great Britain and the United States) and silver standard countries (such as China and India).

7. In 2011, the federal government convicted a man of counterfeiting for selling silver coins that have the appearance of its copper-nickel coins.

8. George Selgin, *Good Money: Birmingham Button Makers, the Royal Mint and the Beginnings of Modern Coinage, 1775–1821* (Ann Arbor, MI: University of Michigan Press, 2008).

9. In the English money system prior to 1971, there were 12 pence in a shilling and 20 shillings in a pound; and, thus, there were 240 pence in a pound. As a pound was worth something more than 4 U.S. dollars, a British half-penny was the equivalent of about one U.S. cent. Taking inflation into account, a British half-penny or an American penny of the 19th century would be worth about 5 U.S. cents of today.

10. Buffalo Nickels that are not worn were either never in circulation or soon removed from circulation.

11. In 1933, it was made illegal for Americans to own gold (except in the form of jewelry and collectible coins). But, the U.S. government stood ready to redeem its money in gold to foreigners. This connection of the dollar to gold was ended in 1971. Shortly after this, ownership of gold was re-legalized within the United States.

12. To be a little more honest, the United States attempted to devalue the dollar relative to gold but Germany declined to participate in the inflationary policies of the United States and floated the German mark. That's actually how the Bretton Woods fixed rate system ended.

13. Governments can also spend newly printed paper money indirectly, through loans and loan guarantees.

14. The total inflation is partially obscured by three currency reforms in which outstanding currency was exchanged old for new at ratios ranging from 1,000-to-1 to 1 trillion-to-1. Even with these exchanges, the amounts written on Zimbabwe currency reached 100 trillion dollars.

15. Today there are three official rates, preferential exchange rates 6.3 bolivars = US$1 and 12 bolivars = US$1 for purchases approved by the government, and 172 bolivars = US$1 for other purchases. Profits on the latter subsidize losses on the preferential exchanges. There is also a black-market rate in which 450 bolivars = US$1 during June 2015.

Chapter 9

Determination of Exchange Rates

In 1971, with the end of the Bretton Woods fixed exchange rate system, the world embarked on a new system of exchange rates. For about 2,000 years, the civilized nations of the world relied primarily on silver for money. Then, for about a hundred years, gold played the primary role. When it was introduced, paper money was merely a claim on metal. The paper money was not itself money. The referenced metal was money. To be sure, this long history was tinctured by inflation, from the debasement of coins to the suspension of convertibility of paper money into metal as often happened during times of war and financial crisis. But, these times of inflation were exceptions to the rule. The rule was that money was something of intrinsic value, which value served as a reference or standard of value for all other prices.

Beginning in 1703, with Sir Isaac Newton's report on the value of gold relative to silver, there were attempts to get gold and silver to serve simultaneously as money, by using the force of government to fix the value of one relative to the other. The first attempt—Great Britain's—served only to shift that country from a silver standard to a gold standard. A subsequent attempt—France's—worked well enough for about seventy years. But, such are the vicissitudes of prices, France's attempt was always doomed to failure. The failure of the French bimetallic standard was followed by the British gold standard, a standard that prevailed for about forty years. Skipping over the failed attempt to re-establish a gold standard between World War I and World War II, toward the end of World War II, there was another attempt to re-establish a gold standard, the Bretton Woods Agreement. This system of fixed exchange rates lasted only twenty-five years.

The breakdown of the Bretton Woods Agreement ushered in a floating exchange rate system. In this system, each of the currencies of the world has no value domestically except as is indicated by price indexes; and, money has no value internationally except the exchange rates determined by the supply and demand for currencies. That is, money has no intrinsic value; or, to put it another way, the intrinsic value of money is zero, and any actual value of money comes from essentially political decisions to limit its supply.

This chapter investigates the determination of exchange rates when currencies do not have intrinsic value; that is, when they fluctuate or float in their values.

ABSOLUTE PURCHASING POWER PARITY

If the cost of transportation is zero, if there are no tariffs or other barriers to trade, if all goods are tradable, if all goods are commodities, and if there is no lag or delay in the adjustment of trade patterns, then it would be easy to demonstrate that exchange rates would simply reflect differences in price ratios. To be sure, there are a lot of "if's" involved in absolute purchasing power parity. Because of these "if's," absolute purchasing power parity is not thought to hold in the short run. It is, instead, thought to be only a long-run tendency. Some of these "if's" are explored below. But, whether or not absolute purchasing power parity is correct in either the short- or in the long run, the model is a good starting point.

Let's say the price of a barrel of crude oil is $60 in the United States and 480 pesos in Mexico. If absolute purchasing power parity holds, what must be the exchange rate of the U.S. dollar to the Mexican peso?

$$E_{MXN,US\$} = P_{MXN} / P_{US\$} = 480 / 60 = 8$$

Comparability of Prices

While crude oil may sound like a commodity, crude oil differs according to sulfur content and in other ways. West Texas oil is described as "light, sweet oil" because it is low in sulfur, making it excellent for refining. European or North Sea oil, also known as "Brent oil," is higher in sulfur. The OPEC oil price is an average of oil prices from seven countries (Algeria, Indonesia, Nigeria, Saudi Arabia, Dubai, Venezuela, and Mexico), which crude oil is, on average, yet higher in sulfur. Comparing crude oil prices across countries therefore requires adjustment for sulfur content. West Texas oil usually sells for a small premium relative to Brent oil, and for a larger premium relative to OPEC oil. The adjustment for sulfur content is well known within the oil industry and is not really a problem for comparing the prices of crude oil around the world. But, it is often difficult to adjust prices for differences in quality because many goods and services are more heterogeneous than crude oil.

The Big Mac Standard

In 1986, in a humorous attempt to compare prices around the world, the *Economist* developed the Big Mac standard. The Big Mac is a hamburger sandwich sold by the multinational corporation MacDonald's. The ingredients of the product are, according to the company's famous jingle, "two all beef patties, special sauce, lettuce, cheese, pickles, onions on a sesame seed bun." Plus, there is the energy needed to cook the meat, the wages of the workers who prepare the hamburger sandwich, and the rent of the space used by the restaurant. The Big Mac is therefore a convenient internationally standardized set of goods and services.

If the Big Mac standard is to be taken seriously, it indicates that prices differ considerably from what would be implied by absolute purchasing power parity. According to the July 2011 issue of the *Economist* magazine, exchange rates range from half the exchange rates implied by the Big Mac standard to twice those rates. The cheapest Big Macs in the world are to be found in India, China, Hong Kong, Thailand, and Malaysia. The most expensive Big Macs are to be found in Norway, Sweden, Switzerland, and the Euro area. What these price differences might mean is not clear.

International Price Surveys

Since 2005, the international price comparison program of the World Bank enables precise comparisons of the purchasing powers of the currencies of the world. The program involves the compilation of an internationally standardized set of prices of goods and services. This price index is part of the World Bank's continuing effort to measure economic development. In this case, to adjust measures such as GDP per capita for differences in the purchasing power of currencies. These data can be used to investigate the extent to which exchange rates reflect prices. While there is a strong positive correlation between exchange rates and the purchasing power of currencies, the variances from a 1-to-1 ratio are too large to be explained by problems with adjustments for quality differences. Something else must be affecting exchange rate in addition to price ratios, at least in the short run.

Non-traded Goods

The most obvious non-traded good is land. As a result, the price of land and the rental cost of residential and nonresidential real estate vary significantly. This is true *within* countries, where exchange rates are not involved, as well as between countries. According to the large commercial real estate company Cushman & Wakefield, annual commercial rents averaged $35.86 per square within the United States in 2011, but were as high as $50.00 in Washington, DC, and $63.35 in Midtown Manhattan in New York City.

Because of differences in the price of land and in rents, other prices are affected. For example, because rent is high, the overall cost of doing business in certain places is high, which impacts the cost of all goods and services produced in these places, and also impacts wages in these places. As to how these higher prices and wages can be sustained, it must be because of some competitive advantage of the place (such as a harbor) or by the competitive advantage that comes along with a concentration of people in a particular place.

Relative Purchasing Power Parity

Relative purchasing power parity concerns changes in exchange rates. It says that *changes* in exchange rates are determined by *changes* in prices.

Let's say that the inflation rate in the United States is 4 percent and the inflation rate in the Great Britain is 12 percent. Then, if relative purchasing power parity holds, over the course of a year, the U.S. dollar will appreciate against the British pound by 8 percent.

$$\%\text{change}E_{US,GB} = \%\ \text{change}P_{US} - \%\text{change}P_{GB} = 4\% - 12\% = -8\%$$

If, at the beginning of the year, it took $5 to purchase 1£, then, at the end of the year, it will take $4.60. Relative purchasing power parity, like absolute purchasing power, is generally thought to hold *in the long run*. In the short run, exchange rate changes can be quite different from relative rates of inflation.

Because it only applies to *changes in* prices, relative purchasing power parity allows for permanent differences in prices due to non-traded goods, tariffs and other barriers to trade, and transportation costs. It is, therefore, a bit more flexible than absolute purchasing power parity.

Real Exchange Rates

Real exchange rates are related to the concept of relative purchasing power parity. Real exchange rates are exchange rates adjusted for the relative rates of inflation. Because an internationally standardized set of prices has not been available until recently, the calculation of real exchange rates has involved an essentially arbitrary choice of a base year or base period. If purchasing power parity held during the base period, then changes in exchange rates should reflect relative changes in prices.

In the above example, where the inflation rate is 12 percent in Great Britain and 4 percent in the United States, the U.S. dollar should appreciate by

8 percent against the British pound. If the U.S. dollar appreciated by more than 8 percent, we might expect the U.S. dollar to be overvalued relative to the British pound; and, the British pound undervalued relative to the U.S. dollar.

Over the long period from 1879 to 2016, the geometric means of the rates of inflation were 3.17 in Great Britain and 2.25 in the United States, a difference of 0.92 percent. Over this same long period of time, the dollar appreciated against the pound by an average of 0.89 percent per year, almost exactly the same number.[1] The closeness of these two calculations argues in favor or real exchange rates. However, from time to time, the ratio of prices in the United States versus Great Britain deviated significantly from the exchange rate of the dollar versus the pound. These deviations indicate that real exchange rates only hold in the long run.

This history of the U.S. dollar relative to the British pound suggests that, in the long run, changes in exchange rates reflect changes in prices. But, it also suggests that deviations from purchasing power parity can be large and persistent. That is, at times, one of these two currencies was significantly overvalued; and, the other significantly undervalued.

Case Study: Argentina

Argentina has always had problems with debt. It is not surprising that, upon the breakdown of the Bretton Woods Agreement, it resorted to massive inflation.

During the mid-20th century, Juan Perón ascended to power. His wife was the beautiful Eva Perón, "Evita." The government he established was characterized by favored industries, powerful labor unions, central planning, high taxes, and heavy regulations. Under Perón and during subsequent administrations, the rate of inflation was in a range of 20 to 30 percent per year. Then, following the breakdown of the Bretton Woods Agreement, the rate of inflation accelerated to hundreds of percent per year. During the 1990s, a currency reform was implemented that put an end to the massive inflation.

With such massive inflation, it is easy to see the correlation between the exchange rate of the Argentine peso for the U.S. dollar, with the ratio of prices in Argentina and the United States, as measured by each country's index of consumer prices.

Case Study: Indonesia

During the rule of President Suharto, Indonesia made significant advances in industrialization, standards of living, and health. But, his administration was marred by authoritarian rule and corruption. During the 1980s, the currency of the country was pegged to the U.S. Dollar and, for a time, this seemed to further the country's economic development. Then, in 1997, the country's currency collapsed, the exchange rate rose very dramatically, and the country fell into a terrible recession.

There is a rough correlation between the movement of the exchange rate between the Indonesian rupiah and the U.S. dollar, with the ratio of prices in the two countries. But, there are also some noticeable deviations. In the case of Indonesia, the rate of inflation was not so massive that it dwarfed all other influences on exchange rates.

Case Study: Germany

Compared to many other countries, the United States has not suffered much inflation. Germany is an exception. Germany has had less inflation than the United States. Probably because of the disastrous hyperinflation that followed World War I, the German people adamantly oppose inflation. Upon the end of the Bretton Woods Agreement, the German mark tended to *appreciate* against the dollar. Therefore, the mark tended to appreciate against the dollar.

A Recap of the Section

The chapter has barely gotten started with the determination exchange rates, and already this section has come to its conclusion. This discussion will continue in the next section. The following summarizes what has been covered thus far:

The Bretton Woods fixed exchange rate system broke down in 1971. This happened because the United States failed to restrict its issue of paper money so as to maintain the value of the U.S. dollar at $35 equals 1 ounce of gold.

Exchange rates tend in the long run to reflect the ratio of prices in local currency of goods that are traded. For example, if the price of a barrel of crude oil is $60 in the United States and 480 pesos in Mexico, it can be supposed that the exchange rate of the Mexican peso is 8-to-1 against the U.S. dollar. This condition is called "Absolute Purchasing Power Parity."

For various reasons, exchange rates differ from the ratios of local prices. Among these reasons are problems with comparing the prices of goods that are not exactly similar, and the existence of non-traded goods. There are also tariff and nontariff barriers to trade, the cost of transportation, and the time and cost involved in the adjustment of trade patterns to changes in exchange rates. Nevertheless, it is useful to think that *changes* in exchange rates will tend to equal *changes* in prices in the long run. This condition is called "Relative Purchasing Power Parity."

THE ADJUSTMENT MECHANISM

This section examines the process by which exchange rates and prices are brought into equilibrium. As a starting point, equilibrium is defined to be when the funds flowing into a country are equal to the funds flowing out, so that the current account is in balance (and necessarily the capital account is in balance). Equilibrium is achieved when the exchange rate and the price ratio together result in the current account being in balance.

As was seen in Figure 6.1, the current account turned significantly negative twice since the 1960s; first, during the 1980s, and a second time, during the first decade of the 2000s. Each time was preceded by a strong dollar. With a strong dollar, consumers find that imports are a bargain, and producers find it difficult to sell overseas. A weak dollar would have the opposite effects on trade and the current account balance.

Because the United States issues the world reserve currency, it can be argued that equilibrium occurs not a current account balance of zero, but at a small negative number such as 1 percent of GDP. When the U.S. dollar is overvalued, as occurred during the 1980s and the first decade of the 2000s, the U.S. current account deficit increases. Either the dollar would have to weaken relative to other currencies or prices in the United States would have to fall so as to encourage exports and discourage imports and reduce the current account deficit. The next several sections explore how this adjustment takes place.

Adjustment within a Currency Union

The analysis of adjustment can start with a situation in which there is no exchange rate. This could refer to a currency union, as is the case of the Eurozone, and this could refer to a large country all the parts of which use the same currency, as is the case of the United States.

Let's say that producers in the state of Texas are able to make goods and services at a low cost relative to producers in the other states in the United States. Then, the state of Texas would tend to sell more goods in the rest of the country, and would tend to buy less goods from the rest of the country. The state of Texas would generate a current balance surplus with respect to the rest of the country. Since the state of Texas uses the same currency as the rest of the country, changes in the exchange rate cannot be part of adjustment process bringing the current account of the state of Texas into balance.

Ignoring movements of capital and labor across state borders, prices within Texas would have to rise and prices in the rest of the country would have to fall in order to bring about this balance. This happens automatically as money flows into Texas from the rest of the country, to pay for Texas's surplus of exported goods. The additional money in Texas would tend to raise prices there, and the reduced amount of money elsewhere in the country would tend to lower prices in the rest of the country.

Much the same thing happens in the Eurozone when a country's current account is not in balance. Let's say that producers in Germany are able to make goods and services at a low cost relative to producers in the other countries of the Eurozone. Then, Germany would tend to sell more goods in the rest of the Eurozone, and would tend to buy less goods from the rest of the Eurozone. Germany would generate a current account surplus with respect to the rest of the Eurozone. Since Germany uses the same currency as the rest of the Eurozone, changes in the exchange rate cannot be part of adjustment process bringing the current account of the Germany into balance. Ignoring movements of capital and labor across national borders, prices within Germany would have to rise and prices in the rest of the Eurozone would have to fall in order to bring about this balance.

There is a big problem with relying on price adjustments alone to bring the current account into balance. Prices are very difficult to lower, especially wages, the price of labor. In addition to the normal resistance to wage cuts, there may be wages set by union contracts, minimum wage laws and equal pay laws that make wage cutting nearly impossible. If the only mechanism for bringing the current account into balance is prices, massive unemployment may result from a current account imbalance, and the imbalance may persist.

The United States has relatively free labor markets. In addition, it is relatively easy for labor and capital to flow from one to another part of the country. Flexible wages, aided by labor and capital flows, usually work well enough within the United States to prevent severe regional imbalances.

The same things cannot be said of the Eurozone. Labor markets in Europe are highly unionized and regulated. While labor can relocate within the European Union, language and other differences inhibit labor flows across countries. Capital flows are inhibited by the rise of populist-left governments in certain countries, which make tenuous the rule of law. As a result, following the Financial Panic of 2008, massive unemployment opened up in the countries of southern Europe. This problem was anticipated by Milton Friedman when the euro was being introduced.

The Mundell-Friedman Debate

Robert Mundell is called the father of the euro, the shared currency of the members of the Eurozone within the European Union. Upon the introduction of the euro, in 2000, the *Financial Post* featured a debate, adapted below, between him and Milton Friedman. Friedman advocated floating exchange rates long before the breakdown of the Bretton Woods Agreement, and was skeptical concerning the euro.

Robert Mundell: The euro demonstrates that a well-planned fixed exchange rate zone can be successful. Speculation against the lira and the mark, the franc and the peseta, and all the other currencies are now a thing of the past. Uncertainty over exchange rates and destabilizing capital movements has ended.

The euro suggests that other currency areas can work when prospective members agree on a common inflation rate and a coordinated monetary policy. It is important, however, to distinguish between a single-currency monetary union that involves each country ending its own currency, and a multiple-currency monetary union, such as preceded the euro in Europe. The latter suffered recurrent speculative attacks that eventually undermined that approach and necessitated an approach based on a shared currency.

Milton Friedman: Robert Mundell and I agree that the euro has no historical precedent. We also agree that its achievement was driven by political, not economic, considerations, by the belief that the euro would contribute to greater political integration that would in turn render war among the states of Europe impossible. Political integration would, eventually, make the monetary and political areas coterminous, which is the historical norm.

But, Ireland requires at the moment a very different monetary policy than, say, Spain or Portugal. A flexible exchange rate would enable each to have the appropriate monetary policy. With a shared currency, they cannot. With a shared currency, adjustment requires changes in internal prices and wages, and movements of people and of capital. These are severely limited by differences in culture and by extensive government regulations in Europe. As the members of the Eurozone experience asynchronous shocks, economic difficulties will emerge.

Adjustment with Fixed Exchange Rates

In theory, it is simple to maintain a fixed or pegged exchange rate. When a country has a current account deficit, it should reduce the domestic money supply; and, when the country has a current account surplus, it should increase the domestic money supply. Following this rule, many countries have maintained the peg of their currency to the reference currency for long periods of time. But, many other countries have run into difficulties. Let's follow the chain of cause and effect that is *supposed* to happen with fixed or pegged exchange rates:

Current account deficit *is supposed to lead to a reduction* in the money supply *and a fall in* prices that will result in a current account balance

Current account surplus *is supposed to lead to an increase* in the money supply *and a rise* in prices that will result in a current account balance

This chain of cause and effect looks similar to what happens automatically within a currency union. What is similar is that the adjustment mechanism requires prices to change in order to bring about equilibrium. As stated in the case of a currency union, relying on prices only requires prices (and, in particular, wages) to be flexible, and this may be a problem. What is different between the adjustment mechanism with fixed exchange rates is that changes in the money supply are discretionary with fixed exchange rates (being the result of decisions of the central bank), while changes in the money supply are automatic in a currency union.

With a currency union, the shared money supply simply flows from one to another region as regions run current account surpluses and deficits. Regions that are gaining money have stronger economies, and prices tend to rise. Regions that are losing money have weaker economies, and prices tend to fall. Labor and capital flows can help facilitate the adjustment process.

With fixed exchange rates, the central banks of the countries involved are supposed to make the changes in the money supply that happen automatically with a currency union. When a central bank subordinates its monetary policy to maintaining fixed exchange rates, the fixed exchange rate will be maintained. When a central bank attempts to have an independent monetary policy, the fixed exchange rate will fail.

Why do Countries have Problems with Fixed Exchange Rates?

It seems simple enough to maintain a fixed or pegged exchange rate. And, many countries are successful at it. But, many other countries are unsuccessful. Three reasons for failure can be identified.

Sticky Wages. As stated above, adjustment with either a common currency or with fixed or pegged exchange rates requires flexible prices and, in particular, flexible wages. Without flexible prices, a country risks persistent high unemployment when there is a current account deficit. Inflexible prices result from "money illusion." Money illusion refers to the perception that monetary values have meaning aside from purchasing power. If all wages and prices and all monetary values—including those in long-term contracts—change proportionately, there would be no change in purchasing power. But, prices and monetary values don't change that way. Many prices and monetary values are fixed by long-term contracts; for example, long-term bonds and mortgages, leases, and multiyear labor contracts. In addition, unionized and government workers are in a good position to resist wage cutting; and, many wages are regulated by minimum wage laws and equal pay laws and such. As a result, prices may not be very flexible, especially wages. Instead of adjustment, maintaining fixed exchange rates results in massive unemployment.

Inflationary Finance. Many governments have limited ability to borrow and yet have persistent budget deficits. They resort to printing money to finance these deficits. The tendency of certain governments to spend more than they raise in revenue undermines their commitment to maintain a fixed or pegged exchange rate for its currency. These governments invite speculative attacks on their currencies such as those that undermined the monetary arrangements in Europe that preceded the Euro, and that undermined those of east Asia at the time of the East Asia Currency Crisis.

Bubble Economy. Some countries wind up with bubble economies. This situation is where opportunities look bright and induce an unsustainable level of investment. As to where the financing of this investment comes is an important question. Is the financing coming from savings or from the creation of new money? This question will be addressed in the chapter on international financial crisis. At this time, the possible role of fixed or pegged exchange rates in a bubble economy will be examined.

Bubble Economy: When economic activity is based on an unsustainable level of investment. Often, the original impetus for the bubble economy is something valid, such as a breakthrough technology (the dot.com bubble) or the prospect for the demand for housing giving expanding standards of living (the housing bubble). But, at some point, economic activity becomes separated from economic reality. At that point, the economy seems to rise on its own. Synonyms: Speculative Bubble, Financial Bubble, Price Bubble, Balloon Economy.

A fixed or pegged exchange rate can contribute to a bubble economy by facilitating the financing of investments denominated in the local currency by borrowing money in the reference currency. For example, Thai banks lending money to finance investments in Thailand, denominated in Thai baht, with money raised overseas, denominated in U.S. dollars. As long as both the peg of the Thai baht to the U.S. dollar holds and as long as the loans are repaid, this arrangement will work and actually feed into the bubble economy. But, when the peg fails and/or the loans are not repaid, the bubble will burst possibly with disastrous consequences.

Currency Boards

A possible solution to the problems some countries face with fixed or pegged exchange rates is a currency board. Currency boards have worked well in francophone Africa and in certain other places. Fourteen countries of west and central Africa use the "CFA franc," which today is pegged to the euro and formerly was pegged to the French franc. Specifically, 100 CFA Francs = 1 former French franc = 0.152449 euro.

In concept, a currency board is a completely automatic process. To get local currency, you deposit the reference currency with the board and receive the local currency. The board holds the reference currency or invests it in high-quality, short-term securities denominated in the reference currency. To get the reference currency, you deposit the local currency with the board and receive the reference currency. The board either disburses the reference currency from its cash or else liquidates part of its investment portfolio. Also in concept, the currency board is located outside the country (e.g., in France) so it cannot be corrupted by the local government. In practice, details often differ.

Argentina used a currency board to end the massive inflation it suffered from the 1940s to the 1990s. For a time, the currency board worked well. But, the government started to manipulate it. Instead of investing the funds of the currency board in short-term, high-quality debt denominated in the reference currency, it invested its funds in local debt of questionable creditworthiness. The market became suspicious of the ability of the currency board to convert local currency into the reference currency. In 2002, there was a run on the currency board that forced it into suspension. Since then, the Argentine peso has floated against the dollar.

Dual Exchange Rates

Some countries use dual exchange rates to help maintain fixed or pegged rates and for other purposes. In some cases, there is an official rate, at a low exchange rate, and a commercial rate, at a higher rate. In some cases, there is also an unofficial or black-market rate, sometimes described as a gray-market rate if the market is tolerated by the government. Venezuela is a country with all three of these rates.

- Official Rate: 6.3 Bolivars-to-US$1;
- Commercial Rate: 12 Bolivars-to-US$1;
- Black-market Rate: 815 Bolivars-to-US$1 [1].

[1] from: DolarToday.com 11/6/2015.

Dual Exchange Rates: When a country has two or more exchange rates. Usually one of these rates is a low rate and reserved for the government and favored industries.

Official Rate: The low exchange rate reserved for the government and favored industries in countries with two or more exchange rates. This rate is usually a fixed or pegged rate.

Commercial Rate: A second legal exchange rate, higher than the official rate, in countries with two or more exchange rates. This rate can be fixed or floating. If this rate is fixed, then there is either a black-market rate or there are quantitative controls on foreign exchange.

Black-market Rate: An illegal rate in countries with two or more exchange rates. Black-market rates are floating rates.

Gray-market Rate: An illegal but tolerated rate in countries with two or more exchange rates.

ADJUSTMENT AND TRADE

To say that a currency is overvalued is to say that at its exchange rate, domestic prices are high relative to foreign prices. This makes it easier for foreign producers to export to the country, and more difficult for domestic producers to export to foreign countries. Just the opposite occurs when a currency is undervalued. In this case, given the exchange rate, domestic prices are low relative to foreign prices. This makes it more difficult for foreign producers to export to the country, and easier for domestic producers to export to foreign countries.

Consider the case of tourism. When the dollar is overvalued, it may be cheaper for Americans to travel internationally than to travel domestically (and more expensive for foreigners to travel to the United States). Conversely, when the dollar is undervalued, it may be cheaper for Americans to travel domestically (and cheaper for foreigners to travel to the United States).

In the following example, we will suppose that at $1 = 1€, Las Vegas and Paris appear as equally attractive vacation destinations to a person living in Washington, DC. If the euro were to strengthen against the dollar, so that it takes $1.20 to buy 1€, Vegas looks like a bargain. And, if the dollar were to strengthen against the euro, so that $0.80 buys 1€, its goodbye showgirls, and hello Louvre art museum. Since tourism is part of the Balance of Services, shifts of tourism from domestic to international, or from international to domestic, impact the current account balance.

Times of an undervalued dollar are times when Americans goods and services *in general* are cheaper than foreign goods and services. These are times when it is relatively easy for American companies to sell their products

Table 9.1   Vegas or Paris?

	Vegas	Paris	Paris at 1:1	Paris at 1.2:1	Paris at 0.8:1
Airfare	$800	€1,000	$1,000	$1,200	$800
Hotel	$400	€400	$400	$480	$320
Food	$200	€200	$200	$240	$160
Entertainment	$400	€200	$200	$240	$160
TOTAL	$1,800	€1,800	$1,800	$2,160	$1,440

abroad, and when it is relatively difficult for foreign companies to sell their products in the United States. The opposite is true when the U.S. dollar is overvalued.

Trade Patterns in General

During the 1980s, as the real exchange rate of the U.S. dollar increased, the current account went massively into deficit. These trends were reversed following the Plaza Accord of 1985. Following this accord, the U.S. dollar weakened (or, corrected), and the U.S. trade account approached balance. The *Plaza Accord* was an agreement among the governments of five major countries (United States, United Kingdom, Germany, France, and Japan) that the U.S. dollar was overvalued. The agreement was named for the luxurious Plaza Hotel in New York City, where leaders of these governments met.

During the first decade of the 2000s, the U.S. dollar again strengthened, and the U.S. current account fell into an even more massive deficit. While there was nothing like the Plaza Accord to precipitate a correction, and while the U.S. government seemed to simultaneously support both a strong dollar and a weak dollar, there was another reversal of real exchange rates. From the mid- to late 2000s, the U.S. dollar was weakening (or, correcting), and the U.S. current account was approaching balance.

These swings in real exchange rates and trade and other flows in the current account are the adjustment mechanism when there are floating exchange rates. When exchange rates for a currency are strong, so that prices for goods and services within the country are high relative to prices outside the country, the country will have an adverse balance of trade, exports will be low and imports high. The country will exhaust its foreign currency reserves, because it is not earning sufficient foreign exchange in trade. As foreign currency reserves become scarce, the value of foreign exchange will rise.

The adjustment process for an overvalued currency can be viewed as a case of supply and demand. The supply of foreign currency falls as a country exhausts its foreign currency reserves when a country is importing more than it is exporting. Therefore, the price of foreign exchange will rise, which is the same thing as saying that the value of the domestic currency in the foreign exchange market will weaken. The weakening of the domestic currency will correct its overvaluation and restore balance to its current accounts.

The J Curve

There is some indeterminacy in the adjustment process preventing or delaying correction for an over- or undervalued currency. The four main reasons for this indeterminacy are:

- The country might not allow its currency to freely float, but might have a managed floating exchange rate by imposing exchange controls. This was previously discussed in the case of China.
- The central bank of the country might engage in the purchase or sale of foreign currency. This is called a dirty float.
- There can be private-sector capital flows, such as borrowing in foreign currencies that offset the flow of goods and services. A prior chapter explored international capital flows.
- It takes time for established patterns of trade to change in response to under- and overvaluations of currencies.

In international economics, the J Curve refers to the possibility that the patterns of trade may be so slow to change following a devaluation. As a result, the effect of a devaluation is initially to worsen the current account balance (the down part of the "J"), and only later to improve the current account balance (the up part of the "J").

Let us suppose that all imports and exports are in physical commodities. For example, a country imports corn and exports oil. And, because it takes time for patterns of trade to change, we will assume that initially there is no change in the physical volume of imports or of exports. At the time of devaluation, the initial impact is simply that people within the country pay more for imports (because it takes more units of the currency of the country to buy corn), and people outside the country pay the same amount (in domestic currency) for the oil they are buying. This means that the initial effect of the devaluation is to make the trade deficit worse and make the current account balance a bigger, negative number. This is the down part of the "J."

Over time, the pattern of trade can change. People within the country react to the higher price of corn (in terms of the domestic currency) by reducing the quantity they demand. People outside the country react to the lower price of oil (in terms of foreign currencies) by increasing the quantity they demand. The combination of the reduced physical quantity of imports and the increased physical quantity of exports can, over time, change the pattern of trade so as to eliminate the current account deficit. This is the up part of the "J."

The Half-life of Adjustment

Considering the several problems listed above making difficult the adjustment of floating exchange rates, a good rule of thumb is that the "half-life" of the adjustment process is two-and-a-half years. This means that the adjustment process is quite slow. On average, only half of any discrepancy between exchange rates and purchasing power parity is closed in thirty months. In the meantime, people's jobs and investments are subject to risks unrelated to their actual competitiveness in the global economy. This does not seem fair.

Speaking candidly about exchange rates, the renowned economist Kenneth Rogoff says that while it is abundantly clear that purchasing power parity is a strong force in determining exchange rates in the long run, we have almost no ability to forecast short run movements in exchange rates.[2]

The Plato-Aristotle Debate

Debates concerning money go back a long, long time. What follows is an imagined debate between the Greek philosophers Plato (427–347 BC) and Aristotle (384–322 BC).

Plato, in his work *The Republic*, imagined that there could be a "philosopher king" who would exercise absolute power for the good of the people. With such a ruler, there would be a utopia. In *The Laws*, Plato argued that the money supplied by the state, while valuable to the people of the state in exchange, should be objects of "no worth amongst the rest of mankind." Furthermore, so as to force the people of the state to use only the state-provided money, "no private person [should] be permitted to own gold or silver."

Plato actually got at least one ruler to try to implement his utopian plans—the dictator of the Greek city-state of Syracuse. The dictator of Syracuse issued tin coins at four times their value as metal, and silver coins at two times their value as metal.

Aristotle is attributed with introducing the term "economics." In his work *Politics* (and elsewhere), Aristotle envisioned society as involving "households" within a "polis." The word translated as "households" refers to families and other voluntary associations. People within households share values, whereas from one household to another, values may differ.

The word "polis" is usually translated as "city-state." The people within a "polis" share only a very minimal set of values, such as the need for defense, internal order, and certain municipal services. The polis enables people with different values to cooperate with each other, through trade and cultural exchange, even though they may have different values.

In *Politics*, Aristotle said that money should be "something which was intrinsically useful and easily applicable to the purposes of life—for example, iron, silver, and the like."

The Twin Deficits

During the 1980s, there was talk of a connection between the budget deficit and the current account deficit. This "connection" was based on two arguments, a logical argument and an empirical argument. The logical argument concerns two approaches to the national income identity:

- GDP = Consumption spending + Investment spending + Government spending + Net Exports (Exports + Imports), or GDP = C + I + G + NX.
- GDP = NI + Capital Consumption Allowance = Consumption + Gross Saving + Taxes, or GDP = C + S + T.

From these two equations, the "sectoral balances identity" is derived:

- (S − I) + (T − G) = NX; or, the deficiency of saving to finance investment and the government budget deficit equals net exports.

To simplify this, assume S = I. Then, there is a one-to-one correspondence between the government deficit and net exports. Now, let's look at the empirical argument. From the 1970s to the 1980s, there was a trend of increasing U.S. budget deficits. The U.S. current account was going negative. The budget deficit shrank during the late 1980s, and the current account deficit, a bit later, also shrank. The budget deficit got larger during the early 1990s, and the current account, again a bit later, turned negative again. These movements seemed to confirm that the federal budget deficit and the current account deficit were connected. This was the highpoint of the theory of the twin deficits.

But, during the first decade of the 2000s, the current account got increasingly negative both while the budget was in surplus and also when the budget drifted negative. Then, the federal budget deficit got very big, following which the current account deficit started to diminish. These years contradicted the theory that there is a one-to-one correspondence between the budget deficit and the current account deficit.

One of the problems with the simple or "one-to-one" theory that the budget deficit and the current account deficit are twin deficits is the assumption that savings equals investment. A current account deficit can result from either foreigners financing a budget deficit or foreigners financing investment spending in excess of saving or both.

During the first decade of the 2000s, the United States had a booming stock market and a booming housing market, as well as a budget deficit. Looking back, it is clear that foreigners were financing both investment spending in excess of saving and the budget deficit. Then, as indications developed that a housing bubble was underway, foreigners reduced their financing both of investment spending in excess of saving and the budget deficit. Then, following the Financial Crisis of 2008, foreigners shifted their portfolios from private-sector securities to "safe" government securities. At this time, with conditions returning to normal, it looks that though the simple twin deficits theory is back at work.

To summarize this chapter in two sentences, exchange rates tend, in the long run, to reflect the ratio of prices in countries, at least with respect to traded goods. But, for a variety of reasons, exchange rates often deviate from purchasing power parity, and short-run changes in exchange rates are almost impossible to predict. The next chapter examines how business can operate in the global economy given the uncertainty regarding short-run changes in exchange rates.

Summary

- In the long run, exchange rates tend to reflect the purchasing power of currencies with respect to traded goods.
- Absolute purchasing power theory says that exchange rates tend to equal the ratio of prices of traded goods in the two currencies.
- Relative purchasing power theory says that changes in exchange rates tend to equal the difference in the inflation rates in countries.
- International price surveys show that there is a strong correlation between exchange rates and the purchasing power of currencies. However, the deviations of exchange rates from purchasing power are too large to be explained by measurement error. There must be slow adjustment to purchasing power parity, non-traded goods, cost of transportation and tariffs, and other barriers to trade.
- When a country's currency is overvalued, it exports will be less competitive, and imports will be more competitive. In the long run, this will tend to lower the prices of the goods it produces and raise the prices of the goods it imports. These tendencies will, eventually, eliminate the overvaluation of the country's currency.
- The opposite occurs when a country's currency is undervalued.
- Because it usually takes time for the physical volumes of exports and imports to respond to changes in exchange rates, a devaluation of a currency's exchange rate will initially only make exports less valuable and imports more valuable; and, worsen a country's balance of trade and services. Only over time, as physical volumes change, will the devaluation improve the country's balance of trade and services. This pattern is called the "J curve."
- In the case of a shared currency, there are no exchange rates that can resolve imbalances of trade. Resolution of imbalances of trade requires adjustment of wages and prices, which is often a difficult thing.
- In the case of fixed exchange rates, resolution of imbalances of trade is supposed to involve changes in the money supply by the central bank of the country. While some central banks implement monetary policy so as to maintain their fixed exchange rate, some do not.

- In the case of floating exchange rates, adjustment of exchange rates can, over time, help to resolve imbalances of trade.
- Some countries use a currency board to maintain fixed exchange rates. Currency boards (freely) exchange national currency for the reference currency at the fixed exchange rate. The better currency boards have been operated independently of the national government.
- Some countries feature dual exchange rates. With dual exchange rates, one—the official exchange rate—is for the government and favored industries. This rate is subsidized. The other exchange rate is for other industries. This rate is taxed.
- Some countries feature a black market or a gray market in foreign exchange. These black and gray markets reflect currency controls (quantitative limits on foreign exchange) or an unrealistic official exchange rate. A black market is an illegal market that the government attempts to suppress. A gray market is an illegal market that the government tolerates.

NOTES

1. The data for these calculations are from Lawrence H. Officer, "Exchange Rates Between the United States Dollar and Forty-one Currencies," MeasuringWorth, 2017.

2. "Interview with Kenneth Rogoff," Minneapolis Federal Reserve Bank, December 2008.

Chapter 10

Managing Exchange Rate Risk

The unpredictable nature of changes in foreign exchange rates seems to add another element of risk to conducting business in the global economy. In addition to normal business risk, such as natural disasters, the business cycle, competition, and adverse changes in taxes and regulations, there is the risk of adverse changes in foreign exchange rates. With this additional risk, it might seem that international trade must require a higher profit margin, and that this additional profit margin would inhibit international trade. Yet, international trade is growing by leaps and bounds. According to the World Bank, at the time of the breakdown of the Bretton Woods Agreement in 1971, international trade was 24 percent of world GDP. In 2016, this figure reached 58 percent. How could international trade have grown so much during a period of floating exchange rates?

The one word explanation of the growth of international trade in the face of exchange rate risk is hedging. Through hedges such as forward exchange, companies involved in international trade can avoid foreign exchange risk. *Hedging* refers to eliminating or at least reducing risk by taking a position in a security or set of securities that has the opposite risk.

Let's say Pier 1 Importers enters into an agreement to acquire 12,000 angora sweaters from Chile during the next year, taking delivery of the sweaters 1,000 per month at a price of 70 million pesos (currently equal to $100,000, at an exchange rate 700 Chilean pesos to $1) with payment due upon delivery in Chilean pesos. Pier 1 expects to sell these sweaters at a retail price of $200 each, in line with a goal, it might be supposed, of a 50 percent gross margin. But, what if the Chilean peso were to appreciate against the dollar during the upcoming year? Then, Pier 1 would fall short of its assumed goal of a 50 percent gross markup. Pier 1 can eliminate this risk by using the forward exchange services of a bank.

This chapter looks at how companies can deal with exchange rate risk beginning, in this section, with the forward market, and continuing in the next with foreign exchange futures, and concluding in the third section with foreign exchange options and swaps.

FOREIGN EXCHANGE RISK

Two kinds of foreign exchange risk are often distinguished: transaction risk and translation risk. *Transaction Risk* occurs when changes in exchange rates affects the firm's net worth by changing the profitability in its transactions. *Translation Risk* occurs when changes in exchange rates affects a firm's net worth by changing the values of its assets and/or liabilities.

The foreign exchange risk faced by Pier 1 with respect to its contract for angora sweaters is an example of transaction risk. If the Chilean peso appreciates against the U.S. dollar, Pier 1 will make less profit. This kind of foreign exchange risk is the focus of the first two plus sections of this chapter.

An example of the other kind of foreign exchange risk—translation risk—would be the revaluation of the assets and liabilities of a foreign subsidiary. This other kind of foreign exchange risk will be part of the third section of this chapter.

Foreign Exchange Risk Exposure

The first step in dealing with foreign exchange risk is determining a company's exposure. A company's exposure is usually understood to be its *net* exposure, taking into account any internal offsets. In the case of Pier 1 and its contract for angora sweaters, if this were the only exposure of the company's net worth to changes in the value of the Chilean peso relative to the U.S. dollar, it would have a negative exposure. That is, if the peso appreciates against the dollar, the company would make less profit. To illustrate this exposure, let's say that the peso appreciates from 700-to-1 to 600-to-1 against the dollar. Then the cost, in dollars, of a sweater rises from $100 to $117. With the retail price remaining at $200, the gross profit margin falls from 50 to 42 percent.

Today's large multinational corporations often have some transactions with negative exposure to a particular foreign currency, and other transactions with a positive exposure. Let's say a U.S. trading company buys products in Chile for sale in the United States and also buys about the same value of products in the United States for sale in Chile, what would be its exposure—meaning net exposure—to the Chilean peso? The answer is about zero. The negative exposure this company has by reason of buying products in Chile is offset by the positive exposure it has by reason of its selling products in that country.

It is not unusual for a trading company to have two exposures from a single transaction. This happens when a company buys in one foreign country and sells in a second foreign country. Let's say a U.S. trading company buys products in Chile for resale in Japan. Then, it would have a negative exposure to the Chilean peso and a positive exposure to the Japanese yen.

Calculating the firm's (net) exposure to all the currencies in which it deals is the first step in managing the firm's exchange rate risk.

Choice of Currency

It is natural to presume each company in an international transaction would prefer that the transaction be denominated in its currency; yet, this clearly cannot be. In the example of Pier 1 buying angora sweaters from Chile, it was supposed that the transaction is denominated in pesos; that is, the seller's currency. But, it is possible the transaction is denominated in dollars; that is, the buyer's currency. It is also possible that the transaction is denominated in a third currency (in which case both the buyer and the seller would have a foreign exchange exposure).

The choice of denomination can be determined by any of the following factors:

- The more stable of the buyer's and the seller's currencies;
- A third, stable currency if neither the buyer's nor the seller's currency is stable;
- The currency of the party to the transaction from a country with the better developed banking system (that can finance the transaction); and
- The convertible currency (meaning, the currency is not subject to exchange controls) of one of the parties to the transaction.

Often, the transactions are denominated in dollars because that is the custom in particular industries (such as crude oil).

The United States accounts for 14 percent of world trade, but the U.S. dollar is used in 36 percent of international transactions.[1] In contrast, China accounts for 11 percent of world trade, but the Chinese yuan (which is not convertible) is used in only one-quarter of 1 percent of international transactions.

Spot and Forward Exchange Markets

The spot market in foreign exchange is the market for immediate delivery (meaning fulfillment of the transaction occurs within one day or so, if not immediately). The forward market is the market for future delivery. It is a contract today, at a price that is fixed today, for a transaction that will be conducted in the future. The *Spot Exchange Rate* is the price of a foreign currency for immediate delivery. The *Forward Exchange Rate* is price of a foreign currency (today) for delivery in the future.

For example, let's say you are an American who will receive ten million Japanese yen in three months, and that you want to avoid the risk associated with the possibility of the Japanese yen falling in value during the next three months. Let's also say that the spot exchange rate of Japanese yen for U.S. dollars is 77.03; the three-month forward exchange rate is 76.86; the annual interest rate in Japan is 0 percent; and, the annual interest rate in the United States is 0.88 percent.[2]

There are several ways to avoid the risk associated with changes in exchange rates. One way is to enter into a forward contract today, to buy U.S. dollars with the amount of yen you will receive in three months.

$$3 - \text{month forward rate} : 76.86 \text{ yen} = \$1$$
$$\text{Therefore, 10 million yen} = \$130,106.69$$

In this case, you have locked-in the value you will receive in dollars, and transferred the risk of exchange rate fluctuations to your bank. (You can be sure that the bank is continually reviewing its own exposure to changes in exchange rates and eliminating excessive risks through its own hedging operations.) This method is illustrated in the first column of Table 10.1.

Another way to avoid the risk associated with changes in exchange rates involves simultaneously exchanging currency in the spot market with money that is borrowed in one currency and invested in another currency. This alternate method is more complicated. It involves three steps:

• Borrow money from a Japanese bank having the present value at the Japanese interest rate equal to ten million yen in three months;
• Exchange the Japanese yen you have borrowed for U.S. dollars in the spot market; and
• Deposit the U.S. dollars you receive in an American bank, earning the U.S. interest rate.

For simplicity, we will assume the Japanese interest rate is 0 percent. *Step 1* is to borrow ten million yen. In three months, when you receive ten million yen from the buyer, you pay off this loan.

Step 2 is to buy U.S. dollars in the spot market with the ten million yen you have borrowed.

Table 10.1 Creating a Synthetic Forward

	Forward Market	Synthetic Forward Market
	Sign contract to sell goods in 3 months for ¥10 million	
Beginning of Month 1	Enter three-month Forward Contract	Borrow ¥10 million; Convert in Spot Market at 77.03; Receive $129,819.55, Invest at 0.88%
End of Month 3	Receive ¥10 million from buyer; Use Forward Contract to convert at 76.86; Receive $130,106.69	Receive ¥10 million from buyer; Pay off ¥ loan; Receive $130,106.69 from investment

Spot rate : 77.03 yen = $1

Therefore, 10 million yen = $129,819.55

Step 3 is to deposit this money in an American bank. For this method to be in equilibrium with the first method, $129,819.55 must be equal in future value to $130,106.69 in three months. This is the case if the U.S. annual interest rate is 0.88 percent. The second method is illustrated in the second column of Table 10.1.

Interest Rate Parity

The relationship discussed above between spot and forward exchange rates and interest rates is known as interest rate parity. Interest rate parity occurs when the forward premium (equal to the percentage difference between the forward and the spot rates) approximately equals the difference between the domestic interest rate and the foreign interest rate.

$$\text{Forward Premium} = (F - S)/S = R_D - R_F$$

Where F is the Forward Exchange Rate, S the Spot Exchange Rate, R_D the domestic interest rate, and R_F the foreign interest rate.

During the 1970s and 1980s, Great Britain suffered a higher rate of inflation than the United States. As purchasing power parity implies, the British pound tended to weaken against the dollar. The market came to expect the British pound to continue to weaken, and forward rates of the pound against the dollar were at a discount. That is, if it took $1.50 to buy 1£ in the spot market, it might take $1.45 to buy 1£ in the forward market. In addition, interest rates on deposits and loans denominated in pounds tended to be higher than interest rates on dollar-denominated deposits and loans. All this is consistent with interest rate parity.

In normal times, countries that have balanced budgets and increase their money supply at a moderate rate, comparable to the growth of real economic activity, do not have much inflation. These countries tend to have low interest rates, currencies that appreciate over time against other currencies, and have a forward rate premium as opposed to a forward rate discount. There are strong economic forces to bring about interest rate parity.

In theory, companies can create their own hedge against exchange rate risk. This method of hedging is described as a synthetic forward exchange in Table 10.1. But, for most companies, it is much simpler to hedge exchange rate risk by entering into forward exchange contracts with a bank. In the example of Pier 1, the company's competitive advantage is in offering interesting and curious things for sale, assembled from all over the world. Necessarily, Pier 1's business requires that it enters into international transactions and some of these transactions will expose the company to foreign exchange risk. Pier 1 can rely on the competitive advantage of banks in the area of money management to deal with this risk.

CURRENCY FUTURES

The prior section looked at foreign exchange risk, what it is and how to calculate it, and one of the methods for dealing with foreign exchange risk, namely, forward exchange. This section looks at a second method, currency futures. These futures contracts are derived from foreign exchange, which is considered to be the underlying asset, and are an example of a class of securities known as derivatives. Derivatives are securities whose values are derived from other securities. In truth, all securities are derivatives. The stocks, bonds, and other debt instruments issued by corporations are derived from the underlying assets and earning power of the corporation. Individuals don't issue equity claims (they are self-owners), but they do issue debt. The debt issued by individuals is derived from their assets and earning power. Likewise, the debt issued by governments is derived from the government's assets and ability to tax.

Emergence of the Futures Market

While a futures market in rice existed in Japan in the 17th century, and there are some indications of futures markets before then in China, the modern futures market was born in Chicago, Illinois, during the mid-19th century. At that time, Chicago was the dominant transfer point for agricultural commodities originating in the west and bound for the east. With only a few exceptions, the major railroads terminated there. The major eastern railroads had their main western terminal there. These included the New York Central, Pennsylvania, Baltimore and Ohio, and Erie railroads. The major western railroads had their main eastern terminal there. These included the Chicago and Northwestern; Chicago, Burlington, and Quincy; Chicago, Milwaukee and St. Paul; and, Chicago, Rock Island, and Pacific. Notice the prominent position of "Chicago" in the names of the western railroads. Chicago, said the poet Carl Sandberg, is the "City of the Big Shoulders."

Hog Butcher for the World,
Tool Maker, Stacker of Wheat,
Player with Railroads and the Nation's Freight Handler;
Stormy, husky, brawling,
City of the Big Shoulders.

Carl Sandberg, "Chicago"

Transshipment of goods at Chicago was costly. There was the cost of unloading and reloading railroad cars, and possibly also the cost of storing grain in silos and maintaining livestock in stockyards. So, naturally, there was a search for ways to avoid these costs such as by arranging in advance of delivery for sale and purchase. There were efforts to arrange for the swap of railroad cars loaded with agricultural goods arriving from the west and headed east, and for railroad cars loaded with manufactured goods arriving from the east and headed west. To facilitate the swap of railroad cars, the railroad companies developed special terminal operations and certain accounting practices. A futures market emerged from efforts to facilitate the sale and purchase of agricultural products prior to delivery.

A futures market requires the development of standards for goods such as bushels of wheat, along with a credible system of inspection. Standards specify the commodity's type, quality and place where the commodity will be delivered (e.g., a bushel of Chicago soft red winter wheat). Actual shipments would be compared to the standard, possibly with a scale of discounts and premiums for small deviations from the standard. In such manner, the heterogeneous stuff of nature was turned into commodities.

Once the concept of futures contracts was developed, the application of the concept to other situations became straightforward. Futures trading expanded from agricultural goods to metals and energy commodities. In New York, futures trading developed in products imported into this country such as coffee and tea, as well as products that were shipped south-to-north such as cotton and oranges. Following the end of the Bretton Woods fixed exchange rate system, futures trading extended to gold, foreign currencies, and interest rates.

Spotlight: "Trading Places"

In the movie *Trading Places*, Dan Aykroyd and Eddie Murphy trade orange futures in New York's World Trade Center. The movie is an adaptation of Mark Twain's classic *The Prince and the Pauper*. It also parodies the disastrous attempt by the Hunt brothers to corner the silver market.

Currency Futures

Currency futures are exchange-traded *standardized contracts* for the purchase and sale of currencies in the future. Liquidity is gained by the standardization of the contract. This standardization involves amount and date (e.g., contracts for each of the third Wednesdays of the next several months). By concentrating trading on relatively few contracts, the volume of trading is increased on those contracts so that prices almost always reflect healthy competition among buyers and sellers. This increases the likelihood that a counterparty will be available at a price that reflects the information available at that time.

Futures differ from forward contracts in several ways. Futures are standardized as to amount and date, while forward contracts are tailored to the particular needs of customers of banks. Futures are guaranteed by a deposit of money into a "margin account," while forward contracts depend on banks wanting to maintain their reputations.

In a typical forward contract, a customer of the bank hedges against foreign exchange risk in its transactions. In the example of Pier 1, the company uses forward contracts to hedge against the risk that the Chilean peso appreciates against the U.S. dollar during the next twelve months.

If there were a futures market in the Chilean peso, Pier 1 could do approximately the same thing by buying futures contracts on the Chilean peso. Then, if the Chilean peso appreciated against the dollar, Pier 1 would lose in the transaction (bad!), but win in the futures contract (good!). Conversely, if the Chilean peso depreciated against the dollar, Pier 1 would win in the transaction (good!), but lose in the futures contract (bad!). Either way, Pier 1 wouldn't care about changes in the exchange rate between the Chilean peso and the U.S. dollar, and shouldn't be distracted by the ups and downs in exchange rates. Instead, Pier 1 should focus on selling products that have a greater value to its customers than their cost of production.

The Intercontinental Exchange (ICE) was founded in 2000 with an original focus on energy commodities. It subsequently absorbed the New York Board of Trade in 2007 and many other exchanges. The ICE has offices, today, in New York, London, Chicago, Houston, Winnipeg, Amsterdam, Calgary, Washington, DC, San Francisco, and Singapore; and is open for business practically twenty-four hours a day. It makes markets in futures and options in commodities, currencies, interest rates, and more, including carbon emissions. The provisions of the U.S. dollar-Mexican peso contract on the ICE are:

- Contract size—500,000 Mexican pesos;
- Contract settlement dates—third Wednesday of March, June, September, and December;
- Margin (representative figure)—$700 per contract;
- Last trading day—two business days prior to contract settlement date.

Let's say it's November 16, 2015, and you buy one contract for delivery of Mexican pesos on the third Wednesday of December (December 16). You have to deposit at least $700 into your margin account. This is your money. It's not a payment for the contract. It's there to make sure you can cover a loss during the next day. You now control a contract for 500,000 pesos, worth $29,886.44 dollars at an exchange rate of 16.73 pesos per dollar.

Let's say that over the next day, the Mexican peso appreciates against the dollar by 1 percent. With this change in the exchange rate, it takes only 16.564 pesos to buy a dollar. Your 500,000 pesos are now worth $30,188.31, a gain of $299.51. This amount of money ($299.51) is transferred to you from the margin account of the loser on the contract. You now have $999.51 in your margin account. As for the loser, if he now has less than $700 in his account, he has to make an additional deposit in order to be ready for the next day or else the exchange will sell his side of the contract. In such manner, one day at a time, the buyers and the sellers of the Mexican peso contract evolve to the third Wednesday of December. Those who are winning see the money in their margin account rise, and those who are losing see the money in their margin account fall or have to make additional deposits into their margin account or see their side of the contract sold.

If the Mexican peso winds up stronger against the dollar on the third Wednesday of December, those who bought the contract are the winners and they will have more money in their margin account than they deposited into it. If they bought the Mexican peso contract in order to hedge a transaction in Mexican pesos that exactly matched the amount and date of the contract, then the additional money in their margin account will enable them to exactly cover the loss in their transaction.

Let's say a company has entered into transactions requiring 70,000 Mexican pesos per month for each of the next twelve months, a total of 840,000 pesos. Notice that these transactions do not match the amounts and dates of the futures contracts traded on the Intercontinental Exchange. The company could create *an approximate* hedge against its exchange rate risk by buying two Mexican peso futures contracts, a three-month contract and a nine-month contract. Or, it could rely on its bank, which will happily tailor the terms of its forward exchange to exactly meet the needs of its customers.

Commodity Futures and International Trade

Many people produce and sell commodities with prices that fluctuate significantly. An example is a farmer that produces and sells wheat. Others buy such commodities. An example is the American food company General Mills that acquires wheat and other grains for its cereal products. The risk of price fluctuation these people and companies face is similar to exchange rate risk. In addition, the exports of many developing countries consist mostly of commodities with prices that fluctuate significantly. For example, the main exports of Peru are copper, gold, zinc, crude oil, and coffee. The main exports of Ghana are gold, cocoa beans, and crude oil. Fluctuations in the prices of these commodities can affect the entire economy of these countries. These fluctuations in prices can also affect buyers. Both the sellers and the buyers would be interested in hedging their risk of adverse price fluctuations and can do so in futures markets. Hedging frees both sellers and buyers to focus on their comparative advantage such as producing copper.

In the United States, wheat is harvested from May to September. Historically, from September until May, there was great uncertainty about the next year's crop. During this time, wheat prices tended to be fair in the sense that not enough was known about the next crop to tell whether it would be plentiful (with the consequence of low prices) or not plentiful (with the consequence of high prices). As information is revealed about the next crop, the price of wheat would rise or fall. Variations in crop yield—as could be affected by drought, flooding, other variations in the weather, by swarms of insects and crop disease—made the price of wheat uncertain; and, this uncertainty was resolved only as the crop began to be harvested.

Over time, the flow of rivers was brought under control, insect swarms were eliminated, and crops were made more resistant to disease. So, variation in crop yields decreased. Furthermore, the wheat markets of the United States became tied together through internal transportation networks. So, local fluctuations in yield had little impact on local supply. In addition, the risk of price fluctuation that remained could be hedged in the futures market. The result is that food supplies became very stable throughout the United States. We now have more of a problem with people eating too much and the wrong kinds of food, than we have of a shortage of food.

Today, the market in wheat is becoming global. The northern hemisphere's harvest season of May to September is complemented by the southern hemisphere's opposite harvest season. Wheat crops are almost always coming to market, and from very diverse places. Since the mid-20th century, all mass starvation in the world has essentially been due to political events; for example, the North Korean famine of the 1990s, when hundreds of thousands and possibly millions of people died from starvation. The 1980s famine in Ethiopia in which 400,000 people died was because the dictator Mengistu Haile Mariam decided to use starvation as a weapon against those who resisted his rule.

Venezuela used to export food. Then, the government started to control the price of food. The purpose was to lower the cost of food for the urban poor on which the government relied for votes. Farmers reduced production and eventually abandoned their farms. Food fell into short supply and began to be rationed. Conditions became increasingly desperate with reports of starvation among the elderly, the sick, and children.

In the emerging global economy, futures are used to manage risks such as adverse changes in prices. The production of the entire world is integrated so nobody is put at risk because of a local crop failure. But the spread of market-oriented economies and liberal, democratic governments has been uneven and remains incomplete.

OPTIONS AND SWAPS

This chapter has thus far looked at foreign exchange risk, what it is and how to calculate it, and two methods for dealing with it, namely, forward exchange and foreign currency futures. This section examines a third method to deal with exchange rate risk, namely, foreign currency options. It also looks at swaps and other long-term strategies.

Call and put options are traded on the major currencies of the world, as well as on stocks, stock indexes, commodity futures, and many other financial instruments. Call options involve the right but not the obligation to buy the underlying asset at the agreed-upon price; and, put options the right but not the obligation to sell the underlying asset at the agreed-upon price. With both, the buyer of the option pays a premium for the right.[3]

Call options are sometimes considered to be a way to lever or multiply the potential gain from an up-move in the price of the underlying asset. Put options are sometimes considered to be a way to insure against a loss from a potential down-move in the price of the underlying asset. In truth, with currency options, the purposes of buying or selling options may be to hedge a complex risk associated with doing business involving foreign currencies.

Let's consider the seller and the buyer of a call option on the euro. For simplicity, assume that the current exchange rate between the dollar and the euro is 1-to-1, the call option has an exercise price of $1.10 per €1.00, and the time-to-expiration is three months.

This call option is currently "out of the money." Nobody would exercise an option to buy euros at $1.10 per €1.00, when euros can be bought at $1.00 per €1.00 in the spot market. But, things may be different in the future.

Spotlight: Mullah Nasruddin

Mullah Nasruddin is a Persian wise man known for his charming, witty, or foolish stories. It is not clear whether these stories are true or merely attributed to him, or even that he is Persian. In one of these stories, Nasruddin is called before the Sultan. Unfortunately, the Sultan did not find Nasruddin charming or witty, and ordered he be executed. Nasruddin implored the Sultan, "If you will give me one year, I will make your horse talk. Many rulers have beautiful horses, but none has a horse that can talk. The Sultan considered the offer, and ordered the execution be delayed for one year." A friend asked Nasruddin, what chance did he have of escaping execution. Nasruddin replied, "I have four chances. In a year, the Sultan might die, I might die, the horse might die, and the horse might talk."

Let's say that the odds of the euro changing by 10 percent or less, either up or down, during the next three months is 6-to-10. Let's also say that the chances are equally 2-to-10 that the euro will fall against the dollar by more than 10 percent, and that the euro will rise against the dollar by more than 10 percent. Finally, let's say that if the euro were to rise by more than 10 percent relative to the dollar during the next three months, on average it will rise by 20 percent to $1.20 per €1.00.[4] With these assumptions, the value of this call option can be calculated:

Value of call option = Odds of a sufficiently large up-move times the average
 profit upon such an up-move = (0.2)*($0.10) = $0.02

There are many reasons why people buy and sell options. In the case of hedging, it can be supposed that the buyer can handle small changes in the exchange rate of the euro relative to the dollar, but risks a devastating loss if the euro rises by a lot. Therefore, the buyer is willing to spend a small amount of money to hedge against that possibility. Think of buying call options as "insurance," and the cost of buying call options as an "insurance premium."

Case Study: Call Options on Oil Futures

On January 17, 1991, the United States and its European and Arab allies charged across the border between Saudi Arabia and Iraqi-occupied Kuwait. In a mere 100 hours, the allies achieved a total victory over the Iraqi military. Subsequently, the allies negotiated a truce that left Saddam Hussein in power in Iraq, but with conditions that were thought would contain his belligerency. Was this quick and decisive outcome expected by the financial market?

The concern of financial markets for uncertainty in the price of crude oil—and indirectly, for the speed and decisiveness of the Persian Gulf War of 1991—can be abstracted from the spot and futures prices of crude oil, and the prices of call options on the crude oil futures contract.[5] When Saddam Hussein invaded Kuwait, it is reasonable to think the financial market became more concerned that the supply of crude oil might be disrupted and that the price of oil could spike. Because of the increased chance of a spike in crude oil prices, the value of call options would increase even if the spot and futures prices of crude oil did not change. This is exactly what happened. The value of call options spiked even though the spot and futures prices were kept from changing much by the willingness of Saudi Arabia to increase oil production during the crisis.

Only with the success of the counterattack did the value of call options on crude oil futures fall. The market was not convinced that the war would be quick and decisive until this actually happened. That the war was quick and decisive was largely a surprise. The market's assessment of risk during the Persian Gulf War of 1991 should have been a lesson that wars should not be presumed to be quick and decisive. But, instead, it appears that many people concluded that because the Persian Gulf War of 1991 was quick and decisive, that a future war in Iraq would also be quick and decisive.

Currency Swaps

Currency swaps involve the exchange of a financial liability denominated in one currency for a financial liability denominated in another currency. An example would be the exchange of a Japanese yen bond for a U.S. dollar bond. Large multinational banks act as market makers in these swaps, similar to the way they make markets in foreign exchange.

To illustrate the potential usefulness of a currency swap, think of a Japanese manufacturing company that has a well-established relationship with Japanese banks. The company seeks to build a manufacturing facility to support production of goods that will be exported to the United States. Suppose that the company is able to raise capital on favorable terms from Japanese banks, denominated in Japanese yen. In particular, the Japanese bank would normally be able to use the manufacturing facility to secure the loan through a mortgage. But, the future earnings of the company will be in U.S. dollars, not in yen, and it is risky to borrow in one currency (yen) when future earnings will be in another currency (dollars).

In this case, a market maker in swaps may be able to exchange the yen-denominated liability for a dollar-denominated liability at a modest fee,

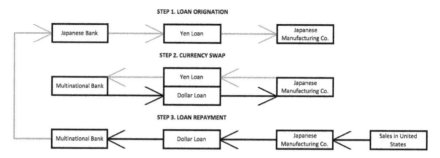

Figure 10.1 Schematic of a Currency Swap. *Source*: Created by author.

eliminating the risk that the future earnings (in dollars) won't be sufficient to pay a liability denominated in yen.

The driving force in swaps is that the cost of entering into a conventional loan plus the cost of swapping out of it and into a loan whose payments better match the future revenue of a company is less than the cost of directly entering into a foreign currency loan. As to why the indirect method would be cheaper, it can be because the indirect method involves already established banking relations, being able to identify property to secure a loan in the local legal system, and being able to legally enforce a loan denominated in the local currency in the local legal system. Other popular swaps include fixed-for-floating interest rate swaps and commodity swaps.

Exchange Rate Risk in Swaps

It may be thought that currency swaps are more risky than conventional loans, or that risk is merely being swapped or transferred to multinational banks. With regard to the borrower (the Japanese manufacturing company in the above example), the riskiness of the swap depends on whether the swap is being used to hedge risk or to leverage (increase) risk. In a swap that is a hedge, risk is reduced. This is the only kind of swap that multinational banks should make.

What if the yen strengthens against the dollar? With a conventional (yen) loan, the company would have a difficult time repaying its loan because the dollars earned from sales in the United States will buy fewer yen. With a swap, the company doesn't need to exchange its dollars for yen. It pays its new debt in dollars. It will breakeven instead of suffering a loss.

What if the yen weakens against the dollar? With a conventional (yen) loan, the company will be happy repaying the loan because the dollars earned from sales in the United States will buy more yen. With a swap, the company doesn't profit by earning dollars worth more yen, because it needs the dollars to pay its debt. It will breakeven instead of enjoying a profit.

This is the nature of a hedge. A hedge reduces risk defined as the volatility of returns. Profit or loss depends more on the competitiveness of the company's products and services than on the ups and downs of exchange rates.

With respect to the multinational bank making a market in swaps, to avoid exchange risk, it needs to keep its total claims and obligations in each currency roughly in balance. To keep its (net) exposure to each currency at or near zero, the multinational bank needs to continually monitor its transactions, summing its assets and liabilities in each currency in which it does business. And, the multinational bank needs to either price its services so as to bring about a neutral position from its operations or hedge any (net) exposure that develops.

Raising Capital Internationally

It often makes sense to raise capital internationally, in places where a company conducts its business and in currencies in which it expects to generate future revenue. Two examples include:

- A Japanese subsidiary in the United States that assembles automobiles for sale in the United States: This subsidiary should develop banking relationships in the United States to use the automobile assembly plant in the United States to secure a dollar-denominated loan.
- A U.S. subsidiary in Indonesia that sells tractors made in the United States: This subsidiary should develop banking relationships in Indonesia to use the sales offices in Indonesia to a secure a loan denominated in the currency of Indonesia.

The first example involves two countries both of which are highly developed. Each of these countries has a well-established rule of law and a highly developed financial sector. Accordingly, the Japanese subsidiary in the United States should have no problem establishing banking relationships in the United States so as to be able to use its U.S. assembly plant to secure a dollar-denominated loan.

The second example involves a country (Indonesia) that is an emerging economy. While Indonesia has made tremendous progress in recovering from the East Asian Currency Crisis of 1997, capital remains relatively scarce, and its financial sector is not highly developed.[6] In the case of Indonesia, capital flow is inward, especially foreign direct investment. Subsidiaries of foreign corporations generally rely on capital raised in their home country or elsewhere in the developed world. Until all countries are developed, there will be countries, like Indonesia, relying on foreign capital.

During the time that countries are developing, they offer good opportunities for investment, but there also are risks. Among the risks is political risk. Because much of the capital is foreign, it is tempting for the country's political leaders to think the country can gain by nationalizing or heavily taxing capital. In fact, nationalizing or heavily taxing capital is shortsighted because it will cut off the flow of new capital into the country. When the country joins the ranks of developed countries, it will have capital invested overseas, and can see capital both from the standpoint of a lender as well as a borrower.

Summary

- The choice of currency in international transactions is often determined by the more stable of the buyer's and the seller's currencies. Sometimes a transaction is denominated in a third country's currency because the currency of neither party is stable. Other factors that are sometimes involved in the choice of currency include: which party's banking system can best finance the transaction, which currency is more liquid and (freely) convertible, and by convention in certain markets such as the oil market.
- The U.S. dollar is the currency of a much larger fraction of world trade than is the fraction that U.S. exports and imports constitute of world trade. The Chinese yuan is the currency of a much smaller fraction of world trade than is the fraction that Chinese exports and imports constitute of world trade. The reason for this difference is that the U.S. dollar is convertible while the Chinese yuan is not.
- A company has a transaction risk when the profit in a transaction can be affected by changes in exchange rates (due to money to be disbursed or received being denominated in a foreign currency).
- A company has a translation risk when the net worth on its balance sheet can be affected changes in exchange rates (due to assets and liabilities being denominated in a foreign currency).
- Calculation of foreign exchange risk involves determining a company's exposure (or net exposure) equal to the sum of its assets and liabilities denominated in each foreign currency. If this sum is near zero in a particular foreign currency, the company is naturally hedged. If the company is not naturally hedged, it should consider using the forward exchange market or a foreign exchange derivative to hedge its exposure.
- To deal with foreign exchange risk, banks offer their customers both spot and forward exchange. Spot refers to immediate fulfillment of the contract; and, forward refers to delayed fulfillment of the contract; for example, three months from the date of the contract.

- Forward rates reflect spot rates and differences in interest rates in the two currencies. The forward premium is equal to the difference of the forward and spot exchange rates as a percent of the spot rate. The forward premium will approximately equal the difference between the foreign interest rate and the domestic interest rate. This is called interest rate parity.
- Since interest rates usually reflect the expected rate of inflation, one of the factors determining the forward premium is the difference in the rates of inflation in the two countries. Countries that have relatively low rates of inflation tend to have forward rate premium. Countries that have relatively high rates of inflation tend to have forward rate discount.
- Exchange-based derivative instruments include futures, call options, put options, and swaps.
- Currency futures are exchange-based instruments (as opposed to forwards, which are offered by banks), providing for the fulfillment at a future date of a contract for the purchase and sale of foreign currency at a fixed price. With futures, standardized contracts are bought and sold by floor traders and brokers operating on behalf of their clients. For example, contracts for five million yen for delivery in one year.
- Currency call options are the right, but not the obligation to buy a foreign currency at a future date at a price set in the contract. For example, the right to buy five million yen in one year at the exchange rate of 120 Yen = US$1. If yen can be acquired at a more favorable rate in the spot market in one year, the buyer of this option should simply allow the call option to expire.
- Currency put options are the right, but not the obligation to sell a foreign currency at a future date at a price set in the contract. For example, the right to sell five million yen in one year at the exchange rate of 120 Yen = US$1. If yen can be sold at a more favorable rate in the spot market in one year, the buyer of this option should simply allow the put option to expire.
- Currency swaps involve the exchange of a financial obligation (such as a loan or a bond) in one currency for a financial obligation in a different currency. Currency swaps usually occur because borrowers have well-established relations with lenders in their home country, who lend money in their national currency, when the borrowers desire to match the currency of their debt to the currency of the income to be generated in the future by sales in a foreign country.
- It is advisable for multinational corporations to raise capital in the currencies in which they generate their revenue. As a practical matter, it may only be possible to raise capital in the currencies of highly developed economies. Because it may not be possible to raise capital in the currencies of developing economies, a higher risk attaches to investments that generate revenue in those currencies, requiring a higher expected rate of return for those investments.

NOTES

1. Marc Auboin, "Use of currencies in international trade," World Trade Organization, 2012. p. 10.

2. The spot and forward rates are from the WSJ Market Data Center for November 15, 2011. The Japanese interest rate is made zero percent for simplicity; and, the U.S. interest rate is made to have equilibrium.

3. In one type ("European"), the buyer can exercise the option only on the expiration date and in another type ("American"), the buyer can exercise the option on or before the expiration date.

4. The now standard formula for valuing options (the Black-Scholes options pricing formula) involves mathematics beyond the scope of this book.

5. In the discussion that follows, "value" refers to the average of the implied volatility of the first "in-the-money" and the first "out-of-the-money" call options on the next-to-deliver futures contract, using the Black-Scholes options pricing formula.

6. "Summary of Indonesia's Finance Sector Assessment," Asian Development Bank. December 2015.

Chapter 11

International Financial Crises

> I can calculate the movement of the stars, but not the madness
> of men.[1]

Economic bubbles, alchemy, witch-hunts, and prophesy are among the "popular delusions" examined by Charles Mackay in his classic book *Extraordinary Popular Delusions and the Madness of Crowds*.[2] Men, he argued, are susceptible to herd mentality, as when one member of a herd, grazing or watering at the time, starts running, and the entire herd joins in. How else can you explain the witch-hunts of 16th- and 17th-century Europe,[3] in which "thousands upon thousands" of people were executed? According to Mackay, the witch-hunts were initiated as a way of settling disputes with neighbors, in which the accusation of practicing witchcraft combined with gossip and suspicion to condemn the first poor soul that was accused. After the first execution, subsequent condemnations were increasingly easy and, soon, nobody was beyond condemnation. Then, there was an intervention. A civil authority or a church leader conducted an investigation into the witch-hunt, demonstrated the flimsiness of the evidence, and put an end to the witch-hunt. Only then was the panic of the crowd replaced by reason.

In the case of economic bubbles, Mackay looked at three: the Tulip Bubble of 17th-century Holland, the Mississippi Bubble of 18th-century France, and the South Seas Bubble of 18th-century England. Table 11.1 summarizes these bubbles. Consider the Mississippi Bubble. The Mississippi Company was granted a monopoly for the development of France's colony in North America known as Louisiana. This colony encompassed approximately the middle third of today's continental United States.

According to John Law, the founder of the Mississippi Company, money does not have to be backed by gold or silver. Instead, money can be backed by other valuable things, such as land. By this reasoning, the vast and fertile lands of the Mississippi Valley of North America could support an enormous issue of money. The banknotes issued by the Mississippi Company were guaranteed by the king.

John Law's argument appealed to many people. The banknotes of the Mississippi Company gained wide acceptance. The company had a practically unlimited license to issue paper money. Eventually, the paper money caused an inflationary spiral; but, in the meanwhile, the company appeared to be profitable, and its shares started to rise in price. This rise in price engendered expectations of further increases in price and a speculative bubble got underway. Soon, the shares were being bought not on the basis of their intrinsic value (such as earning power), but on the projection of share price increases. People were mortgaging their farms, homes and businesses to buy shares of the company, expecting the shares to rise further in value. This is why the word "bubble" is used: share prices were no longer tied to intrinsic value and share prices were rising simply because they were rising. Then, the bubble bursts.

The specific reason for the bursting of the bubble is actually unimportant. If the specific thing that pricked the bubble hadn't, then something else would have. With the bursting of the bubble, the entire economy collapsed. Those who had borrowed to buy shares were forced into bankruptcy. Because so many people were forced into bankruptcy, the normal working of the economy was disrupted. Because the normal working of the economy was disrupted, even those who had not participated in the speculative orgy were hurt. In the case of the Mississippi Bubble, there were three fatal errors:

- Land cannot be used to redeem banknotes. Because of its heterogeneity, land is highly illiquid. Forced sales of land, as would be needed to redeem banknotes, can only be made at an enormous sacrifice relative to intrinsic value.
- The intrinsic value of land is not a constant relative to the value of gold or silver or to the value of goods and services in general. Even if the illiquidity of land could be ignored, the value of land fluctuates relative to gold or silver or other things in general.
- The guarantee of banknotes by the government does not eliminate risk; instead, it *socializes* risk. In fact, because private risk is eliminated, people are less prudent, and risk increases.

In each of the three bubbles examined by Mackay, there was initially a valid reason for optimism. In the Dutch Republic, the emergence of a large middle class meant that large numbers of people would demand things of moderate luxury, such as tulips. Similarly, colonizing the Mississippi Valley and trade with the Spanish colonies of the Americas offered enormous

Table 11.1   The Three Bubbles in *Popular Delusions*

	Tulip Bubble of 17th-Century Holland	Mississippi Bubble of 18th-Century France	South Seas Bubble of 18th-Century England
Initial Cause	Middle-class indulgence	Colonization of Louisiana	Trade with Spanish colonies in Americas
Government involvement	None	Extensive, including guarantees	Extensive, mostly through corruption
Height of speculation	Selected tulips worth several year's wages	Shares worth multiple times intrinsic value	Shares worth multiple times intrinsic value
Following the burst	Not much harm to the economy	Complete collapse of the economy	Complete collapse of the economy

opportunities for profit. But, reason became replaced by herd mentality and bubbles got underway.

In all three cases, the inevitable bursting of the bubble ruined those who had invested heavily in the over-priced asset, especially those who had borrowed to invest. In the two cases in which the government became extensively involved, not only were these investors hurt, the entire economy collapsed.

This chapter reviews the history of international financial crises from the U.S. Debt Crisis of the 1840s to the Financial Crisis of 2008. The chapter explores what is common in the period leading up to a crisis, and what kinds of things precipitate the crisis. It discusses why crises continue several hundred years after the first modern crisis.

THE U.S. DEBT CRISIS OF THE 1840s

The first international financial crises of the modern era were the Latin American Debt Crisis of the 1820s and the U.S. Debt Crisis of the 1840s. These crises involved default by several of the newly independent republics of Latin America, and several states of the United States on debt that was largely owed to foreign investors.

The states of the United States that defaulted or risked default had gotten heavily involved in development projects. Among these were various transportation projects and state banks. The states issued bonds to finance these transportation projects and banks, or else guaranteed the bonds issued by private corporations. In some cases, the investments seemed to be profitable at first. But, these apparently profitable investments were followed up with others that were not. In other cases, the investments were unprofitable even from the start. The crisis is detailed in Table 11.2.

Table 11.2   U.S. State Fiscal Crises of the Early 19th Century

State	Development Projects	Financial Difficulty (year of constitutional amendment to restrict state debt)
AL	State Bank	1842, raised taxes, reformed banking
AR	State Bank	1842, suspended payments, partial repudiation (later full), prohibited banks
FL	State Bank	1841, upon statehood repudiated territorial debt
GA	State Bank, RR	1820, debtor relief, later reformed banking
IL	State Bank, RR, Canal	1842, suspended payments, '47-raised taxes, sold canal, cramdown, resumed payments, ('48)
IN	State Bank, RR, Canal	1841, suspended payments, '47-sold canal, cramdown, resumed payments, ('51)
KY	State Bank	1820, debtor relief, later reformed banking, ('50)
LA	State Bank	1842, reformed banking, ('45)
MD	RR, Canal	1842, suspended payments, '48-raised taxes, resumed payments, ('51)
MI	State Bank, RR, Canal	1842, suspended payments, '46-closed banks, sold RR, cramdown, resumed payments, ('43)
MS	State Bank	1841, repudiation, prohibited banks
MO	RR	1861, suspended payments, later-sold RR, resumed payments, ('75)
NY	RR, Canal	1842, raised taxes, ('46)
NC	State Bank	1820, debtor relief
OH	Canal	1841, paid in scrip, later-raised taxes, resumed payments, ('51)
PA	Canal	1842, paid in scrip, '44-sold canal, raised taxes, reorganized debt and resumed payments, ('57)
SC	Canal	Minor (accumulated some debt)
TN	State Bank	1820, debtor relief
TX	War Debt	1836, nearly full repudiation, prohibited banks, eventually debt paid by U.S., ('45)
VT	State Bank	1809, closed bank, raised taxes
VA	Canal	Minor (accumulated some debt)

No crisis states: CT, DE, ME ('44), MA, NH, NJ ('44) and RI ('42).
Adapted from Clifford F. Thies, "The American Railroad Network of the Early 19th Century: Private versus Public Enterprise," *Cato Journal* 22 (2002): 220–261.

A state that was initially successful with its development projects was New York state. During the period 1817–1825, this state built a canal of 364 miles from Albany on the Hudson River to Buffalo on Lake Erie, known as the Erie Canal. Construction was largely financed by bonds bought by foreigners. These bonds and interest on them were then paid from revenue from the canal in excess of its operating costs and improvement costs, prior to the suspension of toll-collection, making it a break-even investment. The canal attracted farmers and others to the region it traversed, contributing to the economic development of the state. Although the term predates the canal, with the opening of the Erie Canal the nickname "The Empire State" became firmly attached to New York.

The success of the Erie Canal proved intoxicating to the nation. Several of the east coast states envisioned their own canals to the interior. Pennsylvania began to construct what it called the Mainline, a composite canal and railroad from Philadelphia to Pittsburgh. Maryland began to construct the Chesapeake & Ohio Canal, from Washington, DC., westward. Virginia began to construct the James River Canal, from Richmond westward.

States of the interior, including Ohio and Indiana, began their own canal projects. Illinois and Michigan began to build railroads as well as canals. And, New York followed up the Erie Canal with a number of lateral (or, north-south) canals, as well as provided bond guarantees for the New York and Erie Rail Road. In the South, development projects often involved state banks whose capital was provided by bonds issued by the state. These state banks provided loans to planters for the acquisition of land and slaves.

Case Study: Michigan

Exemplifying the enthusiasm of the period is Stevens T. Mason, the "Boy Governor" of Michigan. Mason was appointed Governor of the Territory of Michigan at the age of 22, in 1835. He was elected Governor upon the admission of Michigan to the Union as a state, at the age of 23, in 1836. Mason's vision for the state was very ambitious. His vision involved the construction of several relatively short canals, three great railroads crossing the lower portion of the state, and a "new" form of banking, based on mortgages on land.[4]

To finance these development projects, the state legislature approved the issue of $5 million of state bonds. Mason negotiated the sale of most of these bonds to the Morris Canal & Banking Company of New Jersey, which in turn sold the bonds to investors in England. But, with its development projects generating little income, the state attempted, unsuccessfully, to borrow more money in order to pay the interest on the bonds it had already issued. Not being able to pay the interest, the state defaulted.

With the State of Michigan in default, with work on the state's development projects suspended, and with the collapse of the new banks, the Boy Governor declined to run for reelection and, at the conclusion of his term, relocated to New York state. The state then fell into a long and deep depression.

In 1845 a new Governor was elected, John S. Barry. Under his leadership, the state reduced its debt mainly by selling its uncompleted railroads to private investors for the state's bonds and past-due interest and by restructuring the state's remaining bonds and past-due interest into new bonds on which it resumed interest payments. This restructuring involved a "cramdown" or partial payment on certain bonds.

In addition, the state adopted a constitutional amendment to forbid it ever again from getting involved in development projects, to require it to balance its budget, and to limit it from having any more than a small amount of debt.

Following these reforms, the state found that out-of-state capitalists were happy to invest in development projects in the state as private enterprises, such as by completing the two railroads that the state had started and the third that it had planned.

Reconciliation, Reform, and Recovery

Much the same thing happened in the other northern states that had gotten into financial trouble; and, in select southern states. These states reconciled with their creditors, resumed payments on their bonds, and adopted reforms such as restrictions on borrowing. These states tended to attract new capital from foreign investors, and resumed strong economic growth. Many southern states turned inward, some even to the point of prohibiting banking and repudiating their debts, preferring states' rights and slavery and opposing the capitalist system. Most notable among these states was Mississippi.

With the reconciliation of most of the financially troubled states with their creditors, investors gradually warmed back up to state bonds. Capital again flowed into the states that had reconciled with their creditors. And, along with capital flow, there was migration. The northern states grew tremendously in wealth and population. The armies of the Confederate States fought gallantly during the U.S. Civil War; but, the much larger armies of the Union States prevailed.

The U.S. Debt Crisis of the 1840s was one of the first international financial crises of the modern era. The cause of the crisis could be said to be the enormous potential of the still young United States. Excited by this potential, many state governments issued bonds and/or guaranteed the bonds of private corporations to construct canals, railroads, and turnpikes, and to provide the capital for state banks. But, their plans proved to be too ambitious. And, because these states socialized risk, they undermined private concern for risk and, furthermore, put everyone at risk.

When, as is inevitable, the false prosperity came to an end, some of these states learned from their mistakes, and committed themselves to sound fiscal principles of balanced budgets, limited indebtedness, and relying on private enterprise for economic growth. These states subsequently enjoyed strong capital flows at low interest rates, and quickly developed their economic potential.

Other states reacted to the hard times that followed the false prosperity in a negative way, by turning toward slavery and against the liberal, democratic capitalist system. The next two sections survey the history of international financial crises following the U.S. Debt Crisis of the 1840s, examining in detail the Crisis of 2008 and its aftermath.

FINANCIAL CRISES THROUGH THE 20TH CENTURY

During the early part of the 19th century, there were financial crises involving the newly independent republics of Latin America during the 1820s and the states of the still young United States during the 1840s. Since then, the list of international financial crisis has expanded to include all the major regions of the world and highly developed economies as well as developing economies. Through the 19th century, the main defaults on international debts by developing countries were:

- 1820s—all the newly independent republics of Latin America;
- 1840s—eight states of the United States;
- 1870s—several of the republics of Latin America (again), Egypt and Turkey;
- 1890s—Argentina and Greece.

While these were the main defaults on international debts during the 19th century by developing countries, during that century the largest international capital flows were to the United States, Canada, Australia, and Russia, countries that paid back their debts in full or nearly in full. Regarding the United States, while some of its states defaulted during the 1840s, and the while the country continued to suffer bank panics, stock market crashes and severe recessions, the United States joined the highly developed countries of the world during the 19th century. The United States transitioned from being an international *borrower* to being an international *investor*.

Other international financial crises of the 19th century include the Panic of 1873 in the United States and the roughly coincident collapse of the Vienna Stock Exchange on Black Friday, May 9, 1873. Following these crises there was a prolonged period of depressed economic conditions in much of the world. Contributing causes included the long period of deflation in the United States following the U.S. Civil War and the demonetization of silver first in Germany and then in France.

Spotlight: Black Friday

There are three Black Fridays in the history of finance: September 24, 1869; May 9, 1873; and October 24, 1929. The first concerned an attempt by two Wall Street financiers to "corner" the gold market; second, the collapse of the Vienna Stock Exchange in 1873; third, the New York Stock Market Crash of 1929. In their song, "Black Friday," Steely Dan makes references to the 1873 and 1929 episodes.

The Great Depression

During the early 20th century, the problem of international crises dramatically shifted from the developing countries of the world to all the countries of the world. During World War I, the gold standard was suspended. While the gold standard was in suspension, prices rose.

Then, during the years following the war, an attempt was made to resume the gold standard at the prewar parity (1 ounce of gold = $20). During a short but severe recession, prices fell *part* of the way back to their pre–World War I level. Then, prices were stabilized. During the 1920s, a new era of stability seemed to be achieved. But, prices were inconsistent with gold being worth $20 an ounce. Prices would have to fall further.

As more and more countries returned to the gold standard, deflationary pressure built up. The United States was suffering an international drain of gold. And, the Federal Reserve—to prevent the drain of gold from causing prices to fall and disrupting the new era of stability—"immunized" the gold drain in order to maintain the domestic money supply.

Astute observers perceived the problem with the gold standard. Irving Fisher proposed what he called "the compensated dollar." The Federal Reserve would redeem the U.S. dollar not in a fixed amount of gold ($20 to an ounce) but in a variable amount of gold having a constant purchasing power as measured by a general price index. Fisher's proposal received wide attention and almost led Congress to direct the Federal Reserve to control the money supply so as to keep the producer price level at its 1920s level. But, following the Stock Market Crash of 1929, there was no containing the deflationary pressure.

As prices spiraled down, those who had borrowed money to invest in homes, farms, railroads and other businesses found that they were heavily burdened by their debts. Many of them were forced into default. Many banks, suffering from defaults on loans, were in turn forced to close. Only after several years of deflation did prices approximate their pre–World War I level. But, by this time, the economy was in shambles.

First under President Herbert Hoover, a Republican, and then under President Franklin Roosevelt, a Democrat, the United States dealt with the financial crisis in a number of ways. As shown in Table 11.3, some of these

Table 11.3   U.S. Responses to Financial Crisis

	Great Depression	*Financial Crisis of 2008*
International Trade and Finance	Smoot-Hawley Tariff	–
Monetary Policy	Allowed the banking system to collapse	Expanded Balance Sheet, Quantitative Easing
Bailouts	Reconstruction Finance Corporation	TARP
Spending	Work Projects Administration	Stimulus Package
Taxation	Raise Tax Rates up to 80 percent	–

ways resemble the responses to the Financial Crisis of 2008 under President George W. Bush, a Republican, and President Barack Obama, a Democrat. There are, however, some very big differences.

The responses recently that were similar to the responses to the Great Depression include the bailouts and the increases in spending. The responses that are different are: the second time, the United States did not precipitate a trade war; nor did it raise taxes to confiscatory levels; nor did the Federal Reserve sit idle and simply allow the banks to fail.

In hindsight, it is easy to see that the underlying cause of the Great Depression was the attempt, after World War I, to stabilize prices at too high a level for resumption of the gold standard at $20 an ounce. The Stock Market Crash of 1929 was merely the precipitating cause. It was the needle that pricked the bubble. The subsequent policy blunders such as allowing the banks to fail and Smoot-Hawley Tariff turned what might have been a recession into a depression.

During the 1920s, while the attempt to resume the gold standard at $20 an ounce seemed to be successful, people went about their business, buying homes and farms, starting and expanding companies, and borrowing money to do these things based on prices that were—unbeknownst to them—too high and were bound to fall. Therefore, when the Stock Market Crash of 1929 unleashed the deflationary pressure built into the economy, many of those who had borrowed money were forced into bankruptcy. So many people were forced into bankruptcy that the entire economy was disrupted. The federal government then compounded the problem with one after another policy blunder, condemning the economy to widespread unemployment until the start of World War II.

Financial Crises during the Late 20th Century

During the late 20th century, there were a series of financial crises involving emerging economies and economies in transition from centrally planned economies to market-oriented economies. Among these were:

- The Latin American Debt Crisis of the 1980s;
- The Mexican Peso Crisis of 1994;
- The East Asian Currency Crisis of 1997;
- The Russian Financial Crisis of 1998; and
- The Argentine Financial Crisis of 1999.

While there are many important details about each of these financial crises, the usual scenario is that the country borrowed money in the international financial market in a hard currency such as the U.S. dollar; and, then was unable to earn the hard currency through exports so as to make the promised payments on its debt.

Indeed, a country in which foreign investments are profitable usually never has to pay off its foreign debt. While particular loans are repaid, foreign capitalists reinvest a good amount of that money in the country and continue to provide new capital to the country, so that net capital flow remains positive. It is only countries that are unable to pay off their foreign debt that are required to pay off their foreign debt, except they are unable to do so and, thus, are forced into default.

As to why foreign capital is not profitable, reasons include:

- The use of foreign capital to finance deficits (as opposed to financing development projects);
- The use of foreign capital to finance development projects based on overly optimistic estimates of profitability;
- Adverse fluctuations in the value of the goods produced with the aid of foreign capital relative to the value of the debt in which the foreign capital is denominated;
- Corruption and the re-direction of foreign capital to finance "crony capitalism;"
- Economies in which it is very difficult for companies to be profitable because of high taxes and excessive regulations; and
- The breakdown of the rule of law and, even worse, civil unrest and revolution.

The Latin American Debt Crisis of the 1980s

In the case of the Latin American Debt Crisis of the 1980s, there were two main causes. The first was the potential for economic development in the region that attracted foreign capital during the 1970s; and, the second was the combination of high interest rates and deflation of the early 1980s. It should be noted that "potential for economic development" is often a factor in financial crises involving emerging economies. That's what foreign investors see when countries begin to establish the rule of law. They see potential for economic development. Unfortunately, there often are problems on the path of economic development.

During the 1970s, when foreign capital was flowing into Latin America, there was a moderate inflation in the United States. As a result, interest rates were rising. Because of rising interest rates, many loans involved variable interest rates. A variable interest rate is when the interest rate is periodically re-set. For example, the interest rate might be periodically re-set using a formula such as the three-month U.S. Treasury Bill rate plus 2 percentage points.

Then, starting in 1979, the Federal Reserve tightened money in order to curb inflation. The policy worked; inflation was curbed. But, the immediate effect of the tight money policy was to raise interest rates, even while inflation was falling. Many of those who had borrowed money found that their burden of debt was suddenly very great. This included many homeowners, farmers, businesses, and banks in the United States, as well as the Latin American republics.

The Latin American republics found that they were unable to earn the U.S. dollars they needed by exports of minerals and the fruits of the tropics, because the prices of these commodities were soft. Several of these countries defaulted, which in turn threatened several of the international banks that had lent to them. There followed a period of austerity and lackluster economic performance, as well as various efforts to restructure the foreign debts of the Latin American republics. Following the crisis and afterword, many of the republics of Latin America began to pursue market-oriented economic reform. Today, Latin America features some countries that have embraced market-oriented reform that are doing quite well, and other countries that have turned leftward and inward that aren't doing so well.

The East Asian Currency Crisis of 1997

In the case of the East Asian Currency Crisis of 1997, the promising New Tigers of East Asia—Malaysia, Indonesia, Thailand, South Korea, and Philippines—enjoyed significant capital flows. However, there were some potential problems. The banks of the region were borrowing money in U.S. dollars and lending the money to local business in national currency. This difference in currencies was not supposed to be important, since the countries of the region pegged their currencies to the U.S. dollar. Other potential problems included the lack of transparency in local financial markets and suspicions of crony capitalism (where the government favors certain business based on family relationships and political connections).

To certain politicians of the region, the East Asian Currency Crisis was caused by speculative attacks on their currencies. Currency speculators, sensing that the currencies of the region were overvalued relative to the dollar, borrowed in the local currency and invested in dollar assets. For example, they borrowed twenty-five million Malaysian ringgits and invested in 10 million dollars of U.S. securities, when the peg of the ringgit to the U.S. dollar was 2.5 to 1. Then, when the ringgit fell to approximately 5 to 1,[5] they converted $5 million into ringgits in order to repay the ringgits they had borrowed, and pocketed a $5 million profit.

To try to defeat this speculative attack, the local central bank raised the interest rate very high; but, how does paying a 40 percent annual interest for what you think will only be a few days compare to making an enormous profit? Once the currency speculators sensed that the local currencies were overvalued, it was almost inevitable that they would succeed in forcing a devaluation, at which time they would gain an enormous profit.

While Malaysia, Thailand, South Korea, and the Philippines were hit hard by the East Asian Currency Crisis of 1997, Indonesia was hardest hit. The Indonesian rupiah fell from about 2,000 to 1 against the U.S. dollar, to about 14,000 to 1. GDP, measured in U.S. dollars, fell by about 20 percent in the first four countries, and by about 40 percent in Indonesia. The long-time president of the country, Suharto, was forced to resign, and members of his family were removed from many of the important industries of the country. East Timor, a predominantly Christian, former Portuguese colony that had been taken over by Indonesia in 1976, declared its independence.

The East Asian Currency Crisis of 1997 demonstrated the risk of indebtedness when money is borrowed in one currency and invested in another under the assumption that exchange rates can are fixed. Then, when the link is broken and the local currency falls in value, the country is unable to pay its suddenly much more burdensome international debt. This forces the country into default. It can easily strain relations between countries. In the case of the East Asian Currency Crisis, the countries of the region, for a time, turned away from relations with United States and turned to the Europeans as an alternative source of capital. Today, many years later, it appears the relations between the United States and the New Tigers of East Asia are on the mend. In the case of Indonesia, the very difficult times that followed the crisis lead to inwardness and threatened the unity and budding democratic institutions of the island nation. But, the country lasted through the crisis and is now doing well.

Discussion

It seems fair to ask, after centuries of experience with international financial crises, why do we keep having them? Are the problems of each new; or, is it that people forget the lessons of the past. And, what are the lessons the lessons of the past? Is it that the current generation thinks it is so smart, that it can succeed where others have failed? Is it that debt involves risk?

Among the lessons of the past is that values change, whether the value of gold relative to the value of silver, or the value of one currency relative to another, or whether it is the value of money relative to the value of goods. Debt can provide the financing by which the potential of emerging economies can be developed. But, to ignore its risk is a guarantee of failure.

The involvement of government directly in investment projects or indirectly through guarantees seems to delude people into thinking that there actually is no risk. Just the opposite is true. Because everybody involved thinks there is no risk, investment becomes imprudent, and there is speculative fever. The usual rule of "buy high, sell low," becomes replaced by the rule "buy high, sell higher." More and more people want to get in on what appears to be "a sure thing." Excited by the prospect of easy profit, they willingly borrow in order to invest whether we're talking about shares in the Mississippi Company in 18th-century France, the U.S. canal extravaganza of the 1840s, or the Great Depression of the 20th century. And, because so many become involved, the entire economy is put at risk.

The next section examines the worst international financial crisis since the Great Depression, namely, the Financial Crisis of 2008.

THE FINANCIAL CRISIS OF 2008

In September 2008, President George W. Bush, joined by his Secretary of the Treasury and the Chairman of the Federal Reserve, asked the U.S. Congress for $800 billion to buy and thus support the prices of troubled assets, mostly mortgage-backed securities. The nation, he said, faced a "long and painful recession" unless his proposal was approved. He described the consequences of Congress not approving his proposal as lost retirement savings, job losses, and a collapse of business.

The stock market believed President Bush. From a peak of about 14,164 on the Dow-Jones Industrial Index the year before, the market had fallen by 20 percent by early 2008. During September, as Congress debated the president's proposal and at one point seemed to reject it, the market gyrated with the news from the nation's capital. By November 2008, the market had fallen to 7,552. The market only reached a bottom, at 6,594, in March 2009. This fall of more than 50 percent over a period of about one and a half years was the worst since the Stock Market Crash of 1929.

While the stock market crashed during the Panic of 2008, it subsequently rebounded rather sharply. The stock market recovered much of its lost value during the subsequent two years.[6] In contrast, housing prices, as measured by the Case-Shiller index, which fell 31 percent from their peak in the first quarter of 2006 to the first quarter of 2009, as of 2011 had not yet shown any sign of recovery.

During the years leading up to the panic, real estate and stock prices had increased tremendously. The housing market was propelled by public policies designed to expand homeownership, by a low interest rate policy of the Federal Reserve, and by certain financial innovations.

- During the 1990s, the Clinton Administration lowered the down payment required for government-guaranteed mortgages from 5 to 3 percent; and, during the 2000s, the Bush administration completely eliminated the need for a down payment.
- During this period, the government promoted the extension of loans to households that normally would not qualify for a mortgage, eventually eliminating the need for lenders to verify income and employment histories.
- Also during this period, the government extended its mortgage guarantee program to expensive homes, raising the limit from $360,000 to $625,000.[7]
- Following the 9/11 attack on the country, the Federal Reserve lowered interest rates. The low interest rates raised the market value of long-term assets including stocks and houses.
- The financial industry developed new instruments based on mortgages. These new instruments involved the selling of shares in complex trust funds consisting of many mortgages.

In real time, few recognized the tremendous gamble that was being taken. Since house prices were going up, didn't the house itself guarantee the mortgage? And, if there was any risk involved, wasn't it covered by the government guarantee?

Among those who failed to see the risk, that what was happening was a housing bubble that would eventually burst, were: the banks that originated the loans, their government regulators, the real estate appraisers, the government mortgage guarantor (the Federal Housing Authority), the government-sponsored banks that bought and re-sold mortgages (Fannie Mae and Freddie Mac), the private insurance companies that got involved (most notably AIG), the investment bankers that got involved (most notably Lehman Brothers), the credit rating agencies that evaluated the risk in mortgage-backed securities, and the banks, insurance companies, and pensions that bought mortgage-backed securities.

By 2006, the first signs of trouble were being exhibited. Prices were softening, house sales were slowing down, and foreclosures were starting to rise. By 2007, the government guarantor had lost so much money that it was in need of a bailout. Early during 2008, Lehman Brothers went bankrupt; and the

Federal Reserve was already pumping money into Fannie Mae and Freddie Mac. It was becoming clear that trillions of dollars of mortgages guaranteed by the government were at risk.

The decision was made by the Bush administration to seek authority from Congress to acquire enough of the troubled, mortgage-backed securities so as to bail out the financial institutions that had become involved in mortgages, including the government itself as a mortgage guarantor. While the financial institutions were bailed out, many homeowners found themselves with "underwater mortgages" (meaning that their mortgage exceeded the market value of their home). By propping up housing prices, instead of allowing prices to quickly find their true value, what followed was exactly the deep and protracted recession that the Bush administration had warned against.

Case Study: Ireland

During the 1990s, the Republic of Ireland gained for itself the nickname "The Celtic Tiger." Low tax rates, an open economy and an overall policy of economic liberalization, attracted investment, generated strong economic growth, and lowered the unemployment rate. There seemed to be every reason to be optimistic.

From 1995 to 2006, Ireland—like the United States—experienced a housing bubble. According to one local commentator,[8] house prices in Ireland averaged 105,000€ in Ireland from 1975 to 1995, when adjusted for inflation. Then, house prices started rising, reaching 375,000€ in 2006, before falling back to 200,000€ in 2011. Rising income might have justified an increase in house prices to 175,000€, and rising rents an increase in house prices to 200,000€. Thus, much of the increase in house prices during the bubble was unsustainable. The intrinsic value of housing had not gone up anywhere near as much as house prices had gone up.

As in the United States, low interest rates and zero percent down payments contributed to the speculative boom, as well as widespread confidence in the Irish economy and housing market. Initial warning signals, such as new homes being unsold, were dismissed.

When the bubble burst, the reaction by the government was to attempt to re-inflate the economy by propping up housing prices and by massive deficit spending. This was, basically, the same strategy taken by the United States, except even bigger relative to the size of the Irish economy.

Table 11.4 shows that in 2007, the government was running a small deficit, as a percent of GDP, and the unemployment rate was less than 5 percent. Then, when the crisis hit, the government's expenditure rose and its revenue shrank. Necessarily, the government's deficit increased, becoming more than 10 percent of GDP in 2009. The very large deficits did not—contrary to the

Table 11.4   Selected Economic Indicators, Rep. of Ireland, 2004–2011

Year	Billions of €				% of GDP	Unemployment Rate
	Revenue	Expenditure	Surplus or (Deficit)	GDP	Surplus or (Deficit)	
2004	37.5	37.5	0	158.2	–	
2005	40.8	41.3	(0.5)	167.7	(0.3%)	
2006	48.0	45.8	2.3	176.7	1.3%	
2007	49.3	50.9	(1.6)	186.6	(0.9%)	4.8%
2008	43.0	55.7	(12.7)	180.0	(7.0%)	6.3%
2009	35.3	60.0	(24.6)	166.3	(14.8%)	11.8%
2010	36.2	55.0	(18.7)	156.0	(12.0%)	13.6%
2011	39.3	64.2	(24.9)	161.0	(15.5%)	14.4%

predictions of certain economics—turn the economy around. Instead, GDP remained well below its prior peak (2007) through 2011; and, the unemployment rate grew to over 10 percent.

The Aftermath

Following the Crisis of 2008, countries had varied paths to recovery, with some very slow to recover. Three groups can easily be distinguished.

Relatively fast recovery. Among the countries that were significantly impacted by the Crisis of 2008, Germany was possibly the fastest to recover. Other fast-recovering countries were Canada and Sweden. These countries tended to have balanced budgets going into the crisis, allowed their budgets to go into a relatively small deficit, and then soon returned to a balanced budget.

Canada had a small budget surplus going into the crisis, then let a deficit open up that was never more than 4 percent of GDP, which it brought to near balance by 2014. With the crisis, the unemployment rate jumped, and was subsequently brought back to nearly the prerecession level by 2014.

Reflective of the conservative approach to public finance, housing finance in Canada is conservative. In particular, the minimum down payment in Canada is 5 percent, not zero, and the minimum equity upon a refinancing of a mortgage is 20 percent.[9] Canada largely avoided the housing bubble to begin with, but nevertheless had to deal with the bursting of the housing bubble and ensuing recession in its neighbor and trade partner, the United States.

Germany is another country that has a conservative approach to both public finance and mortgage finance.[10] As the time of the crisis, Germany's budget was moving from a small deficit to balance. Germany's unemployment rate was also falling at the time. These reflect that Germany was still in the process of "reunification," that is, aiding its eastern states that had been communist prior to the fall of the Berlin Wall to be economically integrated with its western states and with the free world in general. Then there was an uptick in unemployment following the crisis and a budget deficit that reached 4 percent of GDP. The budget was subsequently brought back into balance, and the unemployment rate resumed its downward path. By 2014, unemployment was falling even as hundreds of thousands of immigrants were coming into the country.

Relatively slow Recovery. The United States was relatively slow in recovering from the Crisis of 2008. The country entered the crisis with a moderate deficit and with rising unemployment. The deficit then rose to double digits as a percent of GDP, and remained at double digits for three years. Only in 2013 the deficit was brought down to single digits and by 2014 remained at 4 percent. The large deficits of the United States reflect the relaxed approach to debt that characterizes the American people with regard to mortgages, consumer debt, student loan debt, and corporate debt. Debt is promoted by the tax structure and by extensive guarantees of debt by the government. A consequence of the extensive use of debt is that the American economy is fragile. Fluctuations in the economy are likely to throw households and private businesses into bankruptcies and force many state and local governments into financial difficulty. The federal government seems immune to these problems because it can print the money in which its debt is denominated.

The case of the United Kingdom is, in many ways, similar to that of the United States. The major difference is that, by 2014, the United Kingdom had not made much progress in balancing its budget.

No Recovery. In contrast to the countries that had recovered by 2014, albeit at varying speeds, are the countries that had not yet recovered. They are conveniently described as the PIGS of Europe: Portugal, Italy, Greece, and Spain. However, there are important distinctions among these four, and Italy might be miscast as one of the PIGS. Through 2014, these are the figures for the PIGS of Europe. Greece is in the worst shape, followed by Spain, and then Portugal. Italy seems to be okay in terms of its budget, but still has a significant unemployment problem.

- *Portugal*—Unemployment rose to about 20 percent, which has since fallen to about 17; the deficit rose to about 10 percent of GDP, and has since been brought down to 5.
- *Italy*—Unemployment rose to about 12; deficit rose to 5, and is now 3.
- *Greece*—Unemployment rose to the mid-20s; the deficit rose to 16; the deficit was subsequently brought down to 9.
- *Spain*—Unemployment that rose into the 20s, has since fallen to about 20; the deficit rose to about 10, and has since been brought down to 6.

If the United States and the United Kingdom suffered badly from the Crisis of 2008, these countries have suffered much worse, especially Spain and Portugal, and most especially Greece. Yet, in real time, there was a prospect of fast development upon adoption of the euro. These countries—which have never exhibited the saving ethic of the northern Europeans—seemed to instantly gain a stable currency and rules for deficit spending and national debt that made them attractive for foreign investment. Perhaps there is a lesson in this: that rules can help but cannot entirely substitute for the embrace of the work ethic, the saving ethic, and the rule of law by the people of a country.

Summary

- From the bursting of the Tulip Bubble in Holland during the 17th century to the present, there have been financial crises.
- In many cases, the crises have been part of an inter-connected boom and bust in which the good times that preceded the crises involved rising prices of real estate and/or shares of stock financed by extensive borrowing.
- For example, in the Debt Crisis of the 1840s, many of the states of the United States defaulted on bonds issued to finance the construction of canals and in other ways to develop their economic potential.
- Until the Great Depression of the 1930s, financial crises were mostly associated with developing countries. The Great Depression of the 1930s and the Financial Crisis of 2008 involved developed countries.
- Some countries appear to learn from their experience with crises so as to not repeat them. Others seem to not learn and repeat them time after time.

NOTES

1. Sir Isaac Newton.

2. Charles Mackay, *Extraordinary Popular Delusions and the Madness of Crowds* (New York: Harmony Books, 1980 [1841]).

3. Or, the Salem witch trials of 17th-century New England.

4. Considering the Mississippi Bubble, this might not have been a truly new form of banking.

5. The ringgit eventually settled at 4 to 1.

6. Some of what follows is adapted from Bruce K. Gouldey and Clifford F. Thies, "Bubbles and Supply Failures: Where are the Qualified Sellers?," *Cato Journal* 32 (2012): 513–538.

7. The limit was temporarily raised to $729,000 during the financial crisis.

8. Ronan Lyons, "Are we nearly there yet? Finding the new floor for property prices," July 5, 2011.

9. Allan Crawford, Cesaire Meh, and Jie Zhou, "The Residential Mortgage Market in Canada: A Primer," *Financial System Review of the Bank of Canada*, December 2013, pp. 53–63.

10. Jens Tolckmitt, "The German Mortgage Model and the future EU Requirements to the Financial Sector," September 26, 2012.

Chapter 12

Development Economics

At the time of independence, India faced a choice: Either proceed along the path of the Soviet Union, of rapid industrialization; or, proceed along the model of small, largely self-sufficient villages. Either way, political independence would be accompanied by economic independence. Domestic production was to substitute for the importation of manufactured goods from developed nations. For political reasons, the path of a market-oriented domestic economy, open and integrated with the global economy was not an option. Indeed, that path was described as a new model of colonialism, "neocolonialism."

The path of small, largely self-sufficient villages was advocated by Mohandas Gandhi. As part of his advocacy of small-scale production, he started wearing homespun cotton clothing. The path of rapid industrialization through central planning was advocated by Jawaharlal Nehru. Nehru was the first prime minister of India, and served from 1947 until his death in 1964. Under his guidance, India became a democratic socialist state.

Other prominent leaders in newly independent states included Kwame Nkrumah of Ghana, self-described as the Lenin of Africa, and Julius Nyerere, the father of Tanzania. Independence in Africa and Asia was not associated with market-oriented economics, but with socialism. Along with socialism came corruption, increasingly authoritarian rule, civil strife, the deterioration of the infrastructure left by the colonial powers, increased poverty, falling life expectancy, the spread of disease, and increasing dependency of governments upon foreign aid. Some of these countries, being rich in oil, also became afflicted with the "resource curse." In these countries, internal factions vied with each other to receive royalties paid by foreign corporations developing their natural resources.

Table 12.1 presents descriptions, in broad terms, of the three newly independent nations mentioned above. In India, from independence until 1991, the standard of living grew at a modest rate. From 1991 to the present, the standard of living has grown at a much faster rate. Today, India cannot be described as a low-income country (although there remain many poor people within the country). The country is well within the range described as middle income by the World Bank.[1]

Since the 1970s, indexes have become available to quantify the concepts of civil liberty and political freedom and economic freedom. Freedom House, a New York-based think tank, began issuing 7-part scales (where 1 is best and 7 worst), for each of civil liberty and political freedom. Civil liberty includes things such as freedom of speech, religion, and the rights of an accused criminal. Political freedom includes things such as holding free and fair elections.

Table 12.1   India, Ghana, and Tanzania from Independence to 2013

Country	India	Ghana	Tanzania
Independence	1947	1957	1962
First President or Prime Minister	Jawaharlal Nehru	Kwame Nkrumah	Julius Nyerere
Served until	1964	1966	1985
Economics following independence	Socialism with import substitution through rapid industrialization	Socialism with import substitution through rapid industrialization	Socialism with import substitution through rapid industrialization
Politics following independence	One dominant political party	Dictatorship	One dominant political party
GDP per capita at independence [1]	825.42	1,177.45	1,216.53
GDP per capita 1991 [1]	1,722.96	1,937.00	1,442.00
Growth Rate Independence to 1991	1.7%	1.5%	0.6%
Economics following 1991	Mostly free-market, open economy	Mostly free-market, open economy	Partially free-market, open economy
Politics following 1991	Multiparty democracy	Multiparty democracy	One dominant political party
GDP per capita 2013 [1]	5,244.00	3,864.00	2,365.00
Growth Rate 1991 to 2013	5.1%	3.1%	2.2%

[1] 2011 U.S. Dollars-PPP basis.

Since independence, India has mostly respected civil liberties and has always held democratic elections. During the 1970s, Prime Minister Indira Gandhi (daughter of the country's first prime minister and no relation to Mahatma Gandhi) ruled largely by decree. During the 1980s, when Indira's son—Rajiv Gandhi—served as Prime Minister, there was another time of compromise of civil liberty.

Economic freedom involves a market-oriented economy. Among other things, economic freedom means prices are determined and resources allocated by the forces of supply and demand. The Cato Institute, a Washington, DC-based think tank, reduces many aspects of an economy to a ten-part scale. In this scale, 1 is a completely government-controlled economy and 10 is a completely market-oriented economy. Through 1990, India's economy was in the middle of the scale. Then, over the next several years, India moved to a relatively free-market orientation. This transition began during the administration of Prime Minister V.P. Singh, who succeeded Rajiv Gandhi. From independence until 1989, the democratic socialist Congress Party dominated. Since then, India has been a multiparty democracy, with BJP (a center-right party) and the Congress Party (now merely a center-left party), the two largest parties.

During the 1990s, many other low- and middle-income countries began to transition from a relatively socialistic to relatively free-market orientation. Among these were Ghana and Tanzania. Tanzania began implementing free-market reforms a bit later than India and Ghana. Tanzania has not yet secured the level of civil liberty and political freedom found in India and Ghana. Nor has Tanzania accelerated economic growth by as much as India and Ghana. None the less, on all these counts, Tanzania has moved in the right direction.

Julius Nyerere, a follower of Mao Zedung of China, was president of Tanzania from independence until 1984. Nyerere advanced a policy of "Ujamaa," which can be thought of as African socialism. Ujamaa was characterized by rapid industrialization, government control of banking and commerce, and collectivization of agriculture. Political opposition was banned, unions suppressed, and villages that resisted collectivization burned. During this time, Tanzania suffered greatly. Food production collapsed. There was widespread corruption. The government was largely maintained by foreign aid. Government officials became known as "Wabenzi" (People of the Benz, referring to their preference for Mercedes-Benz automobiles).

When Nyerere left office, Tanzania was one of the poorest countries of the world. His successors began the process of moving Tanzania in the direction in economic and political freedom. Nyerere, himself, accepted that his policies needed to be changed. Since then, the country has been on the rebound, but it still has a long way to go.

Kwame Nkrumah was the president of Ghana from independence until 1966. As president, he described himself as a "scientific socialist," and proclaimed himself "the redeemer" of his country. Like leaders of many other newly independent countries, he promoted rapid industrialization. He used "marketing boards" to control exports, and redirected profits from mining and agriculture to the new industrial sector. Nkrumah's greatest achievement was the construction of the Akosombo Dam on the Volta River. The government became involved in hundreds of other development projects, from infrastructure to factories. Most of these projects proved to be economic disasters. Mounting debt and an increasingly autocratic rule led to Nkrumah's overthrow by a military coup in 1966.

From 1966 to 1992, Ghana was involved in a series of military dictatorships interspersed by occasional elections. Then, in 1992, the country embarked on a new path involving a market-oriented economy and a multiparty democratic government. Since then, the country has been making significant progress.

PROGRESS AGAINST POVERTY

The progress made by India, Ghana, and Tanzania since the 1990s has been remarkable. But, is this success representative? Chapter 2 explored the general phenomenon of economic growth since the Industrial Revolution. Figure 2.5 demonstrated a strong correlation between economic freedom and GDP per capita. Figure 2.4 showed that economic growth has been spreading around the world in an uneven manner. In truth, there has been remarkable progress in many areas. In this section, the focus is on poverty.[2] To what extent has poverty in the world been reduced since the 1990s? Based on periodic surveys conducted by the World Bank, poverty, defined as having less than $1.25 per day in income, fell from 36 percent of the population of the world to 18 percent from about 1990 to about 2010.

Pincovsky and Sala-i-Martin have examined progress against an even lower poverty level.[3] While $1.25 per day might be consistent with a subsistence level of income, they looked at the percentage of the population living on less than $1 per day. This standard is more consistent with "slow starvation." It is definitely extreme poverty. They estimate that from 1970 to 2006, extreme poverty practically disappeared outside of Sub-Sahara Africa, and was falling rapidly there.

Some comment is in order concerning the steep decline of extreme poverty in China from 1970 to 1985. To a large extent, this decline marks the recovery of China from the disastrous Great Leap Forward of 1958 to 1961, and the Cultural Revolution of 1966 to 1969. The steep decline of extreme poverty in China from 1970 to 1985 marks the ability of even a totalitarian government to bring order and stabilize income at something like the subsistence level or a bit higher. Since then, with a pragmatic form of socialism, China has rapidly advancing.

Recap of Section

Upon gaining independence, almost all the former European colonies in Africa and Asia embarked on policies of central planning, rapid industrialization, and import substitution. Their desire to be economically independent of their former colonial rulers, as well as politically independent, is understandable. Additionally, practically all intellectuals of the time were socialists of one form or another (democratic socialist or totalitarian socialist), and advocated either rapid industrialization or "small-scale" production in order to achieve economic independence.

The consequences of these policies ranged from disastrous to disappointing. The three examples described in some detail above are among the better experiences. There were worse. During the 1990s, there was a revolution in development economics. Prior to the 1990s, development economics stressed central planning, rapid industrialization, and import substitution. During the 1990s, development economics embraced open, market-oriented economies. With this orientation, civil liberties and political freedom, as well as higher standards of living, were achieved in most of the developing world. Extreme poverty has been practically eliminated, and rapid progress is being made against extreme poverty where it has not been eliminated. Many countries that had been placed in the low-income category have since been re-classified as middle-income countries. Some of these countries have been subsequently re-classified as high-income countries. The next section looks at the problems besetting the countries that remained, as of 2015, in the low-income category.

WAR AND DEVELOPMENT

Since the revolution in development economics of the 1990s, extreme poverty has been eradicated in most of the world. In the Western Hemisphere, there is only one "low-income" country.[4] All other once low-income countries of this hemisphere have transitioned to at least "lower-middle income." To be sure, there are still individuals who are in poverty in a lower-middle income category, just fewer of them. This section examines why some countries still remain in the low-income category. Why aren't all countries at least lower-middle income?

Table 12.2 lists all the countries of the world classified as low income by the World Bank as of 2015.[5] The table includes brief descriptions of the recent history of each country in terms of war (including Civil War), ethnic conflict and genocide, anarchy and dictatorship, and political strife. Necessarily, these descriptions gloss over many details.

As can be seen in the table, it is easy to explain why each country remained a low-income country by reference to a small number of factors internal to those countries: War, ethnic conflict, strife, anarchy, and oppressive government.

Table 12.2   Terse Recent Histories of 31 Low-Income Countries

Afghanistan	Continuous war
Benin	Through 1991 Marxist gov't, then a transition, then in 2006 free and fair elections
Burkina Faso	Continuous strife
Burundi	Continuous war, strife, genocide
Cambodia	Lunatic-form of communism, war, continuous strife
Central African Rep.	Continuous strife, ethnic conflict
Chad	Continuous strife, ethnic conflict
Comoros	Continuous strife
Congo, Dem. Rep.	Continuous war, strife, ethnic conflict
Eritrea	Continuous strife, ethnic conflict
Ethiopia	Through 1991 Marxist gov't, since continued strife and war
Gambia, The	Through 2002 Marxist gov't, since dominant party
Guinea	Through 2006 Marxist gov't, since continuous war and strife
Guinea-Bissau	Through 1994 Marxist, since continuous war and strife
Haiti	Anarchy
Korea, Dem Rep.	Lunatic-form of communism
Liberia	Continuous strife, ethnic conflict
Madagascar	Through 1994 Marxist gov't, then a transition, then in 2013 free and fair elections
Malawi	Through 1994 dictatorship, since dominant party
Mali	Continuous strife, ethnic conflict
Mozambique	Civil war through 1993, since transition
Nepal	Continuous strife
Niger	Continuous strife, ethnic conflict
Rwanda	Continuous strife, ethnic conflict, genocide
Sierra Leone	Continuous strife, ethnic conflict
Somalia	Anarchy
South Sudan	Continuous strife, ethnic conflict
Tanzania	Through 1984 Marxist gov't, since dominant party
Togo	Dictatorship
Uganda	Lunatic-form of dictatorship, continuous strife, war, genocide
Zimbabwe	Dictatorship, continuous strife

Adapted from: Clifford F. Thies, "Not so Great Utopias," *Journal of Private Enterprise* 32 (2017): 63–76.

Looking at the countries in Table 12.2, there can be some confidence that Benin will join the march of progress (if it hasn't already). Indeed, given the new view of development economics, there can be hope for all of the countries in the table, provided that they establish a government that is strong enough to provide order and restrains itself from abusing that strength.

Predation and Defense

In hunter-gatherer societies, people live "from hand to mouth." The concept of property in hunter-gatherer societies is "first possession." An apple belongs to the person who takes it from a tree.

With the development of agriculture there is wealth. Farmers periodically harvest crops and at harvest time have at least a season's worth of production. Ranchers have herds of animals. There are tools and land that is improved through fencing and such. With agriculture, the concept of property shifts from taking from nature to working with nature in order to produce. This new concept of property is sometimes described as the "labor theory of property."[6] Thus, with agriculture there is wealth, there is a new understanding of property, and there is the possibility of theft.

Since the development of agriculture, human life has involved a struggle between those who are productive and those who would take from the productive, whether through plundering (think of the Vikings of Europe) or via enslavement, serfdom, or heavy taxation. Abraham Lincoln once described the conflict between the takers and the makers this way:

> It is the same principle in whatever shape it develops itself. It is the same spirit that says, "You work and toil and earn bread, and I'll eat it." No matter in what shape it comes, whether from the mouth of a king who seeks to bestride the people of his own nation and live by the fruit of their labor, or from one race of men as an apology for enslaving another race, it is the same tyrannical principle.[7]

The first chapter of this book looked at the rise of civilization. The fact that civilizations arose in many places in the world indicates there is an advantage to the productive gathering together. A large part of this advantage is mutual defense. The advantage of mutual defense can be understood as an economy of scale. As more and more productive people join together, they can defend themselves more easily against those who would rob and enslave them.

One way for this economy of scale to occur is through a militia army. In many cultures, all men of military age are expected to join in the defense of the community during times of war. Normally, productive men are more trusting of each other and ready to join into larger groups (such as a militia army or a sheriff's posse) than those who live by stealing. Another way that this economy of scale in mutual defense occurs is through professional armies and law enforcement. A small tax on the productive supports a large-enough, well-trained, and well-equipped army and police force to defend the community.

A problem in this model of predation and defense develops when people join together merely on the basis of race or ethnicity (as opposed to joining together based on the shared value of being productive). When people join together based on race or ethnicity they often do things that are immoral. For example, starting an offensive war to conquer land (which should be seen as theft), or to enslave people (which should be seen as kidnapping).

Race and Ethnicity and the Formation of Nations

Countries are often formed out of particular races and ethnicities. A shared history tends to improve trust within a nation-state. Certainly a shared language improves the ability of people to cooperate with each other in the marketplace and in social relations.

The coincidence of natural geographic borders with language might provide some order to the formation of countries. Spain, for example, has a natural geographic border with France (the Pyrenees Mountains). But, even this border breaks down when examined in detail. Most borders are not so well defined. People join into marriages that cross races, even when laws and social mores prohibit it. There are substantial benefits to cross-border trade, as well as cross-border investment and business formation.

With the formation of nations based on race and ethnicity, those possessing the "will to power" can gain a real advantage. National armies can become much larger than criminal gangs. Should persons who have the will to power attain power within a political entity, they are able to use armies, police forces, and bureaucracies to reduce a part of the population of that political entity to servitude. Furthermore, they can expand that political entity through wars of conquest. Indeed, wars of conquest constitute the major part of what is called "history."

An "Identifiable People" in an "Identifiable Place"

Many national borders are not based on race or some other basis for identify, but on arbitrary decisions made in the past. For example, the Pope draws a line on a map of the Western Hemisphere and "grants" part to Spain and part to Portugal. In addition, migration, intermarriage, trade, and investment have always been significant. The result is that most nations are characterized by some amount of racial, ethnic, and religious diversity.

If the people of a country are secure in their rights by the rule of law, then diversity is not a problem. But, to the extent, nations are formed based on identity, and are not disciplined by equal rights, then people are at risk depending on their identity. Many of the wars and other conflicts since World War II have been wars of independence, civil wars, and ethnic-based conflicts based specifically on identity.

To some extent, racial, ethnic, and religious conflicts can be resolved through the formation of new countries. In recent times, we have seen the formation of several new countries that emerged from racial, ethnic, and religious conflicts:

- East Timor (2002), from Indonesia, Catholic versus Muslim;
- Kosovo (2008), from Serbia, Albanian and Muslim versus Slavic and Orthodox Christian;
- South Sudan (2011), from Sudan, Black African and Christian versus White or Arabic African and Muslim.

The U.N. Universal Declaration of Human Rights indicates that all people have the right to a country. A corollary of this would seem to be that no people should long be kept in a nationless status, and that no people should long be kept in a subjugated status by a country from which they are alienated.

As a practical matter, consideration has to be given to whether an "identifiable people" exists in "an identifiable place." If these elements come together—(1) an identifiable people (2) in an identifiable place that (3) are subjugated by the larger nation—there seems to be a growing consensus that this people and place can be severed from the larger nation.

War and Conflict since 1946

As shown in Table 12.2, war and other forms of political violence are a major reason for the continuation of poverty in the world. Figure 12.1 shows the number and wars and other conflicts, and their magnitudes, that have been ongoing since the end of World War II. From World War II to 1991 (i.e., the Cold War Period), the trend was upward, reaching a peak of forty-nine conflicts. Many of these conflicts were associated (1) with wars of independence during the ending of the colonial period, and (2) with the Cold War.

From 1991 to 2001, the trend line was downward. Among the wars and other conflicts of the period from 1991 to 2001 were some associated with the collapse of the former Soviet Union and the former Yugoslavia. This downward trend was thought by some to signal an end to major wars,[8] and perhaps also to fewer ethnic conflicts.[9] In hindsight, the downward trend came to an end with the emergence of new sources of instability and conflict.

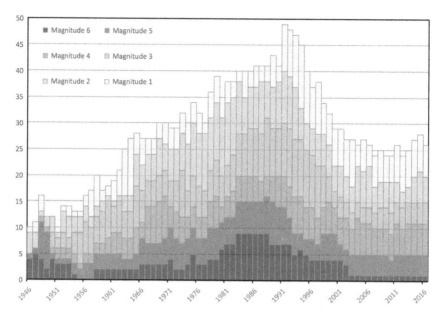

Figure 12.1 Wars and Political Violence in the world by order of magnitude, 1946–2016. *Source*: Created by author. Adapted from: Monty G. Marshall, "Major Episodes of Political Violence, 1946–2016." June 15, 2017.

Since 2001, the number of wars and other conflicts occurring within a year has fluctuated about 25. Among the conflicts of this period are insurgencies that gained momentum following the toppling of certain dictators in the Arab world and conflicts associated with the rise of radical Islamic extremism.

Causes and Consequences of War

There are two dominant views as to the causes of war. One view focuses upon political, economic, and social inequalities, poverty, economic stagnation, poor government services, high unemployment, and environmental degradation.[10] The other focuses upon securing the rights of individuals and identifiable groups, and on provision for peaceful change through open and fair elections. Having said these things, it is difficult to forecast the outbreak of wars. While underlying conditions may set the stage for war, many wars are sparked by seemingly random events. In hindsight, these precipitating causes are often seen as insignificant.

While the causes of war remain a matter of controversy, it is clear that wars cause poverty and frustrate economic development. The next section considers the role of natural resources in economic development.

NATURAL RESOURCES AND DEVELOPMENT

Some developing countries are said to have a "resource curse." They are rich in natural resources yet cursed by low standards of living, corruption, repressive government, political instability, and violence. In a controversial paper, Jeffrey D. Sachs and Andrew M. Warner show that there is a negative correlation between the share of exports represented by oil, metals, diamonds, and other mineral resources and average GDP growth.[11] While there is, in fact, a negative correlation, there is also a wide scatter about the trend line. Not every country that has abundant natural resources is cursed.

Sovereign Wealth Funds

Before investigating why there may be a resource curse, let's examine some places that are blessed by natural resources. The American state of Alaska, the Canadian province of Alberta, and the country of Norway are tremendously wealthy in natural resources. They enjoy high standards of living. Nevertheless, they are also cold places.

Production of resources can generate substantial revenues to the government. These revenues fluctuate wildly with the prices of commodities and will eventually run out when the resources are depleted. To smooth the flow of revenue and to prepare for the day when a resource is depleted, a portion of the revenue can be put into a sovereign wealth fund. A *Sovereign Wealth Fund* is an investment portfolio organized by the government. Often, the fund is financed by revenue to the government from the production of natural resources.

Table 12.3 describes some of the sovereign wealth funds endowed by the production of natural resources. Kuwait and Norway have two of the largest sovereign wealth funds in terms of assets. Considering their relatively small populations, they have the largest funds in terms of assets per capita.

Table 12.3 Selected Sovereign Wealth Funds Endowed by Resources

Country	Fund Started	Source	Assets US$ (millions)	Population (millions)	Assets per capita
Kuwait	1953	Oil	592,000	3.37	175,668
Norway	1990	Oil	825,000	5.01	164,671
Alaska, USA	1976	Oil	53,900	0.74	72,838
Saudi Arabia	1952	Oil	668,600	28.83	23,191
Wyoming, USA	1974	Coal	5,600	0.58	9,655
Alberta, Canada	1976	Oil	17,500	4.15	4,217

Data of funds from: Sovereign Wealth Fund Institute.

It is important that once money is put into the fund only the earnings of the fund are withdrawn. An approximation of this rule is that only 4 to 6 percent of the balance of the fund should be withdrawn in any particular year. By observing this rule, the fund will always be available.

Other good uses of revenue from the production of natural resources include spending on education and infrastructure. These expenditures can increase the productivity of the country, which should outlast the natural resources. In such ways—financial investment and expenditures on education and infrastructure—the bonanza of natural resources is converted into a relatively permanent flow of income.

Spoiled by Easy Riches

Getting back to the problem of the resource curse, many countries use the revenue from the sale of natural resources to support consumption spending rather than investment. By promoting a standard of living beyond the production of the country other than that of its natural resources, an effect of the resources is to promote leisure instead of work. Finding the right balance between working and enjoying life is always a problem. The proper way to find this right balance is to distinguish your (one-time) wealth from the earnings of your wealth.

The Tragedy of the Commons

Another potential problem with natural resources is unclear ownership. When ownership is clear, the owner of the resource has a natural incentive to properly balance current production against future production. But, when ownership isn't clear, the incentive is to maximize current production. Let's say that natural gas is discovered. Usually, this natural gas is found in an underground trap or well, and is discovered by an exploratory drill. In Figure 12.2, the location and size of the deposit are clear enough. But, in the real world, the size and location of the deposit are not known.

When natural gas was first discovered, the law did not recognize claims to the deposit other than the extension, up and down, of claims to the surface land. Therefore, neighboring landowners each had the right to drill into the well and extract natural gas, as long as the drills went straight down. Natural gas, being a gas, would continually expand so as to fill the space, and any drill could empty the entire deposit. The result was a rush by all neighboring landowners to drill into the well and pull out as much gas as quickly as possible. As a result, the market is flooded with natural gas. The price of natural gas is low and the gas is used inefficiently. With the rush to extract, the natural

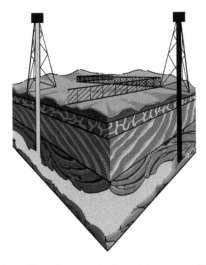

Figure 12.2 The Problem of Underground Natural Resources. *Source*: Daniel Thies.

resource is soon be depleted (meaning the remaining natural gas is at too low a density to extract).

During the Indiana Gas Boom of the 1880s, the enormous Trenton Gas Field covering much of the eastern midsection of the state was tapped into by hundreds of wells. The natural gas taken out was used for almost any purpose, including simply burnt around the clock in "flambeaus," or displays of burning natural gas. By 1905, with the falling pressure of the wells, it was clear that the natural resource was being depleted. It is estimated that 90 percent of the natural gas extracted during the boom was wasted.

The Tragedy of the Commons: When individuals acting independently and rationally according to their self-interest behave contrary to the best interests of the whole group by depleting some common resource. The "commons" at one time referred to the village commons on which residents could graze a cow. Each resident had a private incentive to graze cows, but that would result in overgrazing and the depletion of the grass of the commons.

If there were one owner of the entire deposit, that owner would naturally balance current production against future production. If the current price is low relative to the price expected in the future, the owner would extract less natural gas; and, if the current price is high, the owner would extract more. This is all that is needed to ensure a balancing of current versus future production of natural resources.

The current price of natural gas could be low relative to the price expected in the future if a new, more abundant source of energy is being developed. Such a thing happened when coal supplanted wood, and such a thing seems to be happening now with respect to underground coal mining. Surface mining of coal and natural gas is in such abundance that underground coal mining is in decline. Because of the natural incentives to owners to balance current versus future production, economists do not worry about "running out" of resources that are privately owned. We do worry about the over-use of resources that aren't privately owned, but held in common, such as the atmosphere, the oceans, and the migratory species of this wonderful planet.

Capture of Benefits

Another natural incentive to owners of natural resources is to consider the application of new technologies to improve production. The potential supply of natural resources "in the ground" is only one factor in production. Another factor is the cost of extracting those resources.

In the case of natural gas, "fracking" or the insertion of treated water into wells, enables more natural gas to be pulled out. The water has the effect of pushing the remaining gas in the well into a smaller space, and becoming dense enough in that smaller space to be extracted. If all surface landowners could legally drill into the well, none of them would have a sufficient incentive to frack the well. But, if the law recognized the person who developed the well to be its (single) owner, that person would have a natural incentive to consider the application of new technologies to improve production.

Contested Ownership

In countries where the rule of law is not established, it may not be clear who is the owner of natural resources. It may be said that "the nation" is the owner. But, in practice, the rulers may effectively be the owners. Thus, Saddam Hussein of Iraq enjoyed tremendous personal wealth, while the people of the country suffered in poverty. The same could be said of Mobutu Sese Seko of Zaire (now known as the Democratic Republic of Congo) and Hugo Chavez of Venezuela.

During Mobutu's thirty years as dictator, he amassed a personal fortune estimated to be as high as $25 billion. Much of this money was deposited in overseas bank accounts. When Mobutu was finally forced out of office, he departed with a caravan of trucks taking diamonds, gold, ivory, and leopard skins. The richest person in Venezuela is Hugo Chavez' favored daughter, Maria Gabriela Chavez. She is estimated to have $4 billion in overseas bank accounts. She and the current head of government live in the presidential palace and have personal expenses of $3 million a day paid out of the national treasury, while many of the people of the country starve.

In countries where the rule of law is not established there is a constant struggle for the wealth of the country, especially for the wealth that is in the form of natural resources. Significant amounts of money are spent on armies and other security forces whose main purpose is to maintain the regime in power. Rivals organize themselves into armed insurgencies that sometimes blend into criminal gangs. There are recurrent civil wars and other violence.

In addition to the cost of contending for ownership of natural resources, there is an incentive to hasten production. Since the current ruler cannot be confident of continued rule, he has an incentive to quickly convert natural resources into cash. This can include borrowing against the value of resources in the ground as well as hastening production. Such is the craziness of the resource curse that—instead of using the resource to build up a sovereign wealth fund—rulers of many countries use the country's resource to build up a national debt.

The Foreign Aid Curse

The 2015 winner of the Nobel Prize in Economics was Angus Deaton of Princeton University. Foreign aid, he says, has been mostly a curse. Foreign aid constitutes the majority of revenue of most of the countries that receive foreign aid. These governments do not much rely on the productivity of their people for their revenue. Therefore, why should they care if their people are productive?

Deaton says that if the choice were all or nothing, that it would be better for the people of the poorest countries of the world that the developed countries simply stopped giving their governments foreign aid. Then, those governments would have to adopt policies that actually promote production. Being practical, donor nations are trying to reform foreign aid by tying aid to the adoption of pro-development policies.

Summary

- At the end of the colonial period, the predominant view in development economics was that newly independent countries should adopt policies of central planning, import substitution, and rapid industrialization.
- The results of the policies of central planning, import substitution, and rapid industrialization ranged from merely disappointing (slow growth) to disastrous (corruption, economic decline, and violence).
- By the 1990s, there was a change. International trade and market-oriented reforms became the recommended policies for economic development.

- There followed rapid progress against poverty. The number of people in the world living on less than $1.25 per day has fallen from 36 to 18 percent over the past thirty years.
- By 2016, the number of low-income countries fell to thirty-one.
- Almost every one of these thirty-one countries has been characterized by authoritarian governments or anarchy, and/or has suffered from war, civil strife, and ethnic conflict.
- Wars and other conflicts were on the decline during the 1990s, but the number of wars and other conflicts has stopped falling during the first two decades of this century.
- Many but not all countries rich in natural resources have suffered a "resource curse."
- The countries suffering the resource curse tend to rely on royalty payments from foreign corporations, instead of conventional tax revenue. Therefore, they are not much interested in the prosperity of the people of the country.
- Furthermore, these governments tend to spend heavily on military force in order to maintain power.
- The countries that don't suffer the resource curse often use their natural resources to develop a sovereign wealth fund.
- Analogous to the resource curse is the foreign aid curse. Many governments that receive foreign aid rely on this aid instead of conventional tax revenue. Therefore, they are not much interested in the prosperity of the people of the country.
- Depletable natural resources are subject to "the tragedy of the commons" when freely available to all. The classic problem involves the overgrazing of a town commons by townspeople who keep milk cows.
- One solution to the tragedy of the commons is the extension of the concept of private property to resources such as underground wells of natural gas.
- Other solutions include a regulatory approach such as rationing permits to graze milk cows on the town commons, and a market-approach such as auctioning a sustainable number of permits to graze milk cows to the highest bidders.

NOTES

1. Low income—less than $1,045; Lower-middle income—$1,045 to 4,125; upper middle income—$4,125 to 12,376; high income more than $12,376; United States (2013)—$53,041.

2. Arguments can be made for focusing on the average and on the bottom of the income distribution. But, sustained economic progress usually involves each of the following three elements: an advancing standard of living for the masses of people in

the middle of the income distribution; a rising socially acceptable minimum standard of living; and the unleashing of the creativity of outstanding individuals in various areas such as social, economic, and political decision-making and leadership, scientific inquiry, and artistic expression and performance.

3. Maxim Pinkowskiy and Xavier Sala-i-Martin, "Parametric Estimates of the World Distribution of Income," NBER Working Paper No. 15433, 2009; and, "African Poverty is Falling . . . Much Faster than you think!" NBER Working Paper No. 15775, 2010.

4. Haiti. However, based on PPP, it might be a lower-middle income country.

5. Some of these countries, like Haiti, might be lower-middle income countries on a PPP basis.

6. This approach to the change in the concept of property is found in John Locke's *Second Treatise on Government*, 1690. He goes on to say that, with money, the concept of property can change again, from production to a legal claim.

7. Abraham Lincoln, 1858.

8. John Mueller, *Retreat from Doomsday: The Obsolescence of Major War* (New York: Basic Books, 1989).

9. Lars-Erik Cederman, Kristian Skrede Cleditsh, and Julian Wucherpfennig, "Predicting the Decline of Ethnic Civil War: Was Gurr Right and For the Right Reasons?" *Journal of Peace Res*earch *54* (2017): 262–274.

10. Francis Stewart, "The Root Causes of War," *British Medical Journa*l 324 (2002): 342–345.

11. Jeffrey D. Sachs and Andrew M. Warner, "Natural Resource Abundance and Economic Growth." NBER Working Paper 5398, 1995.

Bibliography

Abramitzky, Ran, and Leah Boustan, 2017. "Immigration in American Economic History." *Journal of Economic Literature* 55: 1311–1345.

Ahmad, Imad-ad-Dean, 2007. *Signs in the Heavens*, 2nd ed. Beltsville, MD: Amana Publications.

Anderson, Benjamin, 1963. *Economics and the Public Welfare, 1914–1946*. New York: D. Van Nostrand.

Anderson, Romola, and R.C. Anderson, 2003 [1926]. *A Short History of the Sailing Ship*. Mineola, NY: Dover Maritime.

Ayittey, George, 1992. *Africa Betrayed*. New York: St. Martin's Press.

Bhagwati, Jagdich, 1988. *Protectionism*. Cambridge, MA: MIT Press.

Barro, Robert, 1991. "Economic Growth in a Cross-section of Countries." *Quarterly Journal of Economics* 106: 407–443.

Bernanke, Ben S., Carol Bertaut, Laurie Pounder DeMarco, and Steven Kamin, 2011. "International Capital Flows and the Returns to Safe Assets in the United States, 2003–2007." Board of Governors of the Federal Reserve System, International Finance Discussion Paper 1014.

Bernstein, William J., 2004. *The Birth of Plenty*. New York: McGraw-Hill.

Black, Fischer, and Myron Scholes, 1973. "The Pricing of Options and Corporate Liabilities." *Journal of Political Economy* 81: 637–654.

Broz, J. Lawrence, 1997. *The International Origins of the Federal Reserve System*. Ithaca, NY: Cornell University Press.

Bruckner, Pascal, 1983. *Tears of the White Man. The Tyranny of Guilt: An Essay on Western Masochism*. Princeton, NJ: Princeton University Press.

Carey, Matthew, 1968 [1822]. *Essays on Political Economy; or, The Most Certain Means of Promoting the Wealth, Power, Resources, and Happiness of Nations, Applied Particularly to the United States*. New York: A. M. Kelley.

Caruso, Raul, ed., 2011. *Ethnic Conflict, Civil War and Cost of Conflict*. Bingley, UK: Emerald Group Publishing Limited.

Cederman, Lars-Erik, Kristian Skrede Cleditsh, and Julian Wucherpfennig, 2017. "Predicting the Decline of Ethnic Civil War: Was Gurr Right and For the Right Reasons?" *Journal of Peace Research* 54: 262–274.

Chalmers, Thomas, 1908 [1821–1826]. *The Christian and Civic Economy of Large Towns*, ed. C.R. Henderson. New York: Charles Scribner's Sons.

Clark, Gregory, 2005. "The Condition of the Working Class in England, 1209–2004." *Journal of Political Economy* 113: 1307–1340.

———, 2007. "The Long March of History: Farm Wages, Population and Economic Growth, England 1209–1869." *Economic History Review* 60: 97–135.

Clendenning, E. Wayne, 1970. *The Euro-dollar Market*. New York: Oxford University Press.

Cohen, Edward E., 1992. *Athenian Economy and Society: A Banking Perspective*. Princeton, NJ: Princeton University Press.

Corsetti, Giancarlo, Paolo Pesenti, and Nouriel Roubini, 1998. "What Caused the Asian Currency and Financial Crisis? Part I: A Macroeconomic Overview." NBER Working Paper No. 6833.

———, 1998. "What Caused the Asian Currency and Financial Crisis? Part II: The Policy Debate." NBER Working Paper No. 6834.

Coyne, Christopher J., and Rachel L. Mathers, eds., 2011. *The Handbook on the Political Economy of War*. Northampton, MA: Edward Elgar Publishing.

Davies. Glyn, 2002. *A History of Money from Ancient Times to the Present Day*, 3rd ed. Cardiff: University of Wales Press.

Davis, Lance E., and Robert E. Gallman, 2001. *Evolving Financial Markets and International Capital Flows: Britain, the Americas, and Australia, 1865–1914*. New York: Cambridge University Press.

Davis, Mike, 2000. *Late Victorian Holocausts: El Niño Famines and the Making of the Third World*. New York: Verso.

de Tocqueville, Alexis, 2012 [1835–1840]. *Democracy in America*, 2 volumes, transl. James T. Schleifer. Indianapolis, IN: Liberty Fund.

Deaton, Angus, 1997. *The Analysis of Household Surveys: A Microeconometric Approach to Development Policy*. Baltimore, MD: Johns Hopkins University Press.

———, 2015. *The Great Escape: Health, Wealth, and the Origins of Inequality*. Princeton, NJ: Princeton University Press.

Diamond, Jared, 1997. *Guns, Germs, and Steel*. New York: W.W. Norton.

Edwards, Sebastian, 1989. *Real Exchange Rates, Devaluation, and Adjustment*. Cambridge, MA: MIT Press.

Eichengreen, Barry, 1992. *Golden Fetters: The Gold Standard and the Great Depression*. New York: Oxford University Press.

English, William B., 1996. "Understanding the Costs of Sovereign Default: American State Debts in the 1840s." *American Economic Review* 86: 256–275.

Fama, Eugene F., 1984. "Forward and Spot Exchange Rates." *Journal of Monetary Economics* 14: 319–338.

Flynn, James R., 1984. "The Mean IQ of Americans: Massive Gains 1932 to 1978." *Psychological Bulletin* 95: 29–51.

————, 1987. "Massive IQ Gains in 14 Nations: What IQ Tests Really Measure." *Psychological Bulletin* 101: 171–191.

Freund, Caroline L., 2000. "Current Account Adjustment in Industrialized Countries." Board of Governors of the Federal Reserve System. International Finance Discussion Paper No. 692.

Friedman, Milton, and Anna Schwartz, 1963. *A Monetary History of the United States, 1867–1960*. Princeton, NJ: Princeton University Press.

Gibbon, Edward, 1983 [1906]. *The History of the Decline and Fall of the Roman Empire*. New York: Modern Library.

Gleditsch, Nils Petter, Peter Wallensteen, Mikael Eriksson, Margareta Sollenberg, and Havard Strand, 2002. "Armed Conflict 1946–2001: A New Dataset." *Journal of Peace Research* 39: 615–637.

Goldsmith, Edward, and Nicholas Hildyard, 1984. *The Social and Environmental Effects of Large Dams*, Volume 1: Overview. Wadebridge, UK: Ecological Centre.

————, 1986. *The Social and Environmental Effects of Large Dams,* Volume 2: Case Studies. Wadebridge, UK: Ecological Centre.

Gouldey, Bruce K., and Clifford F. Thies, 2012. "Bubbles and Supply Failures: Where are the Qualified Sellers?" *Cato Journal* 32: 513–538.

Gowa, Joanne, 1994. *Allies, Adversaries and International Trade*. Princeton, NJ: Princeton University Press.

Griffin, Emma, 2008. *A Short History of the British Industrial Revolution*. New York: Cambridge University Press.

Hamilton, Alexander, 1961–1979 [1791]. "Report on Manufactures." In Harold C. Syrett, et al., ed., *The Papers of Alexander Hamilton*, 26 Volumes, 10: 252–256. New York: Columbia University Press.

Hamilton, Earl J., 1934. *American Treasure and the Price Revolution in Spain, 1501–1650*. Cambridge, MA: Harvard University Press.

Hayek, F.A., 1945. "The Use of Knowledge in Society," *American Economic Review* 35: 519–530.

————, 1954. *Capitalism and the Historians*. Chicago: University of Chicago Press.

Helpman, Elhanan, and Paul R. Krugman, 1985. *Market Structure and Foreign Trade: Increasing Returns, Imperfect Competition, and the International Economy*. Cambridge, MA: MIT Press.

Higgs, Robert, 1977. *Competition and Coercion: Blacks in the American Economy, 1865–1914*. New York: Cambridge University Press.

Irwin, Douglas A., 2003. "New Estimates of the Average Tariff of the United States, 1790–1820." *Journal of Economic History* 63: 506–513.

————, 2015. "The GATT Starting Point: Tariff Levels Circa 1947." Center for Economic Policy Research, Discussion Paper No. 10979.

Johnson, Marion, 1970. "The Cowrie Currencies of West Africa, Part I." *Journal of African History* 11: 17–49.

————, 1970. "The Cowrie Currencies of West Africa, Part II." *Journal of African History* 11: 351–353.

Johnson, Paul, 1991. *The Birth of the Modern*. New York: HarperCollins.

Khaldun, Ibn, 1958 [1377]. *The Muqaddimah; An Introduction to History*, transl. Franz Rosenthal. New York: Pantheon Books.

Kaminsky, Graciela L., 2005. "Internal Capital Flows, Financial Stability and Growth." United Nations Department of Economic and Social Affairs, Working Paper No. 10.

Karatnycky, Adrian, 2000. "A Century of Progress." *Journal of Democracy* 11: 187–200.

Kenny, Charles, 2012. *Getting Better: Why Global Development Is Succeeding—And How We Can Improve the World Even More*. New York: Basic Books.

———, 2014. *The Upside of Down: Why the Rise of the Rest is Good for the West*. New York: Basic Books.

Kinderberger, Charles P., and Robert Z. Aliber, 2011. *Manias, Panic and Crashes: A History of Financial Crises*, 6th ed. New York: Palgrave Macmillan.

Kramer, Samuel Noiah, 1956. *From the Tablets of Sumer, Twenty-five Firsts in Man's Recorded History*. Indian Hills, CO: Falcon's Wing Press.

Krugman, Paul R., 1981. "Intra-industry Specialization and the Gains from Trade." *Journal of Political Economy* 89: 959–973.

LaLonde, Robert J., and Robert H. Topel, 1991. "Immigrants in the American Labor Market: Quality, Assimilation and Distributional Effects." *American Economic Review* 81: 297–302.

Lamppa, Marvin G., 2004. *Minnesota's Iron Country: Rich Ore, Rich Lives*. Duluth, MN: Lake Superior Port Cities.

Lancaster, Kelvin, 1979. *Variety, Equity and Efficiency: Product Variety in an Industrial Society*. New York: Columbia University Press.

Leeson, Peter T., 2007. "An-arrgh-chy: The Law and Economics of Pirate Organization." *Journal of Political Economy* 115: 1049–1094.

Leonard, Thomas C., 2016. *Illiberal Reformers: Race, Eugenics and American Economics of the Progressive Era*. Princeton, NJ: Princeton University Press.

Lerner, Abba P., 1952. "Factor Prices and International Trade." *Economica* 19(73): 1–15.

Lewis, W. Arthur, 1978. *The Evolution of the International Economic Order*. Princeton, NJ: Princeton University Press.

Lynn, Richard, and Tatu Vanhanen, 2002. *IQ and the Wealth of Nations*. Westport, CT: Praeger.

Mackay, Charles, 1980 [1841]. *Extraordinary Popular Delusions and the Madness of Crowds*. New York: Harmony Books.

Maddison, Angus, 1995. *Explaining the Economic Performance of Nations*. Brookfield, VT: Edward Elgar.

———, 2001. *The World Economy: A Millennial Perspective*. Paris: Organization for Economic Cooperation and Development.

Malthus, Thomas, 1960 [1798]. *An Essay on the Principle of Population*, ed. Gertrude Himmelfarb. New York: Modern Library.

McCloskey, Diedre, 2006. *The Bourgeois Virtues: Ethics for an Age of Commerce*. Chicago: University of Chicago Press.

———, 2010. *Bourgeois Dignity: Why Economics Alone Can't Explain the Modern World*. Chicago: University of Chicago Press.

———, 2016. *Bourgeois Equality: How Ideas, Not Capital or Institutions, Enriched the World*. Chicago: University of Chicago Press.

McCuster, John J., 1978. *Money and Exchange in Europe and America, 1600–1775: A Handbook*. Chapel Hill, NC: University of North Carolina Press.

McDonald, Robert L. 2006. *Derivatives Markets*, 2nd ed. Boston: Addison Wesley.

Meade, James Edward, 1951. *The Theory of International Economic Policy*, Volume 1: The Balance of Payments. New York: Oxford University Press.

———, 1951. *The Theory of International Economic Policy*, Volume 2: Trade and Welfare. New York: Oxford University Press.

Melitz, Jacques, 1974. *Primitive and Modern Money: An Interdisciplinary Approach*. Reading, MA: Addison-Wesley: 1974.

Meng, Xin, and Robert G. Gregory, 2005. "Intermarriage and the Economic Assimilation of Immigrants." *Journal of Labor Economics* 23: 135–174.

Mueller, John, 1989. *Retreat from Doomsday: The Obsolescence of Major War*. New York: Basic Books.

Niskanan, William, 1988. *Reagonomics: An Insider's Account of the Policies and the People*. New York: Oxford University Press.

Obstfeld, Maurice, and Kenneth Rogoff, 1996. *Foundations of International Macroeconomics*. Cambridge, MA: MIT Press.

———. 2005. "Global Current Account Imbalances and Exchange Rate Adjustments." *Brookings Papers on Economic Activity* 1: 67–146.

———. 2007. "The Unsustainable U.S. Current Account Position Revisited." In *G7 Current Account Imbalances: Sustainability and Adjustment*, ed. Richard H. Clarida, 339–375. Chicago: University of Chicago Press.

O'Rourke, Kevin H., and Jeffrey G. Williamson, 1999. *Globalization and History: The Evolution of a Nineteenth-Century Atlantic Economy*. Cambridge, MA: MIT Press.

Panizza, Ugo, Federico Sturzenegger, and Jeromin Zettelmeyer, 2009. "The Economics and Law of Sovereign Debt and Default." *Journal of Economic Literature* 47: 651–698.

Pecquet, Gary M., 2017. "The Original Road to Serfdom: From Rome to Feudal Europe." *Journal of Private Enterprise* 12: 45–62.

Pecquet, Gary M., and Clifford F. Thies, 2010. "Texas Treasury Notes and the Mexican-American War: Market Responses to Diplomatic and Battlefield Events." *Eastern Economic Journal* 36: 88–106.

Phillips, William D., and Carla Rahn Phillips, 1992. *The Worlds of Christopher Columbus*. New York: Cambridge University Press.

Pinkowskiy, Maxim, and Xavier Sala-i-Martin, 2009. "Parametric Estimates of the World Distribution of Income." NBER Working Paper No. 15433.

———, 2010. "African Poverty is Falling ... Much Faster than You Think!" NBER Working Paper No. 15775.

Porter, Michael E., 1985. *Competitive Advantage*, New York: Free Press.

Reinhart, Carmen M., and Kenneth S. Rogoff, 2009. *This Time is Different: Eight Centuries of Financial Folly*. Princeton, NJ: Princeton University Press.

Reynolds, Lloyd G., 1985. *Economic Growth in the Third World: 1850–1980*. New Haven, CT: Yale University Press, 1985.

Ricardo, David, 1973 [1817]. *On the Principles of Political Economy and Taxation*. New York: Dent.

Roivainen, Eka, 2012. "Intelligence, Educational and IQ Gains in Eastern Germany." *Intelligence* 40: 571–575

Rostow, Walt W., 1978. *The World Economy: History and Prospect*. Austin, TX: University of Texas Press.

Rothbard, Murray, 1963. *America's Great Depression*. New York: D. Van Nostrand Press.

Sachs, Jeffrey D., and Andrew M. Warner, 1995. "Natural Resource Abundance and Economic Growth." NBER Working Paper 5398.

Samuelson, Paul A., 1948. "International Trade and the Equalization of Factor Prices." *Economic Journal* 58(230): 163–184.

Sargent, Thomas J., and François R. Velde, 2002. *The Big Problem with Small Change*. Princeton, NJ: Princeton University Press.

Sargent, Thomas J., and Neil Wallace, 1981. "Some Unpleasant Monetarist Arithmetic." *Federal Reserve Bank of Minneapolis Quarterly Review* 5(3): 1–17.

Scott, Allen J., 2004. *Hollywood: The Place, The Industry*. Princeton, NJ: Princeton University Press.

Scott, William A., 1893. *The Repudiation of State Debts*. New York: Crowell.

Sedik, Tashin Saadi, and Tao Sun, 2012. "The Effects of Capital Flow Liberalization-What is the Evidence from Recent Experiences of Emerging Market Economies?" IMF Working Paper 12/275.

Selgin, George, 2008. *Good Money: Birmingham Button Makers, the Royal Mint and the Beginnings of Modern Coinage, 1775–1821*. Ann Arbor, MI: University of Michigan Press.

Shleifer, Andrei, 2009. "The Age of Friedman." *Journal of Economic Literature* 47: 123–135.

Sims, Christopher A., 1994. "A Simple Model for Study of the Determination of the Price Level and the Interaction of Monetary and Fiscal Policy." *Economic Theory* 4: 381–399.

Smith, Adam, 1970 [1776]. *The Wealth of Nations*, ed. Edwin Canaan. New York: Modern Library.

———, 1982 [1759]. *The Theory of Moral Sentiments*, ed. D. D. Raphael and A. L. Macfie. Indianapolis, IN: Liberty Fund.

———, 1982 [1763]. *Lectures on Jurisprudence*, ed. R. L. Meek, D. D. Raphael, and P.G. Stein. Indianapolis, IN: Liberty Fund.

Smitten, Richard, 2001. *Jesse Livermore: World's Greatest Stock Investor*. New York: John Wiley.

Sowell, Thomas, 1983. *Ethnic America: A History*. New York: Basic Books.

———, 1983. *Economics and Politics of Race: An Economic Perspective*. Fairfield, NJ: William Morrow.

———, 1990. *Preferential Policies: An International Perspective.* Fairfield, NJ: William Morrow.

———, 1995. *Race and Culture.* New York: Basic Books.

———, 1996. *Migrations and Culture.* New York: Basic Books.

———, 1998. *Conquests and Culture.* New York: Basic Books.

Soucek, Svat, 2000. *A History of Inner Asia.* New York: Cambridge University Press.

Speer, Albert, 1970. *Inside the Third Reich.* New York: Macmillan.

Steckel, Richard H., 2004. "New Light on the 'Dark Ages': The Remarkably Tall Stature of Northern European Men during the Medieval Era." *Social Science History* 28: 211–230.

Stewart, Francis, 2002. "The Root Causes of War." *British Medical Journal* 324: 342–345.

Stewart, Francis, and Valpy Fitzgerald, 2000–2001. *War and Underdevelopment,* 2 Volumes. New York: Oxford University Press.

Stinson, Sarah, Barry Bogen, and Jennis O'Rourke, ed., 2012. *Human Biology: An Evolutionary and Biocultural Perspective.* Hoboken, NJ: Wiley-Blackwell.

Stopler, Wolfgang, and Paul A. Samuelson, 1941. "Protection and Real Wages." *Review of Economic Studies* 9(1): 58–73.

Suter, Christian, 1992. *Debt Cycles in the World-Economy.* Boulder, CO: Westview Press.

Thies, Clifford F. 2002. "The American Railroad Network of the Early 19th Century: Private versus Public Enterprise." *Cato Journal* 22: 220–261.

———, 2007. "Political and Economic Freedom Reconsidered." *Journal of Private Enterprise* 22: 95–118.

———, 2013. "Economic Freedom and Crime: An Examination of the Gallup World Poll's Embedded Victim Survey." *Virginia Economic Journal* 18: 21–29.

———, 2014. "Repudiation in Antebellum Mississippi." *Independent Review* 19: 191–208.

———, 2017. "Not so Great Utopias." *Journal of Private Enterprise* 32: 63–76.

Tomz, Michael, 2007. *Reputation and International Cooperation: Sovereign Debt Across Three Centuries.* Princeton, NJ: Princeton University Press.

Tuckerman, Joseph, 1874. *On the Elevation of the Poor: A Selection of His Reports as Minister at Large in Boston,* ed. E. E. Hale. Boston, MA: Robert Brothers.

Tumlir, Jan, 1985. *Protectionism: Trade Policy in Democratic Societies.* Washington, DC: American Enterprise Institute.

Vinor, Jacob, 1937. *Studies in the Theory of International Trade.* New York: Harper & Bros.

———, 1950. *The Customs Union Issue.* New York: Carnegie Endowment for International Peace.

———, 1966 [1923]. *Dumping a Problem of International Trade.* New York: A.M. Kelley.

Wanniski, Jude, 1978. *The Way the World Works.* New York: Basic Books.

Wicker, Elmus, 2000. *Banking Panics of the Gilded Age.* New York: Cambridge University Press, 2000.

Wilkins, Mira, 1989. *The History of Foreign Investment in the United States to 1914.* Cambridge, MA: Harvard University Press.

———, 2004. *The History of Foreign Investment in the United States, 1914–1945.* Cambridge, MA: Harvard University Press.

Williams, Jeffrey C., 1882. "The Origins of Futures Markets." *Agricultural History* 56: 306–316.

Wiwattanakantang, Yupana, Raja Kali, and Chutatong Charumilind, 2002. "Crony Lending: Thailand before the Financial Crisis." Institute for Economic Research, Hitotsubasi University.

Yeager, Lleland B., 1976. *International Monetary Relations*, 2nd ed. New York: Harper & Row.

Index

Please note that the page locators which refer figures are italicized.

About the Author

Clifford F. Thies is the Eldon R. Lindsey Chair of Free Enterprise and Professor of Economics and Finance at Shenandoah University. He is the author, coauthor, editor, or a contributor to eight books, as well as author or coauthor of ten encyclopedia articles and eighty-eight articles in scholarly journals. Dr. Thies was elected President of the University Faculty Senate at both his current and prior institutions and currently serves on the editorial board of the *Journal of Private Enterprise*. He is a collector of financial memorabilia and he and his wife enjoy traveling.